No.II/15014/4/75-S&P(D-II)
Government of India
Ministry of Home Affairs
(Grih Mantralaya)

New Delhi-110001, the 8th November'75

M E M O R A N D U M

      In accordance with the provisions of
sub-section(4) of section 16A of the Maintenance
of Internal Security Act, 1971 (26 of 1971), as
amended, the Central Government has re-considered
whether the detention of Shri Lal K. Advani
S/o Shri Kishan Chand D. Advani, in respect of whom
a declaration was made on the 16th July, 1975 under
sub-section (3) of section 16A of the aforesaid Act,
continues to be necessary for effectively dealing
with the emergency. On the basis of the facts,
information and materials in its possession, the
Central Government is satisfied that the detention
of the said Shri Lal K. Advani continues to be
necessary for effectively dealing with the emergency.

      (By order and in the name of the President)

Remiss

(R. L. MISRA)
Joint Secretary to the Govt. of India

To

Shri Lal K. Advani
S/o Shri Kishan Chand D. Advani

Received a copy of this memorandum. November 8, the date of this memo, happens to be my birthday. So, I take it to be a birthday gift. Thanks.

L. K. Advani

17. 11. 76.

A PRISONER'S SCRAP-BOOK

TO

A PRISONER'S SCRAP-BOOK

LAL K. ADVANI

Foreword by
MORARJI DESAI

ARNOLD-HEINEMANN

Published by Gulab Vazirani for Arnold-Heinemann Publishers (India)
Pvt. Ltd., AB/9, Safdarjang Enclave, New Delhi-110016 and printed at
Dhawan Printing Works, 26-A, Mayapuri, Phase I, New Delhi-110064

Foreword

The emergency bore out the truth once again of the prison being the only place for a free man in a tyranny. The naked repression of 1975-77 showed how we had not only lost our seven fundamental freedoms which we had won after a long and arduous struggle but had also lost all avenues of legal redress against arbitrary detentions, forefeitures and other excesses. The emergency, which was itself the result of a thirst for unbridled personal power, had sought to punish even the mildest of attempts at the exercise of the right to dissent.

Gandhiji had taught us to resist invasion on our liberty and dignity and to use the term in prison as an opportunity to strengthen the will to resist. The emergency and the days immediately preceding its declaration, enabled a large number of our colleagues in politics to realise the perennial truth of Gandhiji's teaching. We had a new generation of Satyagrahis.

Prison is meant to be a punishment. But the Satyagrahi converts it into a challenge for deepening his political faith and his personal capabilities. Fellowship in prison enabled the detenus to ponder over what the nation needed and inevitably prepared them to work for the formation of a single, viable opposition party. The efforts to form such an alternative party had long been frustrated. But the cussedness of the then Government made it a reality. Thus in life we find that out of evil doth come good.

Shri Advani spent nineteen months in prison. He was arrested in Bangalore where he had gone to attend a meeting of a parliamentary committee. In fact he had the strange experience of being told that he had been arrested even before the emergency had actually been proclaimed. Except for a few days he spent the entire period in the Bangalore prison.

He had the good fortune of having congenial companions in prison, as well as a militant band of younger persons with whom to exchange political ideas. This could by no means be a compensation for the loss of liberty.

The diary reveals a person of singular honesty and dedication, culture and equanimity. It depicts the burning faith with which he withstood the consequences of governmental trickery, and his passion, as an editor, for the freedom of the Press and the mass media. The pamphlets that he wrote for use of the underground which are included in this book show the quality of his learning and are a fine example of political journalism. It is typical of Shri Advani's modesty that he calls it a "scrapbook".

The book, I am sure, will prove to be an important addition to the Library of our second liberation.

Sd/-

Morarji Desai

New Delhi,
April 7, 1978   (Morarji Desai)

Contents

Note from Publisher

Being aware that Lal K. Advani had kept some notes of his jail experiences we had approached him for their publication in the form of a book. But in the aftermath of the March elections to the Lok Sabha and the formation of the Janata Government there was a rash of publications on the emergency and its different aspects. The author, being actively involved in the election campaign and the new Government, was reluctant that anything which looked like adding to the prolific literature on the subject should be done. He also felt that the purpose of his diary had been served as the subsequent events have showed; it was mainly intended for circulation as underground literature.

On our insistence, however, he let us have a look at the manuscript and we felt strongly that it should be published as a book. This book provides an insight into the emergency from a perspective which has not been shared by any of the earlier publications. In this sense, it is unique and fully justifies our interest in seeing it published.

When Advani started jotting down his thoughts and experiences inside the detention camp, he did not mean to maintain a meticulous diary with a view to its eventual publication. What began as a pastime became a regular habit. The circulars and pamphlets widely distributed at that time are also included here. We are keen to preserve them in print because the larger issues involved in the imposition of the emergency and the resistance to it need to be understood and remembered in perspective, not only by the contemporary generations but by posterity as well so that the traumatic nineteen months are never repeated.

PART ONE

A View from Behind the Bars

THURSDAY, JUNE 26, 1975, BANGALORE

It is around 7.30 in the morning. The telephone starts ringing. Shyam Nandan Mishra (Shyambabu) with whom I am sharing a first floor room at the MLA s' Hostel here picks up the receiver, but the next moment hands it over to me saying: "It's for you". We came here yesterday to attend a meeting of a joint select committee of Parliament considering legislation against defections.[1]

The phone call is from the local Jana Sangh office. There is an urgent message for me from Delhi. Rambhau Godbole, one of the secretaries of the Jana Sangh, has telephoned saying that early that morning around 3.30 Jayaprakash Narayan was arrested. So also Morarji Desai, Raj Narain, Nana Deshmukh (this part of the message later turned out to be incorrect because Nanaji remained underground for some months), Chandra Shekhar, Mohan Dharia (this also proved incorrect) and Ram Dhan, the last three prominent Congress M.Ps. The arrests are continuing. Sunder Singh Bhandari, Jana Sangh General Secretary, Godbole himself and several other functionaries of the party are still out. The police, the message concludes, may shortly be calling for Atal Bihari Vajpayee and myself. Atalji, who is also a member of the same select committee had arrived in Bangalore two days earlier than us. I shared the information with Shyambabu and then hastened to Atalji's room to convey the news to him. We conferred briefly and decided that neither of us should evade arrest. Let them come and pick us up whenever they want.

---

[1] Floor-crossing by legislators.

I returned to my room and rang up N. Balu of the Press Trust of India. I had known him when he was posted in New Delhi, where he was involved in a motor accident and lost one of his legs.[2] I had met him only the previous day at a press conference addressed by me at the Woodlands Hotel. After the press conference we chatted and reminisced about common friends.

Balu confirmed the message from Delhi and read out to me the details of a report on the ticker. It gave the names of several other arrested leaders. Chaudhari Charan Singh, Piloo Mody, Biju Patnaik, Baldev Prakash and Balramji Das Tandon (the last two at Amritsar). Even as he was reading out from the ticker, he halted, and remarked, "Here is an interesting report", and chuckled, "The list of those arrested also includes Lal Krishan Advani, President, Bharatiya Jana Sangh".[3] Thus I got the news of my arrest in Delhi even before I was actually taken into custody. Balu volunteered to keep me posted with news, as it came. True to his word, during the next couple of hours, he kept ringing me up after every half-an-hour or so.

At 8 o'clock, I tuned in to All India Radio's main morning news bulletin to see whether it had anything more to say. Instead of the familiar voices of Devakinandan Pandey, Vinod Kashyap or Krishna Kumar Bhargava or any other news reader, I found myself listening to Indira Gandhi's voice. The President had proclaimed a state of emergency under Article 352 of the Constitution to meet the threat of internal disturbances, Indira Gandhi declared and went on to explain how the heavens would have fallen on June 29, if the decision had not been taken. The Lok Sangharsh Samiti had announced at a meeting in Delhi on the previous day its intention to launch a satyagraha from June 29 to demand Indira Gandhi's resignation in the interests of what Justice Krishna Iyer has described as "political conventions and democratic dharma".[4]

---

[2] Three weeks later, he and his family met with an accident in which he lost his life.
[3] The PTI correspondent concerned must have got the names from police sources, as usual.
[4] Justice Krishna Iyer, as vacation judge of the Supreme Court, granted conditional stay of the Allahabad High Court judgment invalidating Indira Gandhi's election to the Lok Sabha.

Soon Atalji arrived and suggested that we have our breakfast and be ready for the police. I had already had my bath. But Shyambabu had still to complete his chores. So Atalji and I went to the hostel canteen on the ground floor for our breakfast. While we were at the table, a party worker came in to tell us that the police had arrived and were waiting outside.

By then, word had gone round the hostel about the impending arrests. Henry Austin, a senior Congress M.P. and a fellow-member on the select committee, came into the canteen to speak to us. "I feel sad that this thing should happen", he said to us. I mentioned to him that Chandra Shekhar and Ram Dhan had also been arrested and suggested that he might condemn the arrests. But with a shrug of his shoulders, Austin expressed his inability to do so.

On emerging from the canteen we were met by a police official who told us that they had come to arrest us. Accompanied by the officials, we went upstairs to our respective rooms to pack our things.

Meanwhile, some half-a-dozen journalists, besides a host of party workers, had assembled in the room. The police said that Shyam Nandan Mishra was also to be taken into custody. Mishra had still to complete his morning *asanas*. That gave us some time to be with the journalists. Atalji and I prepared a joint statement condemning the arrest of J.P. and other leaders, denouncing the emergency and affirming that June 26, 1975 would have the same historic significance in the annals of independent India as August 9, 1942 had in the pre-independence days.

But before going out with the police we asked the officials to show us the warrants for our arrest or orders of detention as the case may be. After some humming and hawing, the officers said that they would be producing them in due course. Mishra said he would not go until a warrant of arrest or a regular written order was produced. After some consultations among themselves, the officers came to us and said that they were arresting us under Sec. 151 (*i.e.* for apprehended breach of the peace) and that no warrant was necessary for it.

It was thus about 10.00 A.M. when we finally left the MLAs' hostel under police escort. Just before our departure, Darbara Singh, chairman of the joint select committee, met us and expressed his personal distress that we should have been arrested like that.

From the MLAs' hostel we were taken to the High Grounds police station. Gopinath, a young Jana Sangh worker of Bangalore, brought us a small transistor radio for our use in jail. Until our release nineteen months later, Gopinath looked after our needs from outside the jail, reaching us inside whatever was permitted by the authorities. He assumed the responsibility from the time he met us at the hostel before we were taken into custody.

We kept listening to the hourly radio bulletins for news of J.P.'s arrest, and the countrywide clampdown but in vain. For Akashvani in those days the arrest of J.P., Morarjibhai, scores of MPs and MLAs and thousands of political activists amounted merely to something like this: "Following the proclamation of the emergency, some persons have had to be taken into preventive custody under MISA (Maintenance of Internal Security Act)".

In the afternoon, we came to know that stringent pre-censorship had been clamped on the Press.

We were kept waiting for the entire day at the Police Station presumably because the State authorities did not know what kind of detention order to serve on us. They had simply been sent a long list of names from New Delhi (we gathered this from a senior police official) and told that if anyone in the list was at Bangalore he or she should be detained under MISA.

The orders of detention were finally served on us at about 7.00 P.M. The orders were signed by the Commissioner of Police, Bangalore, so that in the eyes of the law, the Commissioner of Police, Bangalore, was the detaining authority. As such, it was he who under Section 3 of MISA was personally required to satisfy himself that the detention of the persons held was necessary in the interest of the security of the state and public order. (This, indeed, was a fatal and obvious flaw in the order, which later led to its revocation and the release, though formal, of all of us on July 17. Of course we were re-arrested immediately.)

When we were at the High Grounds police station, we were told that Madhu Dandavate of the Socialist Party had also been

arrested. Dandavate too was a member of the same joint select
committee, but his visit to Bangalore was in connection with
the tour programme of the Estimates Committee of which
he was a member. He was arrested at the Ashoka Hotel where
the members of the Estimates Committee were put up and
brought to the High Grounds police station. All four of us
were taken to the jail at about 8.00 P.M. The jail superintendent, H.L. Chablani, conducted us to our quarters which, he
said, had been hurriedly got ready at short notice but assured
us that bed linen, utensils and other requirements would be
provided on the following day.

I wrote in my diary: June 26, 1975 may well prove the last
day in the history of Indian democracy as we have understood
it. Hope this fear will be proved unfounded.

FRIDAY, JUNE 27

The Inspector-General of Prisons, Karnataka, Mallaya accompanied by the jail superintendent, Chablani, and the deputy
superintendent Desai, came to see us in the morning. They
repeated their assurance that our needs in the shape of bed-
sheets, blankets, kitchenware etc. would be attended to at the
earliest.

Meanwhile, we had a look round our new surroundings.
Two oblong, large-sized rooms facing each other, were to be
our new abode for the next few weeks. Shyambabu and Dandavate occupied one of the rooms and Atalji and I shared the
other. Newly, though shoddily constructed, the rooms formed
part of the jail hospital, intended to serve as segregation wards.
The superintendent told us that we were 'inaugurating' them,
because they had not been occupied until then.

SUNDAY, JUNE 29

It was our fourth day here and we seemed to have settled
down. As promised by the jail authorities, utensils, crockery,
bedding, linen have all arrived. Foodstuffs including cereals
and vegetables were supplied in accordance with the specifica-
tions laid down in the jail manual. Atalji having volunteered to
supervise the cooking (the *Lok Sabha Who's Who* has duly
listed 'cooking' among Atalji's hobbies), the culinary arrangements are as perfect as they can be in a jail. Our food is simple
but wholesome and delectable.

The jail has a small library and a reading room, housed just beneath the circular watch tower located in the centre of the premises. It has a wide range of Kannada books and there are also some English and Hindi books. Even so, this is the best jail library I have seen. It has been very wise perhaps on the part of the State Government to have the library maintained as a sub-branch of the Central Library, Bangalore, rather than run it just as a limb of the jail administration.

MONDAY, JUNE 30

All four of us have borrowed books from the library. The superintendent had meanwhile sent us a pack of cards, and a carrom board. We fitted them too into our routine which included, apart from our daily chores, a two-mile stroll in the evening within the jail compound. For Shyambabu the routine included, besides, an hour's *yogasanas* in the morning.

THURSDAY, JULY 3

The *Times of India* carries an interview with Prime Minister Indira Gandhi in which she gives strange explanations for the curbs on the Press. Indira Gandhi said: "A campaign of hate and calumny was unleashed against me in 1969. But most of our Press did not protest at all". Indira Gandhi's anger against the Press thus dates back to the time of the Congress split! It has not begun with the J.P. movement!

Indira Gandhi goes on to say: "There was no comment when effigies of the Chief Justice were burnt by opposition parties some time ago". This is the first time I, for one, have heard such a canard. There were some reports that the people gathered in front of the Prime Minister's residence in New Delhi, shouted slogans against Justice J.M.L. Sinha and some had even burnt his effigy (we have no means of knowing how true these reports were though the *Hindustan Times* printed photos of posters denouncing Justice Sinha as a CIA agent) but it is preposterous for Indira Gandhi to allege that opposition parties burnt the Chief Justice's effigy. How does the Chief Justice come into this matter?

FRIDAY, JULY 4

The two daily papers provided to us are the *Deccan Herald* and the *Indian Express* (Bangalore edition). We used to see the *Hindu* (Madras edition) also at the library. But following the censorship of the Press, there was hardly any difference between one paper and another. All were dull and drab, inane and insipid—mere reproductions of official handouts.

For news, therefore, the Indian student of public affairs has no option but to tune in to foreign broadcasting media. I took it upon myself to keep track of reports regarding India relayed by the BBC, Voice of America, Voice of Germany and Radio Australia—the four foreign stations which the transistor with us could catch—besides, of course, Radio Moscow, Peking Radio and Radio Pakistan.

At 4.30 P.M. BBC reported that the Indian Government has declared unlawful some 25 organisations. I caught the broadcast only at its conclusion when the headings were being repeated. So for a while we all felt that perhaps all the opposition parties had been declared unlawful. We were sure that the RSS must have definitely been one of the banned organisations. At 6 o'clock we tuned in to All India Radio to learn that the 25 organisations banned did include the RSS but not any political party. The Jamaat-e-Islami, the Anand Marg and its allied organisations, and a number of Naxalite bodies were banned.

SATURDAY, JULY 5

The RSS Sangh Chalak of Bangalore, Narasimhachar, editor of *Vikrama*, Mallya, along with several other swayam sewaks of RSS are brought to the jail and detained under MISA. Also detained are some members of the Jamaat-e-Islami and the Anand Marg.

All these detenus are housed in a ward opposite the central watchtower where some others held on charges of smuggling are kept. The jail authorities put the Anand Marg detenus along with RSS members but accommodated the Jamaat people with those detained on smuggling charges—obviously prompted by considerations of religious homogeneity. The Jamaat detenus resented the classification and requested that they be housed with the RSS men. Some adjustments were accordingly made. It is interesting that a Government which claimed to promote secularism perpetuated religious and other denominations by every one of its acts. Here is a graphic example. Instead of putting all political detenus together, they were sought to be segregated on the basis of religion which led to lumping political prisoners with those suspected of criminal activity. It was by its policy of dividing Muslims and Hindus that the so-called secularism was promoted.

There were some other RSS swayam sewaks arrested under DIR. One of them was a law student who had gone to study along with a classmate residing in Keshava Krupa, where the RSS office was located. He too was arrested in the general swoop.

The MISA detenus are kept segregated from us, as also other prisoners. They are not even allowed to come to the library.

THURSDAY, JULY 10

Three advocates who have gone to Keshava Krupa as counsel on behalf of the Trust which owns the building are arrested under DIR and brought to the jail.

Appa Ghatate, a friend and Supreme Court lawyer, met us and advised us to file habeas corpus petitions in the Karnataka High Court. But he also informed us that at Rohtak[5] the view seemed to be against filing such petitions. A petition filed by Sundari Malkani on behalf of her husband Kewal Malkani, Editor of *Motherland*, has, therefore, been withdrawn. We considered the matter and decided that the petitions should be filed. At the outset Shyambabu was of the view that he would approach the Supreme Court directly but ultimately he, too, decided to go along with the rest and file the petitions before the Karnataka High Court.

FRIDAY, JULY 11

Atalji and I filed our habeas corpus petitions in the prescribed elaborate form. Mishra and Dandavate did so briefly without following the full procedure but merely indicating the relief sought. In our petitions we requested the Court to permit us to argue our cases.

The three advocates arrested under DIR filed bail applications during the hearing of which, they told us, the court-

---

[5] Where Asoka Mehta, Biju Patnaik, Piloo Modi and others were kept.

room was packed with spectators. They thought their applications might be accepted. The Bar, they informed us, was sympathetic to a man. The lawyers of Bangalore also observed a protest against the emergency and boycotted the Courts for a day. The boycott was complete.

SATURDAY, JULY 12

Atalji has been complaining of backache for more than a week, and has been to the hospital several times for a check-up. Immediately after lunch, he complained of acute pain in the stomach. The doctor who examined him said it might be appendicitis. Shortly afterwards, Atalji is removed to the Victoria Hospital.

That evening we met Gundaiah Shetty, President of the Bangalore City Jana Sangh, who has been arrested under MISA. Shetty is also President of the Bangalore Bar Association and seemed to have earned the Government's wrath by organising the lawyers' protest against the emergency.

SUNDAY, JULY 13

The jail superintendent informs us that Atalji has been operated upon for appendicitis. The operation is successful. The rest of us express a desire to call on him. But the superintendent expresses his inability to permit us to do so.

On our return from the evening stroll, I find a neatly packed, very inviting, chocolate cake awaiting us. It has come from the superintendent's office but there is no indication as to who has sent it nor any message with it.

I have a hunch that it's from home and that my family has come to Bangalore to see me. But I am surprised that they have not met me even though an application for an interview had already been given to the superintendent two days earlier (when information was received that they would be visiting Bangalore in a day or two).

MONDAY, JULY 14

The superintendent confirms that my wife and children had come the previous day, but he could not allow them to meet me. Under the prison rules the power to grant interviews with relatives vests with the jail superintendent. But only three days earlier the power, in so far as MISA detenus are concerned, had been withdrawn by the State Government. Interviews with MISA detenus would now have to be permitted by the Home Secretary himself. My family has gone to secure the necessary permission, I am told.

In the afternoon we are taken to the Karnataka High Court. Our habeas corpus petitions are taken up for preliminary hearing by a two-judge Bench presided over by the Chief Justice, Sankara Bhatt.

Byra Reddy, Advocate-General for Karnataka, appearing on behalf of the respondents, said that while two of the writ petitions, namely, those of Atalji and myself, are in order, the other two are not. Shyam Nandan Mishra drew the Court's attention to the severe constraints under which they had to prepare the petitions in the jail, without adequate legal assistance. Dandavate mentioned that so far as habeas corpus petitions are concerned, the Supreme Court has been entertaining even postcards from detainees.

·The Chief Justice appreciated the situation and said all the four petitions would be entertained even though some of them might not have been in the prescribed form.

The Advocate-General then rose to say that as the petitioners had raised a wide range of issues the Government would need plenty of time to file its counter-affidavit. He also referred to the charge of *mala fides* levelled against the Central Government and said that perhaps the Attorney-General might wish to appear personally to rebut the charge.

All the three petitioners present (Atalji could not be present because he was convalescing after the operation he had undergone) opposed the Advocate-General's contention, and pointed out that Parliament's next session was scheduled to start on July 21, that is exactly a week from the day. We, therefore, urged that the matter be heard and disposed of before the Parliament session.

Chief Justice Bhatt seemed to agree with our plea. Addressing the Advocate-General, he said that in the U.K. all habeas corpus petitions are disposed of in 48 hours. As for filing the counter-affidavit he saw no reason why Government should need much time for it. Having detained the petitioners the authorities should be having all the relevant facts in their possession. Without mentioning names, he quipped: "When all the papers needed for the appeal can be readied and printed within 24 hours, what is the difficulty in replying to this?" The reference to Indira Gandhi's election case appeal was too obvious to be missed.

Byra Reddy caught the hint and said sulkily, "That's for the Prime Minister. I can't do that". The Chief Justice said: "You should be able to do that by Wednesday. The hearing can be on Thursday so that the matter can be disposed of in time for the Parliament session".

Byra Reddy intervened, "Parliament is to meet anyhow", provoking the Chief Justice to remark sharply: "What does Parliament mean without opposition parties?"

Touched to the quick by the acerbic observation, the Advocate-General said "Your Lordships, I for one am not at all enamoured of political parties".

"You may not be", the Chief Justice continued his admonition, "but aren't we having in the country the parliamentary system of Government based on the Westminister model?"

The Advocate-General discreetly kept quiet. The writ petitions were admitted, *rule nisi* issued to the respondents, orders passed in respect of legal facilities to the petitioners, and the hearing fixed for July 17, at 10.30 A.M.

At the preliminary hearing, Atalji was represented by Rama Jois, a senior advocate of the Bangalore Bar and formerly Secretary of the Bangalore City Jana Sangh. As mentioned earlier, we had conveyed to the Court in our writ petitions that we would be arguing our cases in person. The Chief Justice, however, kept emphasising the desirability of our engaging legal counsel to represent us. "Apart from other considerations", he said, "would it not be better if one was not an advocate of one's own cause?"

"It is not our own cause that we are pleading for, it is the cause of democracy", we humbly suggested.

"Anyway, I leave it to you to decide", the Chief Justice said.

That very night we decided that none of us would lead the arguments. After the counsel completed their arguments and dealt with the legal aspect of the matter we would, if at all, supplement their points with arguments relating to our charge of political *mala fides*.

For me personally, the visit to the Court yielded a bonus— a meeting with my family. My wife, Kamala, and children,

Jayant and Pratibha, had secured from the Home Secretary
the necessary permission to interview me in jail. But having come
to know about the hearing of the habeas corpus petition they
had come along to the Court.

After the hearing they came over to the jail for the formal
interview. I felt happy and proud that the events had not upset
Kamala, and that she had mentally prepared herself for the
inconvenience resulting from my incarceration.

WEDNESDAY, JULY 16

The two days since the preliminary hearing have passed away
quickly. All three of us kept pouring over the voluminous
law reports sent by our lawyers, Rama Jois and N. Santosh
Hegde (son of the former Supreme Court Judge, Justice K.S.
Hegde), in order to familiarise ourselves with legal precedents
bearing on our case.

My family sought another meeting with me, but the request was
turned down. So they decided to stay on till the disposal of the
habeas corpus petitions. I was told that Intelligence Department
people were pestering the jail authorities for the local address
of my family in Bangalore, presumably to harass the hosts.

THURSDAY, JULY 17

It must have been around 6.00 A.M. when we were all
woken up by deputy superintendent Desai and asked to
get ready to leave. "You have all been released", he told us.
"The superintendent will soon be coming to give you the
details". Desai did not try to conceal the cheerfulness in his
voice. Soon Chablani arrived, wreathed in smiles. He had been
woken up very early, the superintendent informed us, and intimat-
ed that all four of us—including Atalji—are to be released.

The news puzzled us more than it surprised us. We could
visualise three possibilities:

1. All M.Ps are being released in view of the impending
   Parliament session.
2. We are being released only to be rearrested; there are
   some very obvious flaws in the first detention order.
3. The Government of India is upset by the attitude of
   the Karnataka High Court during the preliminary hearing
   of the habeas corpus petitions and so perhaps would like

to detain us in Delhi or some other place outside the jurisdiction of this High Court.

We took our own time packing and had a leisurely breakfast. By the time Shyambabu completed his routine including the *asanas* it was past 9 o'clock. Co-prisoners Krishnappa, Venkata Rao and Shanker Lal who had been assigned duties in our ward as help-mates and who had become personally attached to all of us took leave of us and expressed their joy that our jail term was ending. "Who knows we may be back soon?" I remarked casually.

And it happened exactly that way. We had decided to go to Gopinath's residence. Desai got a taxi for us. But just as the taxi emerged from the jail compound and turned left on the main road, we found a posse of police blocking the way. A fleet of police vehicles lined the road. They had been waiting there since 6.30 A.M., we learnt later. A senior police official Naik, who was to give us company several times later, stepped forward to tell us: "I am very sorry. It is my unpleasant duty to arrest you again". Naik then requested us to board a police car, and directed the taxi to follow his car to the police station.

At the police station, Naik served fresh detention orders on us, under MISA, issued by the Government of India and signed by A.G. Sen, Deputy Secretary, Union Home Ministry. An additional paper delivered to us declared that our detention was necessary "for effectively dealing with the emergency". Both the orders, as also the order revoking the earlier detention, given to us by the superintendent are dated July 16. Thus the new detention order was issued at a time when we were already under detention. Under Sec. 16A of MISA, this declaration dispensed with the need to provide us with the grounds of detention.

Within fifteen or twenty minutes all the formalities were completed and we were driven back to the jail. After our luggage had been off-loaded we were reminded that at 10.30 A.M. we were to be produced in the High Court for the hearing of our habeas corpus petitions. Scene one of the day's farcical drama is over.

The court-room of the Chief Justice of Karnataka was packed. The spectators spilled over into the corridors and the staircase leading to the road. The gathering waved enthusiastically when we arrived. But neither they, nor even our counsel, were aware that the detenus arrested on June 26 by the Karnataka Government had been released, and that we were now guests of the Government of India, albeit in Bangalore.

The information about the change in our status as detenus was officially conveyed to the Court by the Attorney-General, Niren De. He had arrived in Bangalore the previous night. Presumably, he had personally brought the fresh detention orders from New Delhi as well as the decision regarding the revocation of earlier orders. As soon as the hearing began, Niren De rose to submit that he had a statement to make. De told the Court that the detention orders of June 26, 1975, which had been challenged in the writ petitions had been revoked by the Government of India; fresh detention orders had been made out and executed. Therefore, the pending writ petitions had become infructuous and should be dismissed.

Rama Jois, followed by all three of us, protested against what the Government had done and urged that we be permitted to amend our petitions in the light of the new developments.

Jois pointed out that the relief sought by the petitioners was not confined to having their detention orders quashed but also to having the two emergency proclamations declared invalid and to get the Ordinance[6] amending MISA struck down. Revocation of the original detention order met, if at all, only the prayer in respect of the impugned detention. The other issues still remained.

The Chief Justice maintained that filing a fresh petition would be the proper course in the situation. When it was pointed out to him that the detenus were facing difficulty in obtaining legal assistance, he said that necessary orders could be issued in that regard. Turning to the Attorney-General, he said: "I suppose there would be no objection to providing them necessary legal aid". The Attorney-General said he had none.

The Chief Justice thereafter dismissed the earlier writ petitions and issued a direction to the superintendent, Central Jail, Bangalore, that the four detenus be given due facilities for

---

[6] Making detention under the law non-justiciable, and doing away with the earlier obligation to furnish grounds of detention.

consultations with their counsel in order to enable them to file fresh petitions. With this, ended scene two of the day's Act.

In the jail superintendent's office, where we were having a cup of coffee with the jail authorities immediately on our return from the court, Mallaya, the Inspector-General of Prisons, remarked that he had a hunch that we would be transferred from Bangalore. "I am not sure", he says, "but I was asked by the authorities whether Atalji was in a position to move—and this makes me feel that a transfer is in the offing".

Actually, it seems, the Attorney-General had brought with him a transfer order also and while he was assuring the Court that he had no objection to the Court issuing directions to the jail superintendent, Bangalore, with regard to legal assistance for the detenus, he was committing a constructive contempt of the Court by misleading the Court.

This fact was agitated in the High Court the very next day through an application filed on behalf of Atalji the transfer order in respect of whom could not be enforced because the doctors would not permit his shifting. When the application came up before the High Court, the Court took a very serious view of the development and issued orders forthwith restraining the Government from transferring Atalji.

By lunch time, the transfer order arrived. It stated that we were to be "transferred to Rohtak by air".

A special Air Force plane took the three of us to Delhi. We were accompanied by the jail superintendent, Chablani, District Surgeon, Sadasiva Reddy, and Assistant Commissioner of Police, Naik.

The plane took off from the Air Force landing ground at Yerlanka at about 4.30 P.M. It was a Dakota and the weather was far from fair. So the flight was quite bumpy. We had a brief halt at Hyderabad for tea. The Air Force station at Hyderabad also supplied us with our dinner which we had on board.

It was around 11.30 P.M. when the aircraft landed at Palam technical area. The tarmac was wet with rain. It was drizzling when we got off the plane.

The Central Government's reception to us at Delhi was in sharp contrast to the Karnataka Government's sendoff. The three State officials accompanying us must have found it very conspicuous. A police inspector of the Delhi Administration

was sent to the airport with bald instructions that three prisoners
were to be transported from Palam to Rohtak. The inspector,
Inder Jeet Singh, told us later that he did not have even the
ghost of an idea who the prisoners were, or even as to the
category they belonged. The impression he had was that three
alleged smugglers were being transferred.

As we alighted from the aircraft, the officer stepped up to
inquire joyfully *"Kaun Kaun aaye hein?"* (Who all have come?)
As we came closer, he identified me and said a little more
deferentially *"Advani Sahab ko janta hoon; aur kaun Sahib hein?"*
(I know Advani; who are the others?). I introduced Shyambabu
and Dandavate to him. He then asked us to board a ramshackle truck that he had brought.

"Are we to go to Rohtak tonight or tomorrow?" we asked
him. "I do not know", he replied and added, "We shall be
going to the Palam police station first, and there we shall get
further instructions. Board the truck."

In contrast with the correct and courteous treatment shown
to us in Karnataka, the attitude of officialdom in New Delhi
was cavalier and even boorish. We all felt it, including the
Karnataka officials. Shyambabu was particularly annoyed. He
gave uninhibited expression to his annoyance by lashing out at
the police inspector. "I cannot go tonight; my health does
not permit it", he curtly told the officer. "And you must
arrange some other vehicle; we shall not go in this; we are
not prisoners, we are detenus", he added (This last remark of
his was often cited by Dandavate in a lighter vein later).

Inder Jeet Singh was evidently in no mood for a scrape
either with us or with his bosses. But his way of avoiding
trouble was not quite straight-forward. If he really had any
intention of taking us to the Palam police station, he abandoned it after sensing Shyambabu's mood. Without informing
us, he quietly told the driver of the van to take it straight to
Rohtak. He was later apologetic about it, but tried to explain
it away by saying that if we had gone to the police station and
tried for some alternative arrangements it would only have
meant a futile, sleepless night for all of us.

Neither the officer nor any of the three constables accompanying him was familiar with Rohtak. So they had to inquire
at a number of places about the location of the jail. It was
drizzling all through. The streets were naturally deserted at

that unearthly hour. So, it took quite some time, even after reaching Rohtak, to find the jail. It was about 2 o' clock in the morning when we finally reached the place.

Our first encounter with the jail authorities in Rohtak was far from happy. The deputy superintendent of the jail, Saini who was to complete the formalities regarding our entry, asked a convict warder to search our luggage. And what a search it was! Not satisfied with rummaging through our clothes and books, the warder began to examine the soles of our chappals to discover hidden papers. Shyambabu seething with pent up anger over the jerky journey and the sleepless night exploded at the deputy superintendent. Madhu Dandavate flung a good humoured barb at him remarking: "Mrs Gandhi has no doubt called for soul-searching; but that is s-o-u-l, and not s-o-l-e searching".

It was nearly 3.00 A.M. when we finally reached the barracks where Biju Patnaik and others were lodged and where we were to stay for the next ten weeks. Friends there had information that three or four detenus were expected, but they had no idea who they were or from which jail they were being transferred or whether they were fresh arrivals! Thus ended scene three of this day's drama.

FRIDAY, JULY 18, ROHTAK

It was a pleasure to meet friends and colleagues at Rohtak—that is, those of them who were still there. From among the political leaders picked up in Delhi in the first night's swoop, all senior leaders, barring Jayaprakash Narayan and Morarjibhai, had been brought to Rohtak. Chaudhri Charan Singh was not well and was therefore transferred to Tihar Jail in Delhi. J.P. and Morarjibhai had been taken to Sohna from where J.P. was later shifted to Chandigarh for treatment.

Many of those brought to Rohtak had also been transferred just two or three days before our arrival here. Chandra Shekhar has been moved to Patiala, K.R. Malkani to Hissar, and several Haryana leaders like Chaudhri Devi Lal, Mangal Sen and Chaudhri Mukhtiar Singh to other Haryana jails like Ambala and Mahendragarh. Raj Narain was taken to Delhi because of his appeal in the Supreme Court.

A galaxy of senior representatives of all major parties was still there—Asoka Mehta and Sikandar Bakht of the

Congress (O), Biju Patnaik and Piloo Mody of the BLD, Samar
Guha of the Socialist Party, Ram Dhan of the ruling Congress,
Bhai Mahavir of the Jana Sangh and Major Jaipal Singh of
the CPI(M). Besides, there was Bakshi Jagdev Singh, a Sikh
leader of Delhi who for some time seemed to be the odd man
out, but who with the passage of time endeared himself to
everyone by his amicable nature and winsome ways.

SATURDAY, JULY 19

In terms of company, the Rohtak jail had obvious advantages
over its Bangalore counterpart. But in terms of amenities for
inmates it was wanting. In Bangalore we were two in a room.
Here it was a kind of dormitory living with seven of us—
Patnaik, Bhai Mahavir, Ram Dhan, Jaipal Singh, Bakshi,
Dandavate and me in the larger room (which was originally the
entertainment centre of the jail), four others—Asoka Mehta,
Piloo Mody, Sikandar Bakht and Shyam Nandan Mishra—in
the smaller one (supposed to be the jail's library) and the
twelfth, Samar Guha, cooped up in his solitary cell (he had
opted for this in order to be able to write on a subject dear to
his heart, the mystery of Netaji's disappearance).

MISA detenus are covered by rules framed by the respective
States. In Karnataka, MISA detenus are classified into two
categories 'A' and 'B'. We were put in 'A' class which meant
provision of a cot, a mosquito net, a table, a chair and a cup-
board all of which are not available to 'B' class prisoners. In
the matter of food also there was difference. There is a schedule in accordance with which the quantum of cereals, vegetables, sugar, tea and coffee available to a detenu is
determined. In fact we learnt later from the jail authorities
that the food provided to 'B' class detenus cost 10 paise more
per meal than that given to 'A' class detenus. The cost in
the case of 'A' class detenus worked out to be Rs 6.27 (vege-
tarian) and Rs 8.10 (non-vegetarian) per head per day.

Since about a week earlier, interviews with family members
for MISA detenus had been prohibited altogether. Earlier,
one's kith and kin could meet a detenu at Rohtak periodically.
This rule was being observed by all the States under instructions
from the Centre.

In Haryana there was no classification of detenus. All those
held under MISA are placed in a single category entitling

them to a cot, a table and a chair by way of furniture but which in our case could not be provided because there was no space in the room which we occupied. But in the matter of food, instead of prescribing the quantum of each article, the rules laid down that each detenu would be given Rs. 4 per day for food and Re. 1 per day for sundry expenses. Compared to Karnataka, the kitchen we could run on this budget was naturally of a very inferior quality. Even so, Sikandar Bakht, who surpervised the arrangements in our ward, managed the kitchen wonderfully well. Some of the detenus whose indifferent health had prompted the jail doctor, Sen Gupta, to prescribe nourishing foods like milk and curds added their individual provisions to the pool enriching it qualitatively. Some others supplemented it with tinned supplies permitted from outside.

Besides MISA detenus, there were in Rohtak jail, about a hundred others arrested under the Defence of India Rules. Before we arrived, MISA detenus and DIR prisoners could meet but since a few days earlier strict "apartheid" had been in force. The barracks which housed the different categories of inmates were on either side of a spacious park, oblong in shape, with a tarred pathway running round it. Even when one was having a stroll, one was required to keep to the respective side of the quadrangle and not to go round the park and meet the others lest we should hatch a fresh "conspiracy".

MONDAY, JULY 21

The monsoon session of Parliament is due to commence today. It would be the strangest in our Parliament's history. All normal rules of procedure would be suspended. There would be no question hour. No private member would be permitted to raise any matter. Only Government business would be transacted. All this would be accomplished by adopting a formal motion given notice of by the Minister of Parliamentary Affairs, Raghuramaiah in the Lok Sabha, and the Minister of State of Parliamentary Affairs, Om Mehta, in the Rajya Sabha.

Worse still, the proceedings could not be reported freely and faithfully; only ministerial speeches could be published. No formal sanction of either House of Parliament was considered necessary. One does not know whether the Lok Sabha Speaker and the Rajya Sabha Chairman have formally acquiesced in it, or whether their consent was taken for granted by the Government. Ours is a Parliament whose Presiding Officers like the late Vithalbhai Patel put even the British Viceroy in his place, and made it clear to him that within the precincts of the House only one writ could run—that of the Presiding Officer. Now we have Presiding Officers like Goude Murahari, Deputy Chairman of the Rajya Sabha who at Madras the other day tried to justify not only the emergency but the detention of M.Ps as well. The Speaker of the Lok Sabha, G.S. Dhillon, was also going round the country making speeches smacking of cowardly conformity.

In his work "Representative Government", John Stuart Mill spelt out the functions of Parliament thus :

> Instead of the function of government for which it is radically unfit, the proper office of a representative assembly is to watch and control the government; to throw the light of publicity on its acts; to compel a full exposition and justification of all of them which any one considers questionable; to censure them if found condemnable, and, if the men who compose the government abuse their trust, or fulfil it in a manner which conflicts with the deliberate sense of the nation, to expel them from office, and either expressly or virtually appoint their successors.

In a parliamentary democracy, Parliament does not govern; it watches and controls government. It does so by "throw(ing) the light of publicity on its acts" and "compel(ling) full exposition and justification of all of them (such acts) which one considers questionable". The Indira Gandhi Government's anger with Parliament is because Parliament tried to discharge these functions.

TUESDAY, JULY 22 TO SATURDAY, JULY 26

All attention was rivetted on Parliament proceedings. All India Radio and the Indian Press would publish only ministerial speeches and the names of M.Ps who participated in the various debates. Only the foreign media provide other vital information.

Thus the boycott of the session by the opposition parties

except of course the Communists, in the Rajya Sabha on July 22 and in the Lok Sabha on July 23 was covered only by BBC and Voice of America. In the Rajya Sabha, the walk out was led by N.G. Goray and in the Lok Sabha by Tridib Kumar Chaudhry. The two leaders made identical statements protesting against the emergency, detention of Parliament members, censorship of parliamentary proceedings and walked out of the chambers along with almost all opposition members except those of the CPI.

During the week apart from approving the Proclamation of Emergency, Parliament also amended the Maintenance of Internal Security Act to dispense with the constitutional obligation to furnish a detenu with the grounds of his or her detention or to refer his or her case to an advisory board. Yet another amendment made in MISA was aimed at preventing the victim from invoking any natural law or common law right to secure his or her release. The Lok Sabha passed the Bill this week while the Rajya Sabha will adopt it next week.

Another important measure that went through Parliament in the absence of the opposition was the Constitution (39th Amendment) Bill. The Bill made the Emergency Proclamation non-justiciable. The 39th Amendment Bill (when enacted it became the 38th Amendment) protected the President's "satisfaction" from judicial scrutiny not only in the matter of Article 352 (Proclamation of Emergency) but also with regard to Article 123 (Promulgation of Ordinances) and Article 356 (Imposition of President's Rule). The Governors' Ordinance-making power was also similarly protected.

SATURDAY, JULY 26

Appa Ghatate came to meet me. He informed me about the Karnataka High Court's displeasure at the way we were transferred from Bangalore and its stay order with regard to Vajpayee's transfer. He gave me a fresh draft of a habeas corpus petition and suggested that all three of us, moved here from Bangalore, send the petitions from the jail.

MONDAY, JULY 28 TO FRIDAY, AUGUST 1

Parliament's session kept extending itself. This seemed somewhat surprising. The essential business which Government wanted to hustle through has been completed—approval of the emergency, making the emergency non-justiciable, amendment of MISA and the Defence of India Act. Parliament was kept busy this week with innocuous measures such as the Delhi Sales Tax Bill, the Banking Service Commission Bill, the Employees' State Insurance (Amendment) Bill, Agricultural Refinance Corporation (Amendment) Bill—none of which had been announced in the agenda earlier outlined for the session and none of which was in any way urgent.

We kept speculating on the likely reasons for the session being extended repeatedly. Do they propose to push through a radical overhaul of the Constitution itself, while the opposition is kept out?

MONDAY, AUGUST 4

The guessing game ended when in the Punjabi news bulletin put out by All India Radio at 13.40 today it was reported that the Law Minister, Gokhale, had introduced a Bill in the Lok Sabha seeking to amend the Representation of the People Act and the Indian Penal Code to redefine, with retrospective effect :

(a) when a person becomes a candidate in an election,
(b) what assistance given by a government official to a candidate would be deemed corrupt, and
(c) when a Government servant's resignation would become effective.

A couple of friends and I heard the report in Punjabi and again in Urdu (in the 13.50 bulletin). But, curiously, when the entire 'company' in the barracks clustered round the transistor to listen to the English bulletin at 14.00 hrs. they got only a bald statement that the Law Minister had introduced a Bill to amend the Representation of the People Act and the Indian Penal Code (IPC). Not a word was said about the contents of the amendments. The same silence was maintained in all subsequent news bulletins, at 15.00 hrs, 18.00 hrs and 20.45 hrs.

Evidently, some one in the News Services Division of All India Radio had bungled by allowing the Punjabi and Urdu Division bulletins to describe the proposed amendments of the election law. Anyone could see what the Bill was intended to achieve. It was a shameless attempt to undo the Allahabad verdict on Indira Gandhi's electoral corruption. It was like amending the rules of a game and applying the new rules to a match already played with a view to declaring the loser the winner. All the loud-mouthed protests that the emergency has nothing to do with the Allahabad case or with Indira Gandhi's person are now dramatically repudiated by the Government itself with this Bill. No wonder, the Chief Censor promptly clamped down on the radio and the Press and sought to prevent the people from knowing what was happening.

Voice of America, BBC, Radio Australia, and other foreign media, however, reported the contents of the amending measures. They did not also omit to explain their implications and effect on the Allahabad verdict.

We learnt today that rules regarding interviews have been changed again. Detenus would now be permitted to meet family members (father, mother, wife, children—but not brothers or sisters) once in a calendar month. The change followed a writ filed by Morarjibhai's daughter-in-law in the Delhi High Court against the denial of the facility.

TUESDAY, AUGUST 5

The daily papers referred to the Bill introduced by Gokhale in Parliament the previous day but confined themselves to the cryptic description permitted by the Censor, namely that the Bill sought to amend certain provisions of the Representation of the People Act and the IPC. Foreign media, however, feeling protected by the guidelines issued by the Censor at the commencement of the Parliament session, which did not prohibit publication of official Bills, kept giving the full details of the measures and their implications.

WEDNESDAY, AUGUST 6

Sensing perhaps that the position of the Indian media had become ridiculous and untenable, the Censor allowed the publication of the details of the amendments. All India Radio in its afternoon bulletin described the provisions but without any explanation.

THURSDAY, AUGUST 7

The daily newspapers from Delhi published the details of the Election Laws (Amendment) Bill, three days after it had been introduced in the Lok Sabha and two days after it was passed by the house. A former Minister, Mohan Dharia, put up a stiff opposition to the Bill attacking it as meant to subserve the interests of an individual. He moved an amendment seeking to obviate its retrospective application to cases already decided by a High Court. The amendment was supported by Sher Singh.

Despite the opposition, the Bill was passed after a brief debate, the only participants apart from the above two dissentients being Inderjit Gupta (C.P.I.) and G. Viswanathan (A.D.M.K.).

In both the Houses the debate on the Bill which might well be described as the prime legislative measure of the session was deliberately kept short and formal. Not a single Congress member was permitted to speak, except, of course, the Minister. For the sake of form, two members of the pseudo-opposition were made to lend support to the Bill. In the Lok Sabha the duty was performed by Inderjit Gupta and Viswanathan, whereas in the Rajya Sabha, Bhupesh Gupta (C.P.I.) and Kumbhare (Republican) were chosen for the task.

The seeming disinterestedness of members in a matter as vital as the Election Law was in sharp contrast to their enthusiastic participation in the discussion on Salaries and Allowances of Members of Parliament (Amendment) Bill passed by the Lok Sabha on August 6 and by the Rajya Sabha on August 7. As many as 15 members participated in the debate in the Lok Sabha and some 10 members in the Rajya Sabha. It was to raise the emoluments of M.Ps.

Foreign broadcasting media as well as All India Radio had one more surprise for their listeners today—introduction in Parliament of yet another Amendment to the Constitution. This was the 40th Amendment Bill (when enacted it became the 39th Amendment). It was the strangest-ever amendment of the Constitution to be considered by Parliament. It aimed at preventing the Courts from hearing petitions challenging the election of the President, Vice-President and M.Ps holding the office of Prime Minister and the Speaker of the Lok Sabha. These elections, the amendment provided, could be challenged only before a special forum to be created by Parliament.

The most obnoxious feature of the Bill was its clause 4 which declared that all decisions taken by a High Court with regard to the election of any of these four dignitaries would be deemed null and void! Under the cloak of exercising its amending power, Parliament had thus usurped the powers of the judiciary. A Court judgment can be annulled only by a superior Court following the appropriate judicial processes and not by the legislature on the basis of a majority vote. But this is precisely what Parliament did when it incorporated this provision into the Constitution.

We were unable to comprehend the need for such a drastic and crude amendment of the Constitution. Having already amended the Election Law and made sure that the Supreme Court would have no option but to set aside the Allahabad High Court judgment in Indira Gandhi's election case, why did the Government have to resort to this device which suffered from a two-fold infirmity. The amendment to the Election Law could be justified, as it had been, on the ground that it was necessary to iron out ambiguities, whereas this amendment of the Constitution benefited only one individual: Indira Gandhi. Its clause 4 applied to just one judgment, that of Justice Sinha in Indira Gandhi's case. It was an unabashed abuse of a servile parliamentary majority to promote the interests of a single individual. The fig leaf of larger purpose had been dropped. Secondly, on the face of it, the legality of the amendment was very doubtful.

When we were discussing this point, Bhai Mahavir recounted an interesting story. In Western society, the mother-in-law is a common object of ridicule. A person received a telegram saying that his mother-in-law had suddenly died. She had been living with his family but had gone visiting some friends. The wire added: "Should she be buried or cremated? Awaiting instructions". Without a moment's hesitation, so runs the story, the bereaved son-in-law wired back: "Take no chances, do both". The Law Minister, Gokhale, was evidently taking no chances with the law, Mahavir commented.

After adopting the Bill, the Lok Sabha adjourned *sine die*.

FRIDAY, AUGUST 8

Today was to be the last day of the Rajya Sabha session after passing the Constitution Amendment Bill aimed at (as BBC and other foreign media described it) absolving Indira Gandhi of the charges of electoral corruption. The House was to adjourn *sine die*. In theory, the Indian Constitution was still republican. For all practical purposes, however, the law was being so distorted as to make Indira Gandhi like the Queen of England, legally unassailable for any wrong she committed. What else should be done to put the constitutional imprimatur to such an Indira-can-do-no-wrong concept? The Lok Sabha had adjourned. But the Rajya Sabha was still in session. The Government announced today that the Rajya Sabha session would be extended by another day. As had become the practice no one was given a clue to the extension of the session.

If the subject matter of the amendment had been known, Bhupesh Gupta, leader of Her Majesty's loyal opposition, the CPI, would not have spoken the way he did on Friday. When the 40th Amendment Bill was being discussed in the Rajya Sabha, he defended it with zest and gusto, denouncing those who had called upon Indira Gandhi to resign "only because of a High Court judgment". The Prime Minister must be protected, Bhupesh Gupta pompously declared. There should be no need for the person holding this high office to go to court, he said. Blissfully unaware of what the Government proposed to bring to the House the very next day, Bhupesh Gupta added that the Prime Minister after all was not claiming immunity from criminal or civil proceedings if she committed a crime.

SATURDAY, AUGUST 9

On this last day of the Rajya Sabha session, the Law Minister produced the most outrageous of his constitutional monstrosities, the Constitution (41st Amendment) Bill.

That such a measure should have been conceived is itself shocking. It destroys the republican character of our Constitution. On the pretext of protecting the Prime Minister from unnecessary litigation, it seeks to legalise crimes committed by her or him. The same protection is conferred upon the President and the State Governors. At present, Article 361 of the Constitution confers immunity on the President and the Governors in respect of criminal or civil proceedings, but only during their term of office. No such immunity is provided to the Prime Minister or the Chief Ministers who are essentially political officers as answerable to law as other citizens. Equality before the law is an essential ingredient of republicanism.

The rationale for the protection given to the President and the Governors is that they are only constitutional heads of State who do not perform executive functions. Even so, the immunity is only for the duration of their tenure. The new amendment, however, seeks to absolve the President and the Governors of responsibility for any crime they may have committed before assuming the office and after laying it down. The person holding the office of Prime Minister is put on par with them, for purposes of the immunity. It is said that the Bill was thought of after the Lok Sabha adjourned. The House may again be convened for a brief sitting to pass this Bill.

Looking at the 40th and 41st Amendments, one is reminded of Procrustes, the fabled Greek robber who used to stretch or cut his captives' limbs to make them fit his bed. The Constitution is being twisted and tailored, mangled and mutilated to subserve the interests of a single individual.

Appa Ghatate came again to meet me today. Accompanying him were my wife and children who had availed themselves of the changed rules with regard to interviews with detenus. Even so, they had difficulty in obtaining the necessary permission. The amended rules said that only two persons from the family would be allowed. So along with Kamala, it had to be either Jayant (9½) or Pratibha (8) but not both. I was surprised to learn that through a colleague in Parliament, a Minister's intervention was sought to sort out the problem but the minister expressed helplessness. The local officials, it seemed, were more understanding. So both children could accompany their mother.

Appa and Kamala tell me that Atalji has been brought to Delhi. He is at the All India Institute of Medical Sciences.

FRIDAY, AUGUST 15

The Rohtak jail has a television set for the use of prisoners. This is kept in the canteen adjoining the smaller room allocated to us. Early in the morning we all gathered in the canteen to watch Indira Gandhi's performance at the flag hoisting ceremony in connection with our Independence Day. This was her first public meeting since the declaration of the emergency. Her statements and utterances during the past fortnight had been particularly bitter about J.P. and the opposition parties, the Jana Sangh and the RSS in particular. Only the previous night All India Radio broadcast a recorded speech of hers made to a conference of Catholics at Vigyan Bhawan in New Delhi. She lashed out at J.P., and the RSS. J.P. is no Gandhian, she declared. And the RSS wants to wipe out the minorities, she told the Catholics.

We expected to see Indira Gandhi in the same vitriolic mood this morning. But we were happily disappointed. The speech from the ramparts of the Red Fort was in a conspicuously low key. Of course, there was a reference to the opposition at the outset, with Indira Gandhi making a special effort to look enraged. But the worked-up wrath impressed no one. The audience could make neither head nor tail of what Indira Gandhi had in her mind when she spoke about some opposition leader having ridiculed the national tricolour as "a rag". Even we, representing practically the entire political spectrum in the country, could not comprehend the allusion and kept asking one another who the person could be. Ultimately Dandavate had an explanation. He said that a member of the Dalit Panthers, a break-away group of the Republican Party in Maharashtra had once made some remark of that kind. Dandavate added: "So far as I recall, the person belonged to the pro-CPI faction of the Dalit Panthers, and is an Indira supporter!" It is astounding that the Prime Minister found it handy to use against opposition parties which were in no way connected with the group or the person. Since we have no means of repudiating such slander the lies might one day pass for truth. It was the Prime Minister's formal address to the nation, the first major one since she imposed the emergency, which was claimed to have been provoked by the opposition. And the only accusation she hurls at her victims to substantiate the charge of irresponsible and anti-national conduct is this outright lie! It must have given to the thinking sections of our people a measure of the deceit and untruth which marked Indira Gandhi's campaign of calumny against the opposition.

However, but for this initial outburst, Indira Gandhi's speech is surprisingly mellow. As we emerged from the room where we watched the television programme, Asoka Mehta remarked to me : "Why is she so subdued? Why indeed?"

It wasn't long before Mehta's query was answered. At about 8.40 A.M. I casually switched on to the Voice of America. The 8.30 news bulletin was coming to a close and I could only catch the headlines. I was stunned to hear the news reader announce that in an early-morning *coup* in Dacca, Sheikh Mujibur Rahman had been killed and that the army had taken over in Bangladesh! We were at our breakfast then. I shared the news with Asoka Mehta and other friends whose reaction like mine was one of shocked disbelief. "Are you sure the news bulletin

said that?" several of them asked me almost in chorus. The
scepticism was not without reason.

Four days earlier there was an amusing episode. In between
listening to recitals of classical music of which he is very fond,
Dandavate that night hanced to hear a news broadcast
announcing that eight Cabinet ministers had submitted their
resignations to the Prime Minister. The broadcast also said the
Ministers had resigned to help the Government carry out its
economic programme. It was past 11 o'clock and most of us
were preparing for bed when Dandavate brought the news.
Two days earlier when Ghatate met me he also mentioned that
New Delhi was bristling with rumours of an impending Cabinet
reshuffle. Dandavate's report thus fitted in with what had been
talked about. We speculated about the possible dropouts. "Are
you sure they are Cabinet ministers and not simply eight
ministers?" one of us asked Dandavate. He was certain it was
'Cabinet ministers'. And so it was. But where Dandavate had
erred was that the Cabinet was of Argentina, not India ! It was
only the following morning when Asoka Mehta switched on his
transistor—which he did very rarely—that we learnt that eight
Argentine Cabinet ministers had resigned! So when I mentioned
about the Bangladesh *coup*, there was an undercurrent of understandable doubt among my colleagues strong enough to make
me also wait for confirmation of what I had heard.

I began trying to get a medium wave station to see if any
regional language broadcast would be available. Around 8.50
A.M. there was a Marathi news bulletin to which I listened
intently and which said Sheikh Mujib had sent a message of
greetings to the President on the occasion of our Independence
Day! Soon, however, I got Voice of America again and then
BBC also. Both gave full accounts of the gory events in Dacca
that morning. The reports mentioned that Bangladesh radio had
confirmed the killing of Mujib and the takeover by the
military. That solved the mystery which Asoka Mehta had
noticed. It explained why Indira Gandhi sounded so sober in
the morning. When she came to the Red Fort function she was
already aware of the macabre incidents in Dacca. In a democracy hostility to those in power, justified or unjustified,
manifests itself in a variety of ways. There are a number of
safety valves for popular discontent to vent itself. Clog the
openings and you run the risk of explosions. This is exactly
what Mujib did when earlier in the year he threw democracy

overboard, put his political opponents in jail, suppressed the press and declared Bangladesh a one-party state. The fact that Mujib had done so with the full approval of Indira Gandhi, if not, as is widely believed, at her instigation and advice might have been weighing on her mind when she made the speech.

All India Radio's handling of the cataclysmic happenings in Bangladesh was characteristic of the manner in which news media in a totalitarian society function. It took AIR full five hours even to report the *coup*. It reported the take-over by the army at 11.00 A.M. Even then it did not disclose Mujib's murder. There were conflicting reports about Mujib, it merely said.

So we kept listening to foreign broadcasting stations throughout the day for news about Bangladesh. Dacca Radio itself broadcast statements by the three Service chiefs, the head of the police and others swearing allegiance to the new regime with Khondakar Mushtaq Ahmed as the formal Head of State.

In its 6 P.M. news bulletin All India Radio made its first disclosure of Mujib's death. It was a bald announcement without a word of shock or grief over the dastardly event. There was no mention of condolences by the Prime Minister or the President. Worse still, the Independence Day evening party at Rashtrapati Bhawan was held as scheduled.

The BBC and VOA, on the other hand, paid fulsome tributes to Mujib's memory through special bulletins broadcast in the evening. A BBC programme also recalled the affectionate ovation accorded to him when he first reached Dacca after the liberation of Bangladesh and his release from a Pakistani jail.

SATURDAY, AUGUST 16

In its Independence Day Number, "Socialist India" which is the weekly journal of the ruling Congress Party, published a long interview with the Prime Minister. Most of it is a rehash of what Indira Gandhi has been saying day after day. There are, however, some quaint tidbits which are worth taking note of. One of them is: "The Jana Sangh was trying to spread the canard that I drink (liquor). Actually neither my family nor I smoke or take any alcoholic drinks. My sons don't drink even tea or coffee".

No one in the Jana Sangh has ever dwelt on Indira Gandhi's personal habits. But the remark reminds me of a minor fracas between two senior Congress members of Parliament of which I was an eye witness. The incident dates back to July 1972. I was a member of a parliamentary delegation visiting Czechoslovakia led by the Lok Sabha Speaker, Gurdial Singh Dhillon. At a dinner hosted for us at the Indian Embassy in Prague, the Indian Ambassador, Desai, happened to mention casually that when the Prime Minister was in Czechoslovakia a month or so earlier, the toasts at the formal banquet were drunk with water!

The Ambassador's statement evoked a derisive chuckle from one of our colleagues, Buddha Priya Maurya, now a close confidant of Indira Gandhi. "Why water? Why not wine?" he asked. The Ambassador discreetly chose not to reply. But Purabi Mukerjee, another Congress member of the delegation, intervened somewhat belligerently: "For the simple reason that she doesn't drink". Maurya was unimpressed. He persisted: "Who told you? Not that I object to her drinking. I myself am no teetotaller. But I do not indulge in such hypocrisy as 'toasting with water' ".

MONDAY, AUGUST 18

After remaining tongue-tied for three days, the Government of India, through an External Affairs Ministry spokesman, expressed sorrow at the death of Mujibur Rahman and his family.

MONDAY, AUGUST 25

Today is a crucial day. The Supreme Court is to resume the hearing of Indira Gandhi's appeal against the Allahabad High Court judgment. I have been trying to keep track of all news bulletins of All India Radio as well as of foreign media for news of the event. The foreign media in their morning bulletins said the case was due to commence today and also gave a brief resume of the events connected with the judgment. But All India Radio has been keeping quiet. There is no news of Court proceedings either at 6.00 P.M. or 9.00 P.M. We are disappointed when BBC also failed to mention anything about the case in its evening bulletins. At 9.00 P.M., however, Voice of America reports that because of a controversy following the "frisking" of lawyers, the case commenced several hours late. We learnt that the Bar Association, in protest against the humiliating search to which all visitors to the Court including lawyers and journalists had been subjected on the preceding Monday when the proceedings began, decided to boycott the case. The boycott decision was formally conveyed to the Chief Justice who later revoked the search order. But as the revocation decision came late, the Bar had no opportunity of rescinding its boycott decision in time for the commencement of the hearing. So the case had to be adjourned to enable members of the Bar Association to reassemble and formally revoke its earlier resolution! At the meeting where the boycott decision was taken, an angry lawyer had said: "Who is sought to be protected, and from whom? The Prime Minister is not coming to the Court. Is this all for Sanjay?"

TUESDAY, AUGUST 26

All India Radio's morning bulletin carries a brief report on Monday's proceedings in the Supreme Court. We are surprised that the Press also is permitted to publish a brief resume of the hearings. The Government is said to be confident that the 39th Amendment would clinch the issue in Indira Gandhi's favour, and within a few days all would be over. That is perhaps the reason why censorship has been somewhat relaxed in this case.

In the afternoon Jaipal Singh's wife comes to meet him. The major mentions later that his wife is a first cousin of Bhupesh Gupta. Bhupesh met her a couple of days earlier, and, according to her, had been expressing unhappiness over what was happening particularly that Marxists and trade unionists had also been detained. Bhupesh told her that he expected all detenus to be released within a month. The Major's wife also said that official New Delhi was feeling greatly unnerved by the Bangladesh events.

In the evening BBC reports that Kuldip Nayar has been arrested under MISA. The report gives no reason for Nayar's arrest. But it is known that immediately after the imposition of the emergency, Nayar had taken the initiative in convening a meeting of journalists which urged the Government to remove the curbs imposed on the press. Besides, Nayar has been writing articles which though passed by the censor are seen by the authorities as sly attacks on the emergency! On July 3, he wrote an article under the heading "Not Enough, Mr. Bhutto". On July 10, he wrote a piece on the American bicentenary with focus on the civil liberties movement in that country. A more recent article on July 17 was addressed to students exhorting them to work for a cause and not merely their careers.

WEDNESDAY, AUGUST 27

Piloo Mody mentions that in the Central Hall of Parliament stories have been circulating that Piloo and Biju Patnaik are feeling very depressed in jail, that Piloo particularly has been so upset that he has sought permission to have his dogs brought to the jail. These are some of the snippets he got from his wife who visited him a few days ago.

So far as the reports of Piloo's and Biju's depression is concerned, none of us are taken in by it. Far from being depressed, they have been exuding buoyancy and good cheer which are proving infectious. Considering the life-style which they are used to, their adaptability to the inconveniences of prison life is amazing and admirable. To say that jail life has affected their morale is too cheap a jibe to be paid attention to.

"But what's this about the dogs?" I asked Piloo. "When my wife saw me last", Mody explained, "I enquired about the dogs, and told my wife 'why not bring them here when you come next'. Pointing to the Intelligence man in the vicinity, I added 'of course, if he has no objection'."

The dialogue has evidently been reported to the appropriate quarters who avidly jumped to the desired conclusion that Mody was in a blue mood.

THURSDAY, AUGUST 28

Bakshi Jagdev Singh's family comes to meet him in the afternoon. Apart from eatables, they have brought with them a few magazines, and the latest copy of the *Hindustan Times Evening News*.

The *Evening News* is a surprise packet. Its front page carries four items, all relating to Sanjay Gandhi, his views on nationalisation, on the C.P.I., on Opposition parties, on the public sector, on industrial licensing and what not. The views expressed are astoundingly unorthodox. In the suffocating climate of conformism obtaining in the country the latest version of *Sanjaya Uvach*[7] is like a whiff of fresh air merely because it is non-conformist. The merits of the opinions expressed do not matter.

---

[7] "Sanjay speaks" literally. The Bhagavat Gita is narrated as a collection of Lord Krishna's sermons to Arjun, recounted to the Kuru King by Sanjay.

SUNDAY, AUGUST 31

Today is a sad day for Indian journalism. The *Shankar's Weekly*, the only cartoon weekly in the country, has decided to wind up. If Shankar and his journal are to be fitted into an ideological camp, it will be the same camp to which Indira Gandhi claims to belong. But even he feels so suffocated in the present atmosphere that he has chosen to fold his journal. The last issue, dated August 31, carries an editorial captioned "Farewell". Even the word emergency does not find a place in the editorial. But there can scarcely be a more devastating indictment of the emergency than this piece. Shankar writes, inter alia:

> In our first editorial we made the point that our function was to make our readers laugh—at the world, at pompous leaders, at humbug, at foibles, at ourselves. But, what are the people who have developed a sense of humour. It is a people with certain civilised norms of behaviour, where there is tolerance and a dash of compassion.
>
> Dictatorships cannot afford laughter because people may laugh at the dictator, and that wouldn't do. In all the years of Hitler, there never was a good comedy, not a good cartoon, not a parody, not a spoof.
>
> From this point, the world and sadly enough India have become grimmer. Humour, wherever it is there, is encapsuled. Language itself has become functional, each profession developing its own jargon. Outside of the society of brother-economists, an economist is a stranger, floundering in uncharted territory, uncertain of himself, fearful of non-economic language. It is the same for lawyers, doctors, teachers, journalists and such like.

Shankar is not the only journalist feeling uneasy and out-of-depth in the present atmosphere. The *States*, a weekly founded by Durga Das, has also closed down. I am sure the annual report of the Registrar of Newspapers for 1975-76 will have a sorry but significant story to tell. When Hitler assumed power, Germany's tally of newspapers and periodicals was 4,700. By the time the Nazi nightmare ended, the number had dwindled to less than a thousand. The same might happen here if the trend persists.

MONDAY, SEPTEMBER 1

One more *coup* has been reported, abortive though. It is in Ecuador this time. Looking back, August seems to have been a month of *coups*. There have been a series of forcible ousters of established governments.

SATURDAY, SEPTEMBER 6

Kamala, Jayant and Pratibha came to meet me. It is Pratibha's birthday. She has brought a cake for us. My sister Sheela also has come from Baroda to meet me.

Kamala informs me that Nana Deshmukh was arrested on August 29. He is detained in Tihar Jail in Delhi.

Ghatate has gone to Nagpur. He has deputed Shiv Kumar to meet me and apprise me of the progress made in Bangalore in regard to our habeas corpus petition. The preliminary hearing has been fixed for September 10. According to Shiv Kumar, Nanaji was apprehended because a Jana Sangh worker who was being tailed by intelligence men went to meet him without shedding the tail as he ought to have tried to. Arrested along with Nanaji were two other senior party activists, Krishna Lal Maini and Krishan Lal Sharma.

WEDNESDAY, SEPTEMBER 10

BBC reports that arguments in the Delhi High Court in Kuldip Nayar's habeas corpus petition have concluded and that the judgment has been reserved. It is likely to be pronounced within a week.

FRIDAY, SEPTEMBER 12

Biju Patnaik receives a message from New Delhi through a Haryana Minister. The Central Government is concerned that Biju is not keeping good health. The Minister conveys that if Patnaik so desires he can be shifted to Delhi and kept under house arrest. The preceding week Patnaik's wife had come to meet him. She had mentioned that she had had a talk with the Home Minister, Brahmananda Reddy during which he suggested house arrest for Biju Patnaik. Patnaik flared up at her for having met the Home Minister. So the offer is now made through official sources, though informally. Patnaik again rejected it as categorically as before.

BBC reports that Kuldip Nayar has been released. It gives a brief background of the case and adds that it is not known whether the High Court will still pronounce on his petition.

SUNDAY, SEPTEMBER 14

The morning dailies carry an interesting news item. It is reported by all the papers that Sanjay Gandhi has carried out an aerial survey of flood-affected areas of Bihar. The report adds : "Shri Gandhi was accompanied by the Bihar Chief Minister Dr. Jagannath Mishra and the P.C.C. Chief Sitaram Kesari". Significant, isn't it?

Shadows of coming events. "Indira Gandhi's buildup began in an identical manner", Patnaik comments.

MONDAY, SEPTEMBER 15

An interview call comes for Piloo Mody. It's his wife. He returns even more elated than usual. "My dogs also had come", he announces proudly. "All four of them".

BBC reports in the evening that the Delhi High Court has held Kuldip Nayar's detention invalid, and has admonished the Government for breach of courtesy inasmuch as it has failed even to inform the Court in advance about Nayar's release.

TUESDAY, SEPTEMBER 16

The papers carry not a word about the High Court judgment in Nayar's case.

Ghatate comes to meet me. Our case has been posted for September 29, he tells us. The Karnataka High Court has directed that we be taken to Bangalore by September 22. Vajpayee has communicated to the court his inability to be present because of indifferent health. Ghatate also explains how the Government was snubbed by the Delhi High Court in the Nayar case. The Government counsel tried desperately to dissuade the Court from giving an adverse verdict by arguing that as the detenu had already been released, no judgment was called for. The High Court did not accept the Government's contention. It pulled up the authorities for breach of courtesy and pronounced the judgment holding the detention invalid.

Ghatate mentions that M.C. Chagla has agreed to argue our petition in the Bangalore High Court.

After my family met me ten days ago, I am told Kamala has written three letters to me but got no reply. I am surprised because I have not received a single letter. I recall further that I wrote to her on September 8. I enquire from the jail authorities and I am told that there has been a change in the arrangements for censoring our mail as a result of which letters are indeed being delayed. Now all letters from MISA detenus in Rohtak are routed through the censor in Chandigarh. The jail superintendent offered no explanation for the change. Earlier, the letters were being censored at the Deputy Commissioner's office in Rohtak itself.

WEDNESDAY, SEPTEMBER 17

Persistent and probing enquiries made by some of us about the reason for the change in the censorship set-up reveals interesting information.

The Government of India has been led to believe that political detenus at Rohtak are unable to bear the rigours of jail life and are cracking up! The jail authorities have told them that their information is entirely without foundation. The detenus are in excellent spirits. Recent events have, if at all, only hardened their attitude. The conflicting reports are now sought to be sorted out by subjecting the correspondence to expert psycho-analysis. A special department has been set up for this purpose at Chandigarh. An unconfirmed report we got later said that the Chandigarh censor set-up is being run by the Research and Analysis Wing (RAW).

I do not know how fruitful the exercise was for Government. For us, certainly, it was an abominable nuisance. Some letters from Delhi reached me after three weeks. Some letters have not been delivered at all. Immediately after the Karnataka court hearing on September 10, our lawyer Rama Jois wrote a letter, dated September 10, informing us of the next hearing on September 29. That letter reached me on September 21.

FRIDAY, SEPTEMBER 19

As it is now certain that Shyam Nandan Mishra, Dandavate and I would soon be going to Bangalore it has been decided that senior party representatives at Rohtak jointly take stock of the situation and discuss alternative strategies.

Accordingly, we have had three sessions each lasting two to three hours on successive days to discuss the following subjects

on the assumption that after the Supreme Court decision
(which we suspected would be in Indira Gandhi's favour), most
of the detenus would be released:

   (a) What should be our attitude towards the emergency;
   (b) how should we proceed further in the matter of inter-
       party relations (among opposition parties); and
   (c) how should we plan our election strategy.

Participants in this discussion were Asoka Mehta, S.N.
Mishra, Sikandar Bakht, Biju Patnaik, Piloo Mody, Samar
Guha, Madhu Dandavate, Bhai Mahavir and myself. At one
session, Ram Dhan and Jaipal Singh also joined us.

SATURDAY, SEPTEMBER 20

All India Radio and the daily papers report that Nana
Deshmukh has been arrested. The publication of the news is
intriguing. Not a single arrest has been announced in all these
three months, not even that of J P. Publication of names of
detenus is strictly prohibited. Besides, Nanaji's arrest is now
three weeks old. He was arrested on August 29.

It seems reports in the foreign Press of the Lok Sangharsh
Samiti's underground activity have been greatly annoying the
Government. Prominent among the underground leaders are
Nana Deshmukh and George Fernandes. Publication of the
news of Nanaji's arrest is intended to impress foreign audiences
that underground activity is being effectively curbed. Patnaik
thinks that the Government will implicate Nanaji in some
conspiracy cases. We learnt later that Deshmukh is detained
under MISA, but has also been charged under certain provisions
of the DIR.

In the evening, the jail superintendent arrives accompanied
by a police official from Delhi, Jetley, to inform us that we
would be taken to Bangalore by air on Monday, September 22,
morning. The plane would be leaving Delhi around 7.00 A.M.
He asked us whether we would like to leave Rohtak on Monday
morning itself, or whether we would like to go to Delhi on
Sunday, and spend the night there. We decided to leave on
Monday morning itself.

The Delhi police's solicitude this time is in marked contrast
to the tardiness they had betrayed last time. After our arrival

at Rohtak, Mishra and Dandavate addressed a joint letter to the Speaker, Lok Sabha, referring to the cavalier treatment meted out to us. May be, the letter has brought about the change.

SUNDAY, SEPTEMBER 21

The *Sunday Standard*, New Delhi, carries an interesting excerpt from D.P Mishra's recently published autobiography "Living An Era". Mishra who was Indira Gandhi's principal political lieutenant at the time of the Congress split has reminisced about the days of the independence struggle against the British and unwittingly, I presume, sketched for us a striking parallel to recent events. He recalls Mahatmaji's arrest just after the Dandi March, and writes:

> On May 4, at 45 minutes past midnight, the district magistrate of Surat, two police officers armed with pistols and 30 policemen armed with rifles surrounded Gandhi's hut. The British officer woke him up and arrested him under Regulation XXV, an Ordinance of 1827, which empowered the Government of Bombay to intern almost anyone for any period on any charge which could possibly be construed as a menace to public order.
>
> Mirabehn (Miss Slade) remarked: "At the dead of night like thieves they came to steal him away".

On the night of June 25-26, J.P. also had been picked up similarly in a thief-like swoop after the Gandhi Peace Foundation premises in New Delhi had been encircled by the police.

There was a difference, however. Gandhiji's detention was reported the next morning with banner headlines. In J.P.'s case, the news was made a top level state secret, publication of which would entail dire consequences. Censorship orders were issued the next morning for the entire country, but in Delhi where the news could have been reported on June 26 itself, power supply to newspaper offices was cut.

MONDAY, SEPTEMBER 22

We left Rohtak at 5.15 A M. Ram Dhan had been the earliest to wake up in our barracks. He awakened our helpmates in the kitchen to prepare a cup of tea for us and then woke us up. By the time we were ready, everyone was up. They accompanied us to the jail gate to give us a warm send-off. The

superintendent, his deputy and other officials were also there
to bid us farewell. To the extent that the rules permitted, all of
them had been considerate to us.

The vehicle Jetley (the police official) brought this time was
a brand new station wagon. It reminded us of the ramshackle
truck in which we had been brought here.

We reached Palam at about 7.00 A.M. This time we were
to go not by an Air Force plane, but by a Border Security
Force plane. So instead of going to the Technical area controlled by the Air Force we went to the civilian airport. It made
us wish we could go by a commercial flight. It might have
enabled us to meet some acquaintances. But we were forgetting
that we were dangerous persons posing a threat to national
security. Our aircraft—again a Dakota—took off from Palam
around 8.15 A.M. We reached Hyderabad at about 1.00 P.M.
We had lunch at the airport cafeteria, and left at about 2.30
P.M. to reach Bangalore at 4.30 P.M. By the time we reached
the Central jail in Bangalore, our lawyer Rama Jois was awaiting
our arrival at the jail gate. The superintendent and deputy
superintendent who too had been duly informed were also
there. Rama Jois gave us a copy of the Government's 28-page
counter-affidavit. He said he would be seeing us on the morrow
to discuss issues relating to the case.

This time we are housed in the ward specially repaired and
touched up for 'A' class detenus. On reaching the ward we
find we have company, and very pleasant company at that.
Malikarjunaiah, MLC and President of the State Jana Sangh
and Subbaiah, leader of the Jana Sangh group in the State
Legislative Council are there.

TUESDAY, SEPTEMBER 23

Rama Jois interviews us again. We discuss with him the
Government's counter to our writ petitions. We also consider
points for our draft reply statement.

Jois refers to my letter in which I had suggested a change
in the draft petition about J.P's remarks on the army and the
police. The draft had been prepared by Jois at Bangalore while
we were at Rohtak. An otherwise excellent document, it
sounded needlessly apologetic about Jayaprakash Narayan's
call to the army and the police not to obey illegal orders.
There was nothing wrong, legally or morally, in J.P's
call. In our reply, therefore, the point is to be made clear.

Reference should be made to the fact that even under international law a soldier's right to disobey illegal orders is recognised.

WEDNESDAY, SEPTEMBER 24

Held under the DIR, in Class 'B' are 12 RSS swayam sewaks. They have been arrested in connection with the publication and distribution of Lok Sangharsh Samiti bulletins. The underground publicity network in Bangalore seems to have been organised well. Some of the swayam sewaks—like S. Ananthram and Sheshagiri Rao—have been subjected to third-degree treatment by the police to extract from them particulars about the publicity setup.

SUNDAY, SEPTEMBER 28

Precluded from directly criticising the Government and the emergency, writers have taken to historical narratives and references which have a moral for the present. Today's *Illustrated Weekly* carries an article by K.R. Sundar Rajan, entitled "Bhagat Singh and the Terrorist Movement", in the course of which he writes:

One important reason why terrorism ultimately failed to take root in India is to be found in Britain's own imperial policy. . . Dialogue with the nationalists was broken off only for short periods. And for every British official, soldier and policeman bent on keeping Indians in their place, back home there were an equal number of British politicians, trade unionists and journalists eager to defend the cause of Indian freedom and expose the Raj's black deeds.

In July 1908, Secretary of State Morley wrote one of the most meaningful letters to Lord Minto. He said: 'I must confess to you that I am watching with the deepest concern and dismay the thundering sentences which are now being passed for sedition, etc. We must keep order, but excess of severity is not the path to order; on the contrary it is the path to the bomb'.

Even the British-owned *Pioneer* of the then United Provinces wrote in its issue of August 29, 1906: 'The horror of such crimes (assassinations) is too great for words, and yet it has to be acknowledged, almost, that they are the only method of fighting left to a people who are at war with despotic rulers.'

The British rulers provided for other safety valves. Anti-Government writings in the Press invited retaliation only when they incited people to violence, and that too at a sustained level. There was generally no detention without trial; and trials were open, and reported in the Press more or less fully. News travelled quickly from one place to another. For example, Bhagat Singh's execution was known to people in Tirunelveli, in Tamil Nadu, 1500 miles away, within hours if not minutes and a 10000 strong crowd thronged the streets, shouting 'Long Live Martyr Bhagat Singh'.

Even a casual reader of this article would not miss the meaning. It is both a comment and a warning. The comment: the present Government has been behaving worse than even the British Government. The warning: if you do not leave safety-valves open, you will be inviting terrorism. It is very likely that the author had Bangladesh also in mind when he wrote this piece.

In the evening Rama Jois, Santosh Hegde and Appa Ghatate came to meet us. Ghatate had arrived on the same day from Bombay with Chagla. After dropping Chagla at the hotel, the trio of young lawyers came along to discuss with us plans for the Court hearing due to commence tomorrow. It being a Sunday, they had to secure special leave for the interview. Hegde tells us that Venu Gopal, son of M.K. Nambiar, a renowned lawyer of Madras and an outstanding lawyer in his own right, has also agreed to appear on our behalf.

Chagla, who will be formally appearing for Vajpayee, would lead the arguments from our side. He would be followed by Venu Gopal, Rama Jois and Santosh Hegde.

Ghatate had earlier told me that Chagla was keen to deal specifically with the issue whether or not the conditions precedent for the issue of a valid order of detention existed. I stressed that Chagla must deal with the question of emergency also, and attack the Proclamation on grounds of mala fide. Ghatate said today that Chagla had agreed to deal with that aspect also.

MONDAY, SEPTEMBER 29

We reach the Court around 10.15 A.M. On Chagla's arrival, we greet him and express our deep thanks that despite his age and state of health he had taken the trouble of coming to Bangalore for the case. He reciprocated our greetings warmly, and added "For a matter of this kind, I would have come even if I had been on my death-bed". Chagla mentions that his name too was high on the list drawn up by the Government for the roundup. Later, however, it seems the authorities had had second thoughts.

Chagla refers to the suffocating climate prevailing in the country. He tells us about a function in Bombay held to mark the bicentenary of American independence. Chagla was invited to preside. A distinguished scholar had come from the USA to inaugurate it. But the Press blacked out the function completely.

Some friends, he said, had applied for permission to celebrate Gandhi Jayanti. But the permission was not forthcoming. Dandavate quipped: "If it had been Indira Gandhi Jayanti, it would have been permitted".

Punctually, at 10.30 A.M. the two judges arrived. The Bench comprised Justice D.M. Chandrashekhar and Justice B. Venkataswami. At the very outset, V.P. Raman, counsel for the Government (in the course of this case itself he was appointed Additional Solicitor-General in place of Nariman who had resigned immediately after the proclamation of the emergency), raised a preliminary objection against our petitions. Raman's stand was that in view of the Presidential Orders issued under Art. 359(1) of the Constitution we were precluded from moving the Court. Correspondingly the Court had no jurisdiction to hear the petitions. Therefore, these petitions should be dismissed *in limine*, Government counsel urged.

Chagla attacks the preliminary objection as "vexatious, dilatory and without substance". He points out that the counterstatement filed by the Government has raised no such issues of non-entertainability now sought to be made a preliminary objection. Chagla prefaces his remarks with a feeling reference to the general situation in the country and observes: "I sometime rub my eyes wondering whether what I am witnessing is an actuality or a dream. The country is really passing through a nightmare".

Venu Gopal, who follows him, maintains that neither the 38th Amendment nor the latest amendments to MISA could bar an attack on an executive action on grounds of mala fides. Santosh Hegde and Rama Jois supplement the arguments advanced and urge that the preliminary objection be overruled.

After hearing Raman's reply to the arguments advanced by

our side, the Court overruled the objection and called upon Chagla to open his arguments in main. Chagla opens his arguments.

TUESDAY, SEPTEMBER 30

In the morning session, Chagla continues his arguments. In the afternoon, before Chagla could resume his case, the Advocate-General of Karnataka, Brya Reddy, makes a strange request. He objects to our presence in the Court. He says that our presence entails elaborate security and transport arrangements. "I request that the presence of the petitioners in the Court be kindly dispensed with," Reddy says.

Justice Chandrashekhar summarily rejects the plea and virtually snubs the Advocate-General saying: "I am unable to understand this sensitivity. Are they going to run away? After all, they may wish to instruct counsel".

Chagla resumes his arguments; he has not concluded when the Court rises for the day.

BBC reports an interview given by Justice J.M.L. Sinha of the Allahabad High Court to a West German paper *Der Spiegel*. Justice Sinha had agreed to be interviewed on the condition that he would not say anything about Indira Gandhi's election case. He discussed the role of the judiciary in general terms, and said that it was wrong to say that the judiciary was an obstacle in the path of social progress.

WEDNESDAY, OCTOBER 1

When we reach the Court, Ghatate mentions that yesterday September 30, was Chagla's birthday. We offer him our warm greetings. He narrates how his family members were put out when he told them that he would not be home for his birthday, but would be in Bangalore. They tried to dissuade him from going to Bangalore. He said: "What better way can there be of celebrating one's birthday than fighting for civil liberties".

Chagla resumes his arguments, takes the entire morning sitting, and concludes in the afternoon.

Just after the lunch-break, Raman rises to seek the Court's leave to appeal to the Supreme Court against the High Court's rejection of the Government's preliminary objection. The High Court declines to grant leave. After Chagla has completed his arguments, Raman makes another plea. He says that the

Attorney-General Niren De would like to appear in the case. He is indisposed at the moment. So he suggests that the hearing be adjourned for a week.

Justice Chandrashekhar replies that the Court would like very much to be enlightened by De. But he would not like to adjourn a habeas corpus case, he says. Besides, the case would continue yet. So Niren De could appear next week.

Venu Gopal then opens his arguments. He has not concluded when the Court rises for the day. Hearing in this case is to be resumed on October 6.

THURSDAY, OCTOBER 2 (Gandhi Jayanti)

Who could ever have believed that India would one day come to this pass and that celebration of Gandhi Jayanti would be taboo. Chagla told us about what happened in Bombay. Some friends who had organised a "Kavi Sammelan"[8] at the Shanmukhananda Hall to mark the occasion were first granted permission which was later rescinded. They went to court. The Court called for an explanation from the authorities and made it clear to them from its demeanour that it was in no mood to accept any puerile justification. The authorities responded with a duly signed permit. The "Kavi Sammelan" was a grand success.

Elsewhere, things were not as smooth. At many places, people were arrested for celebrating Gandhi Jayanti. At the Gandhi Samadhi at Rajghat itself no less a Gandhian than Acharya Kripalani found himself in the hands of the police when he tried to hold a prayer meeting. Among those physically restrained along with J.B. Kripalani were Rajmohan Gandhi, Gandhiji's grandson and socialist leader H.V. Kamath. Several others were arrested under the DIR on the occasion.

Afternoon brings sad news, the passing away of K. Kamaraj, Congress (O) leader and the darling of millions in Tamil Nadu. Death occurred at 3.00 P.M. We heard about it over the radio at 5.00 P.M.

The Government of India announces a 12-point programme

---

[8] Poetry recital.

as a first step towards total prohibition. It is rather difficult to
decipher the motives behind this move. Is Indira Gandhi
genuinely committed to prohibition? If so, why has she been so
deliberately encouraging anti-prohibition measures over the
last several years. States like Haryana, whose Chief Minister
would not move his little finger unless he felt assured of the
backing of 1, Safdarjung Road have been promoting drinking
with a vengeance. I doubt if any other State has as many govern-
ment-run bars as Haryana. Why then this sudden about-turn?
A sop to Vinoba Bhave?

Anyway, I feel that prohibition is a matter in which half-
heartedness is as disastrous as hypocrisy. If there is any country
in the world where prohibition has a chance of success, it is
India. But more important for its success than even the effi-
ciency of physical restraints is the climate obtaining in elitist
circles. If among politicians, bureaucrats, journalists, industrialists and the like, drinking is the 'in' thing, the chances of prohibition succeeding are bleak.

FRIDAY, OCTOBER 3

BBC quotes an article in the *New Statesman* saying that
the officially admitted number of political arrests in India
is 28,000 (for 20 states), but unofficial estimates vary from
75,000 to 1,50,000. The *New Statesman* correspondent who has
written the article has travelled in six States of India. He writes
that while the leaders of political parties are being generally
treated well in jails the lot of the rank and file leaves much to
be desired. Jail conditions in West Bengal, Bihar, Andhra
Pradesh and Madhya Pradesh are particularly bad, he writes.
BBC also reports the Madhya Pradesh Chief Minister, P.C.
Sethi, as telling a press conference in New Delhi that in his
State, out of 5,100 persons jailed at the beginning of the emergency, 2,600 are still behind the bars. Another news item put
out by BBC is that the Government of India has withdrawn
the accreditation of the New Delhi correspondent of the West
German paper, *Der Spiegel*. The paper has referred the case to
the International Press Institute, Zurich. The report has not
given any reason for the action against the correspondent. I
wonder whether it is not in connection with the publication of
an interview with Justice Sinha in the journal.

SUNDAY, OCTOBER 5

All India Radio reports Indira Gandhi as saying in New

Delhi that Kamaraj was not against the emergency and that in fact he had restrained his followers from criticising the emergency. Sin, they say, has many tools, but a lie is the handle which fits them all. Kamaraj had been ailing for quite some time. He had not moved out of Madras for months. But some political leaders had met him and discussed with him the current situation. Ramakrishna Hegde, Congress (O) leader in the Karnataka Legislative Council who met us later told us that accompanied by Virendra Patil he had met Kamaraj twice after the proclamation of the emergency. Kamaraj was very unhappy about it. His views were formally recorded in the shape of a Tamil Nadu Congress (O) Executive resolution passed on July 4, 1975. The resolution strongly criticised the emergency, the arrest of political workers, censorship and other measures and warned the Government that suppression of civil liberties and fundamental rights might plunge the country into violent disturbances. The resolution was appended to our habeas corpus petition as an exhibit.

When Shyambabu heard Indira Gandhi's remark about Kamaraj, he said it was characteristic of her. After L.N. Mishra's tragic death in January last, a Government employees' rally scheduled to take place in the afternoon and addressed by Jayaprakash Narayan was converted into a condolence meeting. The Congress organised a condolence meeting on the next day. Indira Gandhi was the main speaker. In marked contrast to what J.P. did, Indira Gandhi converted the condolence meeting into a political occasion. She used the platform to make a vituperative attack on the J.P. movement and went to the length of saying that Mishra's murder was a rehearsal for her own killing!

Shyambabu recalls that at the very first meeting of the Congress (O) Executive held after the 1969 split, Kamaraj who was seated beside him said: "Now, our party can have just a single-point programme: Remove Indira!"

MONDAY, OCTOBER 6

The hearing of our habeas corpus petitions is resumed. Venu Gopal continues his arguments and takes the entire day.

TUESDAY, OCTOBER 7

The Courts are closed today because of Id. Newspapers are full of reports about the Congress (O) in Tamil Nadu. They

say that the Congress (O) in Tamil Nadu is likely to merge with
the Congress (R).

Judging from the reports, it seems obvious that Kamaraj's
death has dealt a severe blow to the Congress (O) in Tamil
Nadu. How the party would be split may not be very material.
But one outcome seems apparent: Congress (O) may never be
the same again in Tamil Nadu.

It is evening. Shyambabu, Madhu Dandavate and I are
having a stroll in the foreyard of the jail. There is a lovely
little rose garden here. We enter the narrow pathway that runs
round the garden. The pathway is too narrow to allow more
than one person at a time. Shyambabu leads. I follow him.
Madhu follows, with both of us jointly addressing Shyambabu:
"Please don't lead us into the Congress (R)!"

On our request, the superintendent takes us to the corner
of the jail compound where the gallows are. He explains the
mechanism to us. There are three condemned prisoners in the
jail now. But their appeals are pending before the Supreme
Court. There has been lately some modification in the law with
regard to capital punishment. Earlier, for persons convicted of
homicide the death penalty was the rule and life imprisonment
the exception in mitigating circumstances. Now a life sentence
is the rule. Where murder is attended by savagery or in other
exceptional circumstances the death sentence is prescribed.
An improvement though this is, it is not enough. It is time
India decided to abolish capital punishment altogether. Aboli-
tion of capital punishment in several Western countries has
not led to increase in serious crime, thus disproving the theory
that the gallows act as a deterrent.

We ask the superintendent whether he considered the
electric chair used in the United States as more humane than
the gallows. His reply was a strong "no". He told us that
electrocution caused greater agony than hanging.

WEDNESDAY, OCTOBER 8

At the High Court Venu Gopal continues his unfinished
arguments.

Shortly before lunch, because of Justice Venkataswami's

indisposition, the hearing is adjourned till after the Dussehra vacation, that is, till October 20.

Going through the morning papers, I notice an interesting news item in the *Deccan Herald*. It reports that the C.B.S. (Columbia Broadcasting System) has denied access to President Ford to announce extension of tax cuts over its television network. The C.B.S. President Richard Salant explained that if he allowed Ford he would be legally required to broadcast statements from other candidates for next year's Republican presidential nomination under the equal time provision of the Federal Communications Act.

It is where the media can flaunt the law against the highest executive authority in the land that they really can be deemed to be free.

The External Affairs Minister Y.B. Chavan is reported as saying in Washington that there have been no "mass arrests" in India as reported in the Western Press. He said: "Most of the arrests related to economic offences, hoarding, black-marketing, smuggling or violation of foreign exchange regulations"!

Shortly after the promulgation of the emergency, the Indian Ambassador in Washington, T.N. Kaul, had made a statement which had been widely reported, that political leaders in detention were under house arrest, and that only "bad characters and economic offenders" were sent to jail!

First Kaul; now Chavan. The cheekiness and brazen-faced lying of official spokesmen is astounding. Here in prison I have no way of checking up facts. But I am sure statistics would bear it out that never before even in the British days have so many persons been thrown into prison without trial.

BBC reports in its 8.00 P.M. Hindi broadcast that the teleprinter and telephone connections of *Reuters* in New Delhi have been cut off because of alleged violation of censorship rules. *Reuters* are understood to have reported the beating of political detenus in the Tihar Jail in Delhi. We learnt later that there was a baton charge, then a protest hunger strike in which Chaudhri Charan Singh, Rajmata Vijaya Raje Scindia and Nanaji Deshmukh also participated.

THURSDAY, OCTOBER 9

The Supreme Court hearing of Indira Gandhi's appeal against the Allahabad judgment concludes. The Court reserves judgment.

The arguments till now are confined to the validity of the 39th amendment, and of the latest amendment of the Election Laws. Judging simply from press reports, Shanti Bhushan, counsel for Raj Narain, has done a wonderful job. He has attacked both the Constitution amendment and the changes in the Election Law as invalid. Again, judging by the questions fired from the Bench to the Attorney-General and to Indira Gandhi's counsel, Ashok Sen, the Court is unlikely to uphold the Constitution amendment. It is difficult to say what their view would be on the election law amendment. They did not put any probing queries to counsel in this regard.

The Nobel Committee has announced that this year's Peace Award would go to Soviet writer Nikolai Sakharov. BBC mentions that Moscow has been silent in this regard.

FRIDAY, OCTOBER 10

Rama Jois meets us in the evening and informs us that the Supreme Court yesterday considered the Government's request for special leave. Niren De pressed that the proceedings in the Karnataka High Court be stayed. Appearing on our behalf, Shanti Bhushan opposed the plea. Stay was refused, but an order was issued by the Supreme Court directing that "before entering into the merits of these petitions on other grounds, the High Court should hear the parties and render judgment on the preliminary objections raised by the Government, including the questions whether the objections so raised are preliminary".

Jois mentions that judges here have been feeling somewhat intrigued by the Supreme Court order. After all, the High Court had given its ruling on the preliminary objection. They would have to listen to the objection again and give their judgment afresh. Jois suggests that we wire to Shanti Bhushan and request him to appear for us in Bangalore also. Accordingly, we send a telegram to Allahabad.

BBC covers in its evening bulletin the Supreme Court hearing of the appeal against our petitions and reports that the

Court has upheld the right of the High Courts to consider habeas corpus petitions filed by MISA detenus. It also reveals that this decision follows petitions filed by four opposition leaders in Parliament in the Karnataka High Court.

The Voice of America quotes Tass criticism of the Nobel Peace Award for Sakharov. Tass has questioned his patriotism and described the Nobel Prize as a reward for his anti-Sovietism.

SATURDAY, OCTOBER 11

Chavan is heckled by an Indian audience in Chicago. It is hardly surprising. But what is surprising is the publication of the news in the Indian Press, howsoever briefly. We learnt later that Chavan's visit to the US was virtually blacked out by the American Press. At the Chicago meeting the External Affairs Minister lost his temper and challenged the demonstrators "to show their bravery on Indian soil".

This morning's papers report a Supreme Court judgment in which Justice Krishna Iyer has characterised Government as "the biggest culprit" responsible for delays in the legal process. The pronouncement is noteworthy because one of the grounds on which Government propagandists run down the Courts is "delay inherent in legal procedures". Here in this jail itself, there is a batch of three women satyagrahis who distributed some pamphlets criticising the emergency and the detention of J.P. and other leaders on August 15 and who were arrested under the DIR. They were led by Padma Joshi who is in charge of the women's section of the Karnataka Jana Sangh. It is nearly two months since they were arrested but they have not been charged so far. One of the satyagrahis is pregnant. When her relations sought her release, the magistrate expressed helplessness saying, "If it had been a murder case I could have straightaway granted bail". But in a DIR case of this nature, his hands were tied, he said.

MONDAY, OCTOBER 13

Padma Joshi and her two co-satyagrahis are at last charge-sheeted. One of the charges is that they shouted "Bharat Mata ki jai!" A pamphlet appended to the chargesheet, said to have been distributed by the satyagrahis, recounts the mythological tale of Hiranyakashyap who had obtained a multiple boon to ensure his immortality. It was that neither man nor beast could kill him; he could be slain neither inside a house nor outside, neither on land nor in the air nor in water; neither during the day nor at night, etc. The pamphlet said that Indira Gandhi has likewise sought to arm herself with a constitutional amendment, a changed Election Law. But even so retribution would overtake her and she would be ousted from power. Padma Joshi admitted having distributed the pamphlet. The Magistrate, Chandrasekhar, read out the pamphlet and then addressing the police sub-inspector said: "I do not approve of the pamphlet; but I would like to understand how it is punishable under the Defence of India Rules?"

WEDNESDAY, OCTOBER 15

A high-powered meeting of the Lok Sangharsh Samiti is being held in Bangalore today. Feverish preparations are going on to launch a countrywide satyagraha in November. The exact date would be announced after a meeting in Delhi on November 1. Some senior leaders are in town for the meeting.

THURSDAY, OCTOBER 16

Rama Jois and Santosh Hegde meet us and inform us that Shanti Bhushan has agreed to appear for us in the case. The Attorney-General will also be there to make a determined bid to block the petitions at the threshold itself.

SATURDAY, OCTOBER 18

Nana Gadre, Parmanand, Brij Mohan Mishra, Veer Singh, Chhagan Lal and Prakash Sholapurkar, all prominent Jana Sangh workers of Madhya Pradesh, detained in the Khandwa district jail have sent me a cute little postcard conveying *Vijaya Dashmi* greetings and wishing for the victory of Truth over untruth and Light over Darkness. Its most attractive aspect is a neatly sketched jail house, with bars and padlock, captioned "MISANAGAR". A quotation of Mahatma Gandhi given along with it reads: "It is cowardice to submit to untruth, injustice and oppression". The postcard bears the official "approved" stamp of the jail authorities of Khandwa.

Ganapaiah, President of the Karnataka Bharatiya Lok Dal whose writ petition is being considered along with ours, is released and rearrested under fresh detention orders. The declaration made under Sec. 16A of MISA following the first

detention had said his detention was necessary to deal effectively with the "emergency". The declaration, under Sec. 16A,
obviated the legal need to furnish grounds to the detenu and
to refer the detention to an advisory council. However, in the
course of the hearing of our petitions, Venu Gopal dealt at length
with the implications of the declaration, and it is this that
appeared to have inspired Ganapaiah's release, the phraseology
being the same in our case also.

Venu Gopal drew the Court's attention to the fact that Sec. 16A
of MISA has defined "the emergency" as inclusive of both the
1971 emergency arising out of external aggression as well as the
1975 emergency arising out of the threat of internal disturbance.
He pointed out that as stated in the petitions filed by Vajpayee
and myself, the Jana Sangh had pledged full support to the
country in the wars of 1962, 1965 and 1971. The Government's
counter-affidavit contended that the Jana Sangh's patriotic role
at the time of the wars was no answer to the charge that it
posed a threat to internal security in 1975. Venu Gopal argued
that this meant that the detention of the petitioners had nothing
to do with the 1971 emergency. And if this was so, the declaration ought to have made it clear. By omitting to do so, the
detaining authority was guilty of a misjoinder. He cited several
Supreme Court judgments that if several grounds of detention
are cited and any one is found to be vague or irrelevant and
bad, the detention order would fall in its entirety. That some
other ground or grounds were sound would be of no avail.

The Government of India counsel did not seem to be impressed by the argument. But the Advocate-General of Karnataka, Byra Reddy, obviously was. It seems he has advised the
State Government accordingly. The new declaration given to
Ganapaiah after his rearrest specifically refers to the emergency
declared on June 25, 1975.

Jois tells that Shanti Bhushan has arrived. Niren De also
has come by the same plane.

SUNDAY, OCTOBER 19

In Gujarat a major trial of strength is scheduled for today.
Rajkot is to elect its 51-member Corporation. Press reports say
that the Janata Front is no longer as united as it was during the
Assembly polls. The reports seem prompted. Anyway we
would be keenly awaiting the outcome. Of the two major

parties in the Janata front, the Jana Sangh is known to be particularly strong in Rajkot. Of the three Assembly seats in the city,
the Jana Sangh had won two.

MONDAY, OCTOBER 20

The hearing of our habeas corpus petitions is resumed in the
High Court. Justice Chandrasekhar mentions at the outset
that the Supreme Court had passed an order directing the High
Court to adjudicate on the preliminary objection. He asked the
Attorney-General to formulate his objection. The Attorney-
General says that in view of the Presidential Order under Art.
359, the petitioners cannot seek to enforce their right to
liberty. He maintains that the Supreme Court's order obligated
the High Court to consider only two matters at this stage
namely (a) whether there were materials on the basis of which
the order could be made and (b) whether the detaining authority had applied its mind when making the order. After hearing Shanti Bhushan and Venu Gopal, the High Court opines
that six questions arise for determination from the preliminary
objection, the first two relating to justiciability of the proclamation of emergency, the next two to the validity of the 38th
and 39th amendments to the Constitution, and the last two to
the justiciability of an order of detention under MISA while
a Presidential order under Art. 359 is in force. The Attorney-
General strongly disputed this interpretation and said that if the
High Court proceeds with the hearing on the basis of such an
interpretation, it would be a violation of the Supreme Court's
order and so illegal. De urged that the hearing be adjourned so
that he could get a clarification from the Supreme Court
about the meaning of its order. He is confident that he would
get a "proper" clarification from the Supreme Court.

Justice Chandrashekhar says that he had heard both sides and
would now pass orders which must precede the disposal of the
Government's challenge to the maintainability of the petitions.
If the Attorney-General wished to appeal against the order he
may do so. An elaborate order is then issued formulating the
six questions and giving reasons why the preliminary objection
cannot be decided without answering these questions. The
hearing is then adjourned to October 27, so that the Union
Government may appeal against the order if it wished to.

Shanti Bhushan says Niren De is not at all happy with

the amendments of the election law and the Constitution with retrospective effect. He has told some of his friends that he wants to quit but is afraid of the consequences of such action.

BBC paints a touching picture of how J.P. spent his 74th birthday last week—in solitary confinement, cut off from friends and relations. We learnt that he was kept in a hospital room for months on end, without enough ventilation or moving space. A fortnight ago, a writ petition was filed in the High Court against the treatment being given to him and promptly thereafter he was shifted to a private house in Chandigarh which has a compound and where he is able to move about.

TUESDAY, OCTOBER 21

The morning papers refer to the possibility of a Special Bench of the Supreme Court being convened to review the judgment in the Keshavananda Bharati case. It is obvious that Niren De was aware of this possibility when he was arguing in the High Court yesterday and when he referred to the Keshavananda verdict saying that a Special Bench of the Supreme Court might be constituted for reviewing the judgment. Now in the Supreme Court he will make it an additional ground for seeking stay of High Court proceedings.

We search the newspapers for any report on the Rajkot elections. But there is none. *Nulla nuova, buona nuova.* No news is good news—that's how we feel.

THURSDAY, OCTOBER 23

Papers still have nothing to report about Rajkot. I keep trying for some local bulletin from a Gujarat radio station. I chance upon a Gujarati news bulletin once. But listening to it carefully I discover it is Radio Moscow! I doubt if any other foreign broadcasting network has more Indian language broadcasts than Moscow.

At 1.00 P.M. All India Radio announced the Rajkot civic election results. The Janata Front has secured 39 seats and the ruling Congress 12. The news is included only in that one bulletin, perhaps by mistake, later it was blacked out.

I send a congratulatory telegram to Chimanbhai Shukla (I learnt later that he himself had contested and won). I have no inkling if the wire reached him.

FRIDAY, OCTOBER 24

At last, five days after completion of the polling the newspapers are permitted to publish the results of the Rajkot civic election. It is a signal victory for the Janata Front, belying earlier reports about differences within the Front.

In an interview with the Communist Central News Service, Indira Gandhi says that only top leaders actually engaged in plans to paralyse the Government have been arrested. The rest are all free. An inspired report in the *Hindu* says that 40 to 45 per cent of the detenus are released, and that the State Governments have been directed by the Centre to continue reviewing detention cases. We know about Rohtak and Bangalore. We have been in touch with Delhi and some other prisons. But we have not come across a single case of a political detenu having been released. We have known about the release of quite a few COFEPOSA detainees held for alleged smuggling. From Bangalore jail itself about a dozen such persons have been released. This recurring propaganda about increasing percentage of releases, first 25 per cent, then 30 per cent, now 40 to 45 per cent is a deliberate exercise in deception.

Narasimhachar, RSS Sangh Chalak of Bangalore, is brought back here for medical treatment. At the Belgaum station he happened to meet Jagannathrao Joshi, who told him that he had met Balasaheb Deoras at Yerawada Jail in Poona and that he was keeping well.

BBC and VOA report that Potter of the World Council of Churches has written a strongly worded four-page letter to Indira Gandhi protesting against the state of affairs in India. The Council has been actively helping freedom movements in Africa. The letter is a fervent plea for the restoration of civil liberties. It takes strong exception to the misuse of the preventive detention law and particularly of the fact that a veteran leader like Jayaprakash Narayan has been kept in solitary confinement. Letters have been addressed to the churches in India asking them to exert pressure for a change in the situation.

The Government's special leave petition against the Karnataka High Court's order is to be heard in the Supreme Court today.

SATURDAY, OCTOBER 25

The morning papers have a surprise for us. The *Indian Express* reports that the Supreme Court has rejected the Central Government's special leave petition against us. This is the first time that an Indian paper has made any reference to our case; (of course, no names are mentioned).

Rama Jois who returned only this morning from Delhi gives us a fuller account of the hearing in the Supreme Court. He says that when the Attorney-General sought to protest against the Karnataka High Court order and said that it went against the Supreme Court's earlier directive Justice Mathew snubbed him saying that the Court had been misled by the Attorney-General earlier. When Niren De pressed for adjournment on the plea that the Keshavananda Bharati decision was being reviewed, Justice Mathew replied "Why should any one presume that the decision would be changed? So far as the High Court is concerned, Keshavananda Bharati is the law. If anyone is aggrieved by the High Court's decision he can certainly come to us."

SUNDAY, OCTOBER 26

In the desert of conformist crap that newspapers are these days, Abu's cartoons are like an oasis. The fact that Abu has always been a critic of the J.P. movement makes his incisive cartoons against the establishment's emergency antics all the more effective. Today's *Sunday Standard* has a cartoon depicting the common man with a sleeping board of nails. At first glance, the cartoon does not register. But a second look reveals that the nails are numbered. The sleeping board carries exactly 20 POINTED nails!

Today's *Sunday Standard* carries a bold article by Nayantara Sahgal under the caption: "The call of clean conscience". It speaks of the great martyrs of history, Socrates, Jesus, Apostle Peter and Guru Tegh Bahadur who would rather give up their lives than submit to tyranny. No reader can miss its relevance to the present situation. Lest one might, Nayantara Sahgal underscores it by writing in the concluding paragraph:

Aurangzeb should have learned the lesson that only rebellion rises from the blood of a martyr. But history, it seems, is a bad teacher. We never learn from it.

MONDAY, OCTOBER 27

The Karnataka High Court resumes hearing of our case. Shanti Bhushan has arrived. Understandably, Niren De has not. Venu Gopal concludes his arguments. Shanti Bhushan opens his case. The court is packed to overflowing. We learn later that some magistrates have taken leave from their courts to be able to hear Shanti Bhushan. We notice a foreigner in the court and learn that he is the *New York Times* correspondent from Delhi. We see the State Advocate-General Byra Reddy beckoning to an intelligence official (who used to come to the court regularly and sit behind us obstensibly taking notes, but actually keeping a watch over us) and pointing the foreigner out to him. After a while we see the correspondent being summoned outside by a police official. We are told later that his name and address are noted by the police.

THURSDAY, OCTOBER 30

It has been announced that the Supreme Court would commence reviewing the Keshavananda Bharati judgment from November 10 onwards. Shanti Bhushan mentions that the Delhi Bar is thinking in terms of boycotting the hearings. There is in reality no occasion for review. The Chief Justice has suggested it suo moto. He has added that the Government of India desires such a review. But whatever be the Chief Justice's thinking we need not assume that the Full Bench of the Supreme Court would decide against us, Shanti Bhushan says, and expresses himself against the boycott proposal. We agree. We have understandably no rapport with the executive. We have not concealed our utter distrust of the executive. By boycotting the Supreme Court hearings we would be further demonstrating our distrust of the judiciary as well. It would only weaken our position in the eyes of the world. Besides, we point out, that if there is any organ of the State which has shown courage and integrity in the emergency, it is the judiciary. Shanti Bhushan concludes his arguments. Raman opens his case on behalf of the Central Government.

There is an unusual incident in the jail today, an escape. Krishna, the escapee, is a habitual thief serving a sentence of two years on one count, but simultaneously undergoing trial on more than half a dozen other charges. Krishna was attending to some electrical repairs in our ward. There is a godown in a corner of the ward, abutting on the main prison wall with an opening inside that led out over the wall. He had worked his way into the confidence of the chief warder who had given him the keys to the godown and assigned him the repair work which is not usual in the case of a habitual offender like him. Krishna betrayed the misplaced trust and performed the vanishing trick. The upshot: suspension of the chief warden which is understandable; and confinement in a solitary cell of Krishnappa and Gujrappa, convict warders assigned to assist us, totally ununderstandable and unjustified.

FRIDAY, OCTOBER 31

The hearing of our case is adjourned till Diwali, that is, November 5; Raman has yet to conclude his arguments.

I undertake an exercise in the shape of an article on the probable course of events during the next six months.[9]

SATURDAY, NOVEMBER 1

We receive the first formal notice of the preparations going on for satyagraha outside when Varadaraja Iyengar, Secretary of Magdi Taluk (Bangalore District) Bharatiya Jana Sangh is brought to jail. He was arrested under the DIR.

Iyengar was enrolling satyagrahis. He himself had decided to court arrest along with his wife. He says the response to the satyagraha is excellent. I ask him whether the police have found anything incriminating in his house. He says that the police raided his house and took away pictures of Mahatma Gandhi and Shri Guruji![10]

The Voice of America has an odd report about the Indian Ambassador in Washington, T.N. Kaul. Addressing a ladies' club meeting in Washington, Kaul said it was wrong to say there had been mass arrests in India. Asked if he could give the number of political prisoners, he said glibly, "Fifteen leaders and about 1,000 followers." These fifteen were those who had participated in the June 25 meeting (incidentally, we three were in Bangalore on June 25). Out of them three had been released, he said. The thousand followers arrested were those who

---

[9] See Appendix.
[10] Former RSS Chief, M.S. Golwalkar.

turned out on the streets on June 26, throwing stones. Out of them 300 had been released.

In his *Mein Kampf*, Adolf Hitler has written "The size of the lie is a definite factor in causing it to be believed... The primitive simplicity of their (people's) minds render them a more easy prey to a big lie than a small one, for they themselves often tell little lies but would be ashamed to tell big ones". The Nazi dictator would have found an adept disciple in the Indian diplomat!

We have been eagerly looking for a report on the Commonwealth Parliamentary Conference now going on in Delhi, which would show that our colleagues have not allowed it to be a stifling, suffocating, *sarkari*[11] show. This evening's BBC bulletin says that five opposition members walked out of the conference when their leader Tridib Kumar Chaudhry was denied an opportunity to speak on "Internal Threats to Democracy" and to voice the views of the opposition on the subject in the context of the Indian situation. The walkout was led by Mallur Anand Rao, M.L.C. from Karnataka, who some days later was penalised for it by being arrested under MISA and brought to the Bangalore jail to give us company.

SUNDAY, NOVEMBER 2

In the press there is a long and puerile explanation by Parliamentary Affairs Minister Raghuramaiah why Tridib Chaudhry could not speak. But the fact that opposition delegates to the conference walked out has been suppressed by the censor.

MONDAY, NOVEMBER 3

It is Dipawali today. Among the sheaf of greeting cards I got, there is a special one sent by an anonymous friend in Bangalore. It is inscribed thus:

NO   F R E E D O M
NO   D E E P A V A L I
NO   G R E E T I N G S
                     from A Brother

---

[11] Governmental.

TUESDAY, NOVEMBER 4

The *Times of India* of Bombay reports a "hand clap poll" in Zaire, Africa, on November 2. There were no polling booths, no identity papers and no ballots. Local officials read out the names of the candidates of the ruling party (People's Revolutionary Movement) and the assembled voters were asked to applaud those names which they approve. The results were judged, so runs the reports, from "the level of applause as gauged by the officials"! I wonder if New Delhi would be willing to buy the idea!

WEDNESDAY, NOVEMBER 5

The High Court resumes the hearing of our petition. Raman continues his arguments.

THURSDAY, NOVEMBER 6

Raman concludes his arguments. Advocate-General, Byra Reddy, opens.

FRIDAY, NOVEMBER 7

The Supreme Court is to pronounce today its judgment on Indira Gandhi's appeal against the Allahabad judgment. In the Karnataka High Court, therefore, those in the court-room, not excluding the petitioners and their counsel, are less interested in Byra Reddy's arguments than in reports from Delhi. Around 12.30 P.M. we get a cryptic report that Indira Gandhi's election has been upheld. We enquire about the basis: Constitution amendment or the Election Law amendment? Our source tells us that both have been upheld. Upholding of the 39th Amendment appears shocking to us. It is in a somewhat depressed mood, therefore, that we return to the jail for lunch. We tune in to All India Radio at 2.00 P.M. to be told what we have already learnt, namely, that Indira Gandhi's election has been upheld by the Supreme Court. The report adds that the Court has held the amendment of the Election Law valid. However, that there is not a word in the report about the constitutional amendment seems significant to us. In the courtroom in the afternoon, reports continue to vary. No one is able to say precisely what the Supreme Court has decided about the Constitution amendment. Meanwhile, Byra Reddy completes his arguments departing sharply from the stand taken by the Government of India counsel, Raman, on the scope of judicial review in MISA detention cases.

Raman had conceded some area of judicial scrutiny. He said that an order could be challenged if it is prima facie bad, that is, if, for example, the detention of 'A' has been ordered and 'B' is arrested instead, or if instead of a competent authority signing the order, a petty official does it. Byra Reddy, however, disagrees with him, and argues that so long as the emergency lasts, the Court's intervention just cannot be invoked—not even in cases of mistaken identity or where the order is not signed by a competent authority.

On behalf of the petitioners the "debate" on the preliminary objection is replied to by Rama Jois. He reinforces the arguments already advanced with a plethora of precedents. He has not concluded when the Court rises for the day.

The confusion about the fate of the 39th Amendment is cleared only when in the night we hear BBC and the VOA announcing categorically that clause 4 of the 39th Amendment has been struck down by the Supreme Court as being beyond the legislative competence of Parliament.

SATURDAY, NOVEMBER 8

Since last evening, a stream of greetings telegrams has been pouring in reminding me that it is my birthday today and that I am 48 years old. Among the first to send the greetings are Kamala and the children. From amongst the colleagues here Madhu is the first to get an inkling. Affectionately, he organises an impromptu get-together, and Shyambabu cordially greets me with flowers and a tender hug. Madhu's postcard reads: "Many happy returns of the day! Wish you long life to live in the image of your ideals". May God enable me to measure up to this greeting.

SUNDAY, NOVEMBER 9

The morning papers report Indira Gandhi as saying that in the absence of the steps she had taken, Bangladesh would have been enacted in India too. Now that she has said it one can expect Congressmen all over the country to echo the thesis, knowing well that it is a lie.

J.P., Morarji, Charan Singh, Vajpayee—the four top leaders

of the Janata movement—literally abhor violence. Even to insinuate that they had been scheming a bloody *coup* is a slander, vile and contemptible.

MONDAY, NOVEMBER 10

In the High Court Jois concludes his reply. Justice Chandrashekhar announces that the judgment on the preliminary objection is reserved.

We learn in the Court that a lawyers' conference convened in Bangalore by the Government as part of a scheme for countrywide lawyers' conferences to applaud official policies has ended in a fiasco even though the choice of participants is selective and even though several Bar Associations in the State have formally boycotted it on the ground that it is a *Sarkari tamasha.*[12]

The sponsors had intended to make the conference pass several resolutions including approval of the 20-point programme and demand for restructuring of the Constitution to clip the authority of the courts. But they got a clear measure of the mood of the conclave when they placed before them a resolution congratulating Indira Gandhi on the Supreme Court judgment. Only *eleven* out of the 600 present supported the resolution. Hastily the sponsors decided to drop all resolutions.

Midway through the radio sports bulletin in the evening, the newsreader announces "Tomorrow, at 8.00 P.M. Prime Minister Indira Gandhi will speak to the people". The announcement touches off another round of speculation. Is it going to be a turning point? The announcement is repeated almost every hour.

In the exercise I had undertaken on October 31, I had identified "Possibility C" as the most likely, namely, that because of the satyagraha, there would be no release of detenus and no elections. But I also thought that Indira Gandhi may decide to pre-empt the satyagraha by releasing, either en bloc or in phases, the detenus after the Supreme Court verdict is announced, and before the satyagraha is launched. The announcement about Indira Gandhi's broadcast made me apprehend that it is perhaps this course of action that the Government is going to opt for.

Reports about the preparations for the satyagraha have been

---

[12] Officially sponsored farce.

very good. The satyagraha has as its objectives: (a) lifting of
the emergency, (b) release of detenus, (c) lifting of the ban on
RSS and other organisations, and (d) removal of the curbs on
the Press. Of these the one that evokes the greatest amount of
public sympathy is demand (b), that is, release of detenus. If
Government were to do that on its own, the movement would
be shorn of much of its thrust. Ironically, therefore, the prospect of release appears to me somewhat disturbing. Sharing
my thoughts with friends, I remark: "A release at this juncture
would be as humiliating as the unilateral withdrawal of the
Chinese in 1962". They withdrew from wherever they wanted
to and stayed put wherever they wanted to.

Till now the impression given to the country and to the
world by the Government is that J.P. and thousands of other
political activists were arrested, but there was no protest whatsoever. The proposed satyagraha is to be in the nature of a
peaceful but powerful protest. Our mettle is also to be put to
the test. Our release would cheat us of the opportunity. Tonight
I pray to God that Indira Gandhi should not announce any
such course of action.

The Supreme Court begins consideration of the Keshavananda Bharati judgment.

TUESDAY, NOVEMBER 11

Four Vidyarthi Parishad workers who were arrested while
distributing Lok Sangharsh Samiti pamphlets at the local
Ashoka Hotel, on Friday, November 7, are brought to the jail.
The hotel had been chosen by the workers because delegates to
the Commonwealth Parliamentary Conference on a visit to
Karnataka were staying here. The delegates, we learn, were
given a lot of literature published by the Lok Sangharsh Samiti
first in Delhi and then in Bangalore. Wherever they went in the
State they were witness to protest demonstrations.

The authorities are angry, and understandably so. They have
been feeding world public opinion for the last several months
with the myth that the emergency has not provoked any popular
protest. The demonstrations on the occasion of the Commonwealth Parliamentary Conference have exploded the myth.
According to the law, the students should have been produced
before a magistrate within 24 hours of their arrest. It was not
done. Instead, the police handed them over to the C.O.D.—

Corps of Detectives—for interrogation. The students are subjected to third-degree methods to ferret out of them the source of the literature. On November 10, the mother of one of the students filed a habeas corpus petition in the High Court. That forced the Government's hands. Today, therefore, the students are brought to the jail under MISA.

At 8 P.M. Indira Gandhi delivers her much publicised speech. Considering the kind of build-up given it was an anti-climax, both inane and inconsequential. Ironically, we heaved a sigh of relief that there was going to be no release of prisoners and that the satyagraha would be launched as scheduled. Ravindra Varma, Secretary of the Lok Sangharsh Samiti, has already given notice to Indira Gandhi of the Samiti's decision to begin a peaceful and countrywide satyagraha from November 14.

In her speech, Indira Gandhi describes the emergency as a bitter pill "she had to administer to the country for its health." She spoke of the discipline generated and the cessation of strikes. The question really is: what is health when one thinks of a people? Who decides this question? All dictators—from Napoleon to Hitler, Mussolini and Franco—thought liberty was unhealthy and dissent a disease. They all regarded themselves as the sole arbiters of what was good for their respective nations. Indira Gandhi is no different. It is said of Napolean that once, relaxing in a bath-tub, he remarked to an aide: "An opposition, as in England, was that it? I haven't been able to understand yet what good there is in an opposition. In France there is just a single party, and a single will". About journalists, his opinion was: "A journalist is a grumbler a la Caesar; four hostile newspapers are more to be feared than a thousand bayonets".

When Benito Mussolini took over in Italy, he pontificated: "The truth is that men are perhaps weary of liberty. They have had a surfeit of it. There are other words which move them more deeply. These words are: order and discipline".

Hitler's contempt for the *demos* and democracy is well known. His conception of political ethics was simple. In his *Mein Kampf* he wrote: "Success is the sole earthly judge of right and wrong". But even he resented being called a warmonger. He said once: "I am insulted by the persistent assertion that I want war. Am I a fool? War! It would settle nothing".

Indira Gandhi's protestations are identical. Just as Hitler feigned dislike of war because it would solve no problems so also Indira Gandhi pretends to abhor dictatorship because "dictatorship will not remedy the ills of a country as vast as India".

THURSDAY, NOVEMBER 13

There is a big surprise for us in the papers this morning. A cryptic Press Trust of India message from Chandigarh says that Jayaprakash Narayan has been released "on parole". We tune in to All India Radio for more news on the subject. It says not a word, not even what the papers have said. We switch on to the only source which can give some enlightenment, the foreign media. Both BBC and VOA report J.P.'s release, but do not use the words "on parole". BBC says he has been released "possibly for health reasons". It gives a brief background of his detention and comments that the Government of India has perhaps been worried lest anything should happen to him while in jail, thus causing reactions in the country. VOA also suggests that J.P.'s release is because of health reasons. We send a telegram to J.P. at his Delhi address expressing anxiety about his health.

FRIDAY, NOVEMBER 14

It is D-Day, the day fixed for launching the countrywide satyagraha. In pursuance of a Lok Sangharsh Samiti circular the day is observed as a day of fast and prayers. All detenus and DIR prisoners in the Bangalore jail communicate to the authorities in writing their decision to observe a 24-hour fast as part of the nationwide programme.

We get information that in Bangalore the satyagraha has been a grand success. Some fifty satyagrahis split into batches of six to eight have offered satyagraha at seven different points. Large crowds have gathered to witness the satyagraha and cheer the satyagrahis. The main batch, led by Ramakrishna Hegde, Congress(O) Leader of the Opposition in the Legislative Council, courts arrest at the Mysore Bank Square. The arrested satyagrahis are expected to reach the jail only tomorrow. It is a pleasant surprise, therefore, to find two batches of satyagrahis arrive in the evening. Totalling 28 they are from Doddaballapur in Bangalore district.

There is a very disturbing report that J.P.'s condition is serious. There is no way of confirming it. But it seems to be the only explanation for his release.

Today is Nehru Jayanti. I have had occasion recently to glance through a book on Nehru by D. F. Karaka, entitled "The Lotus Eater of Kashmir". It carries a passage from Nehru's presidential address to the Lucknow Congress in 1936 which applies to the current situation. Nehru said:

Comrades, being interested in psychology, I have watched the process of moral and intellectual decay and realised, even more than I did previously, how autocratic power corrupts and degrades and vulgarises. Of one thing I must say a few words, for to me it is one of the most vital things that I value. That is the deprivation of civil liberties in India.

A Government that has to rely on the Criminal Law Amendment Act and similar laws, that suppresses the press and literature, that bans hundreds of organisations, that keeps people in prison without trial and that does so many things that are happening in India today, is a Government that has ceased to have even a shadow of justification for its existence.

I can never adjust myself to these conditions; I find them intolerable. And yet I find many of my countrymen complacent about them, some even supporting them, some, who have made the practice of sitting on the fence into a fine art, being neutral when such questions are discussed.

Judging the British Government by its onslaught on civil liberties, its reliance on lawless laws, its suppression of press freedom, its outlawing of organisations, and its incarceration of people without trial, Nehru declared it as bereft of "even a shadow of justification for its existence". Nothing that the British Government did in 1936 in the matter of civil liberties can match the crimes committed against democracy by the present government. Nehru expressed dismay over the process of intellectual and moral decay and the debasing influence of autocratic power. He felt pained that while all this was happening some Indians had made a fine art of fence sitting. One wonders what he would have felt about today's Congressmen, most of whom whisper their unhappiness over the present scene in private but indulge in loud-mouthed sycophancy when speaking in public.

The sins of these past few months are not Indira Gandhi's alone. In retrospect, it would be deemed the collective guilt of all Congressmen—those who supported her policy actively, and those who acquiesced in it by remaining silent. Bhishma and Drona were as much responsible for the outrageous disrobing of Draupadi as were Duryodhana and Dushasana.[13]

SATURDAY, NOVEMBER 15

The satyagrahis arrested in Bangalore yesterday are brought to jail. They are charged with breach of the Defence of India Rules. Ramakrishna Hegde is, however, let off after being taken to the police station. This is an index of the general policy towards the Congress(O) in the State. Swetadri, Jana Sangh leader of Bangalore, who led one of the batches yesterday, tells us that following the announcement of J.P.'s release, D.M.K. workers in Madras put up posters in the city showing J.P.'s photos and saying that he was seriously ill.

SUNDAY, NOVEMBER 16

The influx of satyagrahis continues. I hear a striking Kannada slogan being shouted. Subbaiah explains it to me:

Hedotu (Twenty), *Madotu* (Four-twenty,) *Janatege* (for the people) *Tik-20*; which means: "They talk about twenty (points), they practise four-twenty, and for the people, it is all TIK-20"

An Ordinance has been promulgated further amending the MISA. It empowers the Government to rearrest detenus after their release by the court.

In their masterly study of the second world war, "Total War", the authors Peter Calvocoressi and Guy Wint have this comment on the functioning of courts in Nazi Germany:

Justice became a farce. It was, said Hitler, 'a means of ruling.' Illegality was legalised by the invention of the principle of 'hidden right' (of the State). An advocate who got his client acquitted would see him being bundled into a police van as he left the court.

---

[13] An allusion to an episode in the Mahabharata.

MONDAY, NOVEMBER 17

BBC and VOA report J.P.'s remarks to the Press on arrival in Delhi. He is reported to have reaffirmed his demand that the emergency be lifted, press censorship removed, all prisoners released and civil liberties restored. He said that it would be pointless to hold elections on schedule without first lifting the emergency. He also stressed that his campaign against corruption had been entirely peaceful and non-violent.

Rama Jois sees us in the evening. He tells us that Vajpayee was operated upon yesterday for a 'slipped disc'. It has been a major operation, lasting from 7.30 A.M. to 2.00 P.M. Two days earlier, Vajpayee also was released 'on parole'. The operation is successful, Jois tells us. We send a telegram to Atalji wishing him speedy recovery.

THURSDAY, NOVEMBER 20

I receive four Diwali greeting cards sent from different places in Gujarat, but addressed to me "Care of Indira Gandhi, Prime Minister of India, New Delhi." The Prime Minister's Secretariat sent the cards to the Karnataka Government, which in turn has passed them on to the jail authorities for delivery to me. Those who have sent the greetings evidently know that I am enjoying Indira Gandhi's hospitality these days but seem to be unaware of the 'guest house' where I have been lodged. So they thought it would be safe to address the cards to the hostess herself. Anyway, I feel grateful that the cards have been redirected to me.

A memo arrives from the Government of India saying that our continued detention is necessary for effectively dealing with the emergency. The MISA requires a four monthly review of detentions. This memo fulfils the formality. Madhu Dandavate, with his characteristic humour, acknowledges receipt of the memo on the copy (which the jail authorities have been asked to send back to the Home Ministry) and adds that his special thanks may be communicated to the Prime Minister for this 'birthday gift' from her. November 19 is Indira Gandhi's birthday.[14]

---

[14] See Appendix 4.

SATURDAY, NOVEMBER 22

Shyam Nandan Mishra and Madhu Dandavate receive Lok Sabha bulletins informing them that Jagannathrao Joshi has been arrested under MISA. He was arrested on November 11 three days before the commencement of the satyagraha. He has been detained at Tihar Jail, Delhi.

We learn that his arrest followed a stormy session he had with the Home Minister Brahmananda Reddy, at a meeting of the Home Ministry's Parliamentary Consultative Committee. The meeting, we understand, lasted four to five hours. Joshi and Krishna Kant are believed to have given the Minister a very hard time and exposed the government's lies about the condition and treatment of the detenus. It is remarkable that at this meeting too, held on November 7, the Home Minister cheekily claimed that all detenus are in normal health. Did he not know about J.P.'s critical condition at that time? If he is ignorant of it, he is unfit to be the Home Minister. If he knew it he was guilty of telling the committee a deliberate lie.

We learn that Virendra Patil offered satyagraha yesterday. There was a massive turnout and enthusiastic scenes were witnessed at the Mysore Bank Square, where the satyagraha was offered. But in accordance with the policy of dividing the opposition Patil was taken to the police station and released.

MONDAY, NOVEMBER 24

The superintendent tells us in the evening that our telegram to J.P. sent to his office on November 13 (the day on which J.P.'s release was announced) was cleared by the Government only today, that is, eleven days after! We understand that even an innocuous telegram enquiring after J.P.'s health is to be sent to New Delhi for clearance by the Home Ministry!

We tell the superintendent that there is no point in sending the telegram now to Delhi. J.P. has already gone to Bombay. We reframe the telegram and send it to the Jaslok Hospital, Bombay. It will be sent the next day, we are told.

There is a report in the Press on the Prime Minister's address to a rally of primary teachers held in Delhi. The report mentions Indira Gandhi as saying that distributing pamphlets is no act of 'bravery'. The remark is rather odd. Was she referring to the satyagraha in general of which distribution of leaflets is a major feature, or was she referring to any incident on the spot?

TUESDAY, NOVEMBER 25

The question is answered by a BBC report which says that at the rally of primary teachers addressed by Indira Gandhi last Saturday, there was a protest demonstration, and that four persons were arrested. Indira Gandhi's pique is on account of this.

The Press reports that J.P. has been operated upon at the Jaslok Hospital. A prominently displayed box item says that the Prime Minister had sent Uma Shankar Dikshit to Bombay to inquire about J.P.'s health! There is, however, not a word on All India Radio; indeed, there has been nothing in the official news bulletins as yet on J.P.'s health.

Another important news item is about the Janata Front's victory in the Surat Corporation elections. Following Hitendra Desai's joining the ruling Congress some weeks ago and his appointment as President of the Gujarat Pradesh Congress Committee (ruling), there had been a lot of propaganda that Congress(O) members in large numbers were defecting to the ruling party. Surat is Hitendrabhai's home town. Hitendra Desai and Madho Singh Solanki had issued a statement expressing confidence that their party would sweep the polls in Surat and Baroda, and that Babubhai Desai, the Chief Minister, ought to accept the elections as a test of confidence in his Ministry. "We would be the first to garland Babubhai if he resigns", they boasted. Surat has administered to the ruling Congress a resounding slap in the face.

WEDNESDAY, NOVEMBER 26

The ruling Congress suffers another setback in Gujarat. The Press reports that the Janata Front has triumphed in the Baroda Municipal Corporation also.

November 27 is Kamala's birthday. I draft three greetings telegrams, one to Kamala and the other two for Surat and Baroda. I hand them over personally to the jail office. I am told later that the Surat and Baroda telegrams have not been permitted; only the third one has been sent.

Santosh Hegde informs us in the evening that the High Court will deliver its judgment on the preliminary objections on Friday.

THURSDAY, NOVEMBER 27

Jois meets us in the evening. He mentions that doctors who have been to Bombay and seen J.P. feel greatly concerned about his health. His condition is critical, they say. We have already come to know from arrested satyagrahis that J.P.'s brother Rajeshwar Prasad had met J.P. in the first week of November and felt much disturbed by the state of his health. On November 9, without J.P.'s knowledge, Prasad addressed a letter to Indira Gandhi in which he wrote: "I have very serious apprehensions that if his (J.P.'s) condition continues like this he might not survive for more than two months. This is causing us great anguish. I have not discussed my anxiety with J.P. nor mentioned that I would be writing to you, but I feel I must apprise you about his condition so that you can make your own assessment. Apart from the great personal tragedy that this loss would mean to our family, it is for you to decide whether it would be in the best interest of the government, if J.P. dies in jail".

On November 11, J.P. was released. Indira Gandhi obviously agreed with Prasad that it would not be in the best interest of the government, if J.P. died in jail! Neither generosity nor humantarian considerations had prompted his release. The motivation was sheer political self-interest. The parole announcement betrayed it very clearly. It was adding insult to injury.

FRIDAY, NOVEMBER 28

The Karnataka High Court pronounces judgment on the Government of India's preliminary objection to our writ petitions. The Court overrules the objection and holds that our petitions are maintainable. In its earlier order the Court had formulated six questions which it thought had to be answered for a proper disposal of the objection.

The first two questions related to the justiciability of the proclamation of the emergency. The Court's answer to these questions is that a proclamation of emergency is non-justiciable. It based its decisions on the Supreme Court's rulings, particularly Justice Krishna Iyer's judgment in what has come to be known as the Bhoothnath case. In this the Supreme Court had held that "it was argued that there was no real emergency and yet the proclamation remained unretracted with consequential peril to fundamental rights. In our view, this is a political, not justiciable issue and the appeal should be to the polls and not to the Courts. . . ."

The High Court does not agree with our contention that a subsequent observation in the same judgment concedes that in certain situations the Courts can intervene. Justice Krishna Iyer has also said: "Of course, when a problem which is essentially and basically constitutional—although dressed up as a political question, is appropriately raised before the Court, it is within the power of the judges to adjudicate".

Without explaining how, the judgment blandly affirms that "the above sentence does not, in our opinion, detract from the effect of the dictum of His Lordship that a proclamation of emergency is not justiciable".

Our attack on the validity of the proclamation is based on two grounds: firstly, that it is mala fide, and secondly, that it has been in violation of Article 74(1) of the Constitution which makes it obligatory for the President to act only on the aid and advice of his Council of Ministers. If the President acts on his own, or only on the advice of the Prime Minister, as he had done in issuing this proclamation, it is not a constitutionally valid act.

It is significant that the Court has not rejected the argument. It has repeated the legal position affirmed by the Supreme Court that "the requirement of clause (1) of Article 74 that the President should act on the aid and advice of Ministers is mandatory". It has also taken note of the fact that the averment made by the petitioners that the President had acted without the advice of the Cabinet "has not been specifically rebutted in the counter statements filed on behalf of the Union of India". But it has added that in view of clause (2) of Article 74, the Courts cannot enquire whether or not the President acted on the advice of his Cabinet. "In other words", so runs the judgment, "that clause makes that question non-justiciable". It adds: "Even if there is any contravention of the mandatory requirement of Article 74 (1), the remedy is not in the courts but elsewhere". The evident suggestion is that the President may be impeached for that.

Thus to the first two questions formulated, the Court answered in the negative and held that a proclamation of emergency is non-justiciable.

The next two questions pertained to the validity of the 38th and 39th constitutional amendments. The need to answer these questions would have arisen only if the first two had been answered in the affirmation. In this case, the Court has held that

there is no need to pronounce on them. The last two questions
are those that really clinched the issue of maintainability. These
questions are whether a MISA detenu can move a habeas
corpus petition, and whether a High Court can entertain such
a petition, notwithstanding the issuance of a Presidential Order
under Article 359 (1). The High Court's answer is: Yes. The
relevant portion of the judgment reads: "Inspite of the
Presidential order suspending enforcement of the fundamental
rights conferred by Articles 21 and 22 of the Constitution, this
Court can examine whether an order of detention is (a) in accordance with those provisions only of the Maintenance of Internal
Security Act, which constitute the conditions precedent for
exercise of power thereunder (but not those provisions of the
Act which are merely procedural); (b) mala fide; or (c) made
on the basis of relevant material by which the detaining authority
could have been satisfied that order is necessary".

Government counsel seeks leave to appeal, which is granted.
He also urges stay of proceedings which is declined. The case is
however adjourned till December 10.

BBC reports about a *New Statesman* article by a Labour
M.P. who had been to India for the Commonwealth Parliamentary Conference. The article is sharply critical of the conditions in India. The author narrates his own experiences.

MONDAY, DECEMBER 1

Indira Gandhi has reshuffled her Cabinet. The Press front-
paged the changes. Uma Shankar Dikshit's ouster is no surprise.
Swaran Singh's exit is. He was supposed to be a man for all
seasons. Many interpretations are being put on his resignation.
One that he has been unhappy about the emergency happenings
and so has fallen from her grace. Secondly that he continues to
command Indira Gandhi's confidence and that his ouster is only
a prelude to the weeding out of ministers equally senior, but
less loyal.

Today's *Indian Express* has yet another clever piece of news
—this one about Hemvati Nandan Bahuguna. Abu's tall and
short twins have this observation to make on the event:
"Bahuguna had to go. He was interfering in the internal affairs
of U.P".

We receive a report from North Canara that the magistrates there are generally discharging satyagrahis charged under the DIR. In one specific case, the satyagrahis admitted having shouted a list of seventeen slogans like "J.P. Zindabad", "Indirawani Asatya Wani", "Down with Emergency", etc. The magistrate held that shouting such slogans was not an offence under the DIR.

THURSDAY, DECEMBER 4
The 9.00 P.M. radio bulletin announces revocation of the detention order against J.P. Whatever the motivation of the decision, it is welcome. All reports about J.P., formal and informal, cause concern and anxiety.

FRIDAY, DECEMBER 5
Two days hence, on December 7, Balasaheb Deoras, Sarsanghchalak of the RSS, will be completing sixty years of age. Friends in the jail decide to have a get-together and offer prayers on the occasion. Satyagrahis coming from the Court inform us that friends outside would be sending sweets for distribution on the occasion. Meanwhile, a message from outside says that the Lok Sangharsh Samiti has called for country-wide prayers on December 7 for the health of Jayaprakash Narayan. We decide to blend the two functions suitably. Those who had offered to send sweets from outside are advised not do so.

SATURDAY, DECEMBER 6
Raghupati, an M.A. student, is brought to jail after being kept incommunicado for seven days and subjected to savage torture by the Bangalore police. The police authorities are at their wits' end tracking down the source of the Lok Sangharsh Samiti literature. So, any worker found distributing pamphlets is picked up and tortured. Raghupati was apprehended by the police on Sunday, November 30. The law required that the young man be produced before a magistrate on December 1. But the police did nothing of the kind. Raghupati's worried father called on Rama Jois and on his advice, filed a habeas corpus petition in the High Court. Even after six days, that is, on Friday, December 5, when the High Court took up the matter for consideration, the Government counsel stoutly denied that Raghupati had been arrested. When on behalf of Raghupati's

father Jois challenged the veracity of Government's stand, counsel said that the police inspector concerned would be available only at 4.45 P.M. that is after Court hours. The Court decided to sit till 5.00 P.M. The inspector arrived and with a straight face denied that Raghupati had been arrested. As an upshot of all that Raghupati was brought to the jail today with scars and bruises on his body. The chargesheet against him later said that he was arrested on the night of December 5 at 10.00 P.M. when shouting slogans and distributing pamphlets!

Jois comes to the jail in the evening, records a full statement by Raghupati and proposes to initiate contempt of court proceedings against the police officials who had told the Court brazen-faced lies.

SUNDAY, DECEMBER 7

A meeting is held in the jail where prayers are offered for the health of Jayaprakash Narayan. There are recitations from the Upanishads and the Quran. Devotional songs are sung in chorus. Shyam Nandan Mishra addresses the gathering and pays rich tributes to the Sarvodaya leader. He refers to the fact that it was also the 61st birth anniversary of Balasaheb Deoras and prays that God bless the RSS leader with long life for the service of the nation. Earlier, Mishra, Dandavate and myself send a joint greetings telegram to Deoras at Yerawada. Narasimhachar, Bangalore Sangh Chalak, sends another telegram on behalf of all swayam sewaks in jail and on his own behalf.

MONDAY, DECEMBER 8

The newspapers report that J.P. had a heart attack last night. In its 2 P.M. bulletin All India Radio also reports that J.P. had had some breathing difficulty in the morning, but was all right later.

All India Radio announces that three Ordinances relating to the Press have been promulgated. The first Ordinance provides for the scrapping of the Press Council. The second does away with the immunity conferred on the Press in regard to defamation etc. in the reporting of parliamentary proceedings. The third Ordinance, the worst of the lot, tightens the statutory curbs on freedom of the Press by empowering Government to proceed against any paper found guilty of publishing "objectionable matter".

The Ordinances were signed by President Fakhruddin Ali Ahmed while on a tour of West Asia. A special courier secured his signature to the documents and brought them home.

TUESDAY, DECEMBER 9
Completed reading the much-talked-about "Freedom at Midnight" by Larry Collins and Dominique Lapierre. For sheer readability, the book is A1. It's as racy as fiction. The pity is that in a large measure, it is fiction, though it pretends to be history. The only personality to whom the authors have done justice is Mahatma Gandhi. Lord Mountbatten, of course, emerges from the book as a kind of super man. On the whole, history and historical personages have been badly mangled, with the authors' obsession with sex surfacing from time to time.

WEDNESDAY, DECEMBER 10
We are taken to the High Court for our scheduled hearing. We have already been informed by our lawyers that the Supreme Court has stayed High Court proceedings and posted Government's appeal against the High Court judgment for hearing on December 15. In the Court Government counsel formally state this fact and the hearing is adjourned till after the disposal of the appeal by the Supreme Court.

One more victim of police cruelty arrives in the jail. He is Krishnamoorthy, a college teacher who was picked up on Friday (December 5) and tortured by the Special Branch. He has been repeatedly subjected to what is known in police circles as the 'aeroplane treatment'. His feet are tied together. His wrists are tied behind his back, and the rope which binds his wrists is slung round a pulley fixed to the ceiling. This rope is then pulled gradually. The victim's arms undergo an excruciating convolution, often resulting in permanent damage to nerves and muscles. The rope continues to be pulled until the victim is lifted up. He is then kept suspended in mid air with his body in an extremely painful posture and interrogated.

When Krishnamoorthy arrived in the jail, he was so badly shaken that he could not even talk coherently. His face wore a dazed and terrified look. One of the first questions he put to other colleagues in the jail was "They will keep me with you, won't they?"

The police could get nothing out of Krishnamoorthy for the

simple reason that the young teacher had nothing to tell. What really worried us inside was the knowledge that a couple of prominent swayam sewaks actually organising the movement outside had been picked up and despite habeas corpus petitions filed on their behalf in the High Court, they were not being produced before any magistrate.

Incidentally, I note that today itself the U.N. General Assembly approved a resolution sponsored by Greece condemning torture of prisoners, particularly political prisoners. Moving the resolution, Anestis Papasterhanon, Secretary-General of the Greek Ministry of Justice said, "For us, the Greeks, torture is not an abstract topic, but a painful reality", born out of years of suffering under a military regime. The U.N. Assembly then asked the appropriate committee to draft codes "to protect jailed or detained persons against torture and other forms of inhuman or degrading treatment or punishment".

THURSDAY, DECEMBER 11

President Fakhruddin is to return to India from his West Asian tour. It is intriguing why Indira Gandhi sent the Press Ordinances abroad for his signature when they could very well have been signed by him on his return. There is nothing in the Ordinances that could not have waited for three days.

Anyway, I am sure the President is never going to forget Abu's cartoon on him today. It is brutal and irreverent, but well-deserved I must say. It is in today's *Indian Express*, and shows Fakhruddin signing the Press Ordinances in his bathtub, handing them over to a messenger who has intruded into the bathroom, and telling him: "If there are any more Ordinances, just ask them to wait".

Jois meets us in the evening. Jois tells us that Shanti Bhushan and some other senior members of the Supreme Court Bar are going to meet the Chief Justice to impress upon him that the hearing due to commence on December 15 regarding the scope of judicial review in MISA detention cases is very important and so the seniormost judges should be appointed to the Bench which will consider it.

FRIDAY, DECEMBER 12

Dinesh Kamath and two other swayam sewaks apprehended

several days ago are brought to jail under the DIR. They reveal that Sheshu and Srinivasa (about whom we were feeling concerned) are in police custody and are being tortured. Both of them are on a hunger strike for the last four days insisting that they be produced before a magistrate as required by the law. As a result of the hunger strike, the torture has been stopped.

Blitz weekly of Bombay reports that J.P. has categorically turned down suggestions for withdrawal of his movement. Immediately after J.P.'s release the journal itself wrote an editorial suggesting it. In its latest editorial, R.K. Karanjia extols Vinoba Bhave and hopes he will resolve the present political deadlock by bringing about 'national reconciliation'. Vinoba is to end his one-year *maun-vrat* (silence) on December 25, which would also mark the silver jubilee of the Bhoodan movement. Vinoba's speech at the conference to be held at Paunar on December 25 is to be broadcast and telecast. The revenue ministers of all the States are to participate in the conference. The kind of official publicity being given to the conference suggests a measure of Governmental interest in it.

SATURDAY, DECEMBER 13

Rama Jois meets us in the morning and informs us that Chief Justice A.N. Ray has agreed to include the seniormost judges in the Bench which is to consider Government's appeal against us. The Bench will thus comprise the Chief Justice himself, and Justices H.R. Khanna, M.H. Beg, Y.V. Chandrachud and P.N. Bhagwati. Jois is to leave for Delhi in the evening.

One more RSS activist, Arakali Narayan, is held under MISA.

Press reports on J.P.'s health are reassuring. I got a message today indicating that the Lok Sangharsh Samiti is proposing to dissociate itself from George Fernandes, Socialist leader who has been underground since the imposition of the emergency. Some of his activities and writings favouring violent action are not liked by many in the Samiti. I convey to them my reaction that it would be unwise to do so. We may discuss his activities and writings with him but in the kind of struggle we are involved in, anything that smacks of a rift in the movement must be scrupulously avoided.

SUNDAY, DECEMBER 14

The *Sunday Standard* has another delightful piece from Abu. A caged parrot is shown prattling "Work more, talk less; work more, talk less" *ad nauseam*. In a letter to Ghatate, I request him to convey to Abu our sincerest appreciation of his contributions—from his Barefoot Humour to his Bath tub Humour. The same paper reports that Sanjay Gandhi would be presiding over an agricultural conference in U.P. which would "also" be addressed by Kamalapati Tripathi.

MONDAY, DECEMBER 15

Sheshu and Srinivasa[15] are brought to jail. Srinivasa has been very badly tortured. Their hungerstrike, coupled with the habeas corpus petitions filed in the High Court, however, brought the torture to an end.

The morning dailies report the celebration of Sanjay Gandhi's birthday. Evidently, the heir-apparent has been anointed. The dailies also carry a curtain-raiser on the Supreme Court appeal due to begin today. No names are mentioned but the issues to be decided are indicated. Directly in question are three judgments of the Karnataka High Court, one of the Jabalpur Bench of the Madhya Pradesh High Court and another of the Allahabad High Court. In our case, the appellant is the Government of India. In the other two, the appeals are filed by the respective State Governments. But as similar petitions are pending before all High Courts, all Advocates-General have been given notice and are expected to intervene.

All India Radio announces that the next session of Parliament will be held from January 5 and will last four weeks. The report also says that there would be question hour. How very condescending! However, one should be thankful for even small mercies these days.

A batch of Bangalore satyagrahis led by Krishnayya is discharged by a local magistrate. The Magistrate Chandrashekhar, who holds that shouting slogans against the emergency or demanding the realease of leaders through pamphlets is no offence under the DIR.

---

[15] RSS activists.

BBC reports that two Sunday papers of London carried long articles on the Indian situation on December 14. One of them, The *Sunday Times*, published its correspondent's interview with George Fernandes, "the man most sought by Indira Gandhi's Government". Fernandes said that till now there had been three satyagrahas. In each of the first two 10,000 satyagrahis had courted arrest. In the third from November 14 to January 15 one lakh would court arrest. *The Observer* reported the arrival of a Socialist emissary in London. The emissary has submitted a 26-page report on the Indian situation to the Socialist International.

TUESDAY, DECEMBER 16

The Press gives good coverage to the Supreme Court hearing of our case. Justice Khanna points out to Niren De that Article 21 of the Constitution deals with the right not only to personal liberty but also to life. Is it the stand of the Attorney-General that even if a person is killed he has no remedy because enforcement of the right has been suspended? Niren De replies: "It weighs on my conscience. But that is the position in law".

We have a new, and very welcome, colleague—Ramakrishna Hegde, Congress(O) leader in the State Legislature Council, and former Finance Minister of Mysore State (now Karnataka). Hegde had offered satyagraha on November 14 but had not been sent to jail. He has been so active outside that he has made it impossible for the authorities to let him remain out.

WEDNESDAY, DECEMBER 17

All India Radio announces that the Jaslok Hospital would hereafter issue a bulletin on J.P.'s health only once in three days and not daily as until now. The reason given is improvement in J.P.'s health. The news that J.P.'s health has improved is heartening. But this squeamishness about health bulletins is ununderstandable. Someone in the Government is perhaps irked by J.P.'s name appearing in print daily even if it be on account of his ill-health. For five months, he had been a "non-person" as far as the newspapers were concerned. Only the imminence of death has made the authorities allow brief references to him in the Press. Now that that danger has receded, let J.P.'s name also go into limbo: that is how the authorities' mind seems to be working.

THURSDAY, DECEMBER 18

Padma Joshi, her two women colleagues and Prabha, a swayam sewak, who were arrested on August 15, are discharged by the magistrate. They had distributed pamphlets. The magistrate has held it is no offence. But they have undergone more than four months' imprisonment—without being formally convicted whereas some others found guilty have been awarded shorter terms.

BBC states that the International Commission of Jurists has released its annual report in which seven countries have been named where laws impairing the position of the judiciary have been passed. India is one of those seven.

All India Radio reports that in the panchayat elections in Gujarat, Congress is leading over the Janata Front. The report is strange. Normally the radio does not cover panchayat or municipal committee elections. Corporation elections and those to the Assemblies it covers. But while the Surat and Baroda Corporation results were not reported, incomplete accounts of the panchayat poll are being put out.

FRIDAY, DECEMBER 19

The *Hindu* of Madras reports a Bombay High Court decision striking down a prohibitory order against a proposed meeting of lawyers. BBC describes it as another setback for the Government on the judicial front.

The Gujarat panchayat poll results are not complete as yet. But All India Radio continues to crow about Congress victory in every one of its news bulletins.

SATURDAY, DECEMBER 20

There is a perceptible tightening of security arrangements in the case of MISA detenus. This is particularly noticed by those going to the hospital. Dandavate who has been going frequently to the hospital for physio-therapy (for spondylitis) says that while originally the escorting police officials never objected to his purchasing a book or a journal on his way back they seemed somewhat hesitant now. Enquiries reveal that the cause of this strictness is the practice of detainees held under COFEPOSA (Conservation of Foreign Exchange and Prevention of Smuggling

Act) to use their private funds—of which they have no dearth—to get whatever they want during their trips to the hospital.

A curious incident involving one such detainee made the authorities aware of the happenings. The detainee who has been in jail for about a year has been blessed with a son this month! An amusing aspect of the story is that earlier in the month he made an application to the State Government seeking release on parole as his wife was due to be delivered of a child. It was this application that made the State Government conscious of the facilities which COFEPOSA detainees are enjoying. The upshot of this is (a) greater strictness in respect of MISA detenus and (b) transfer of most COFEPOSA detainees a few days later to other Central jails in the State.

Another transfer, of a political detenu, is, however, patently unjust and unwarranted. Ramakrishna Hegde, who had been brought here just four days ago is bundled off to Belgaum for no rhyme or reason. His family is in Bangalore. The detention order specifically mentioned that he be kept in Bangalore. Perhaps the State Government does not relish his being with us.

All India Radio did not miss today also the report of Congress victory in the Gujarat panchayat elections. The results are not complete still.

Prakash Chandra Sethi and Bansi Lal are included in the Union Cabinet. Sethi's replacement by S.C. Shukla appears to have more to do with factional politics in the State than with considerations of New Delhi's politics. But Bansi Lal's induction into the Central Government is clear evidence of Sanjay Gandhi's growing influence. Bahuguna's ouster from U.P. some weeks ago is also believed to be Sanjay's handiwork.

We have been expecting our advocate Rama Jois today. He had gone to Delhi for a case and was due to return today. But he does not turn up. Maybe, he has been held up in Delhi.

SUNDAY, DECEMBER 21

At last the complete results of the panchayat elections in Gujarat are out. Judging by what the radio has been saying all these days one would have thought that the Janata Front has been wiped out and that the Congress party has swept the polls. There are in all 670 district panchayat seats in the State.

Of those the Congress party has won 383 seats. In the taluk panchayats there is a total of 3,942 seats. The Congress has taken 2,024 seats of these. In the Assembly elections last June the position of the ruling Congress in the countryside was decidedly better than this. From the Janata Front point of view, the results indicate that in the rural areas the Front has still not been able to make headway.

MONDAY, DECEMBER 22

Around eleven o'clock in the morning, a convict helpmate comes and tells us that our advocate Rama Jois has been arrested and brought to the jail. The news sounds incredible. We first think our informant is mistaken. Jois must have come to meet us after his return from Delhi. We rush to the deputy superintendent's room where we find Jois, with bag and baggage and accompanied by the Station House Officer of the High Ground police station, Hasabi. The message given to us is correct. Jois has been arrested under MISA.

The police had been to the airport on Sunday to arrest him immediately on his arrival from Delhi. But Jois had gone to Bombay from Delhi and returned to Bangalore by a later flight. So the police missed him at the airport and later apprehended him at the residence. There is no doubt that Jois was arrested because he has been at the head of a team of Bangalore lawyers who are waging a fearless legal battle for civil liberties. It is he who did all the spade work for our case and also mobilised the best possible legal talent for it. That a lawyer should have been arrested for fulfilling his professional obligations is an outrage without precedent in independent India and perhaps without parallel even in the British days. It appears that apart from the general annoyance Jois's activity has caused to the State Government, the series of *habeas corpus* petitions he has filed on behalf of Lok Sangharsh Samiti workers picked up by the police and tortured in custody and particularly his exposure of the police officials indulging in third-degree methods is responsible for his detention.

TUESDAY, DECEMBER 23

Shyama Charan Shukla has been sworn in as Chief Minister of Madhya Pradesh. Newspapers report that his name was proposed by his predecessor P.C. Sethi. It reminds me that four years ago when Sethi assumed the chief ministership of the State, his first public pronouncement which was widely reported and talked about even more had referred to Shukla and his colleagues as "Ali Baba and his forty thieves" whom he had gone to Bhopal from Delhi to hound out of the State's politics: (Sethi was until then a minister-of-State at the Centre). The sentiment was mutual. I recall a few months before the emergency I happened to run into S.C. Shukla at the Palam airport. In the course of a brief chat I asked him how stable the Sethi ministry was. I was literally taken aback by his response. He nearly pounced on me saying that Jana Sangh legislators in the State were not cooperating with him in pulling Sethi down! "Jana Sangh have a soft corner for Sethi", Shukla added in a complaining tone. The incident surprised me, not only because Shukla's grouse was factually baseless, but more because it betrayed how bitter the relations between the two Congress factions were.

This morning's papers carry advertisements by the Handloom House offering 20 per cent rebate "in honour of the Prime Minister's 20 point programme". For once, I wish the programme had 100 points!

BBC carries a review of British Press reaction to six months of emergency in India. The entire Press, BBC reports, has been severely critical of the emergency. From papers like the *Daily Telegraph* which have never been able to reconcile themselves to an independent India to those like the *Guardian* which have been traditionally and steadfastly pro-India, all have condemned the emergency. So have the people. Individuals like Jennie Lee are rare exceptions, BBC notes. But the British Government, BBC says, has avoided formal reaction. The only overt action was the cancellation of a visit to India by the Prince of Wales. No reasons were given to it. At the same time, the largest amount of aid ever given to India by the UK was during the emergency. The BBC commentator for his part makes no secret of his unhappiness at the present state of affairs in India.

BBC also reports that the International Press Institute, Zurich, has published its annual report in which the Government of India has been sharply criticised for the curbs it has imposed on press freedom.

WEDNESDAY, DECEMBER 24

All discussions in the jail are centred round what is likely to be the substance of Vinoba Bhave's speech tomorrow. All India Radio has been publicising the event with a vengeance. Journals like the *Blitz* and the *Current*, supposed to be close to official quarters, have also been writing a lot about the Paunar conference.

THURSDAY, DECEMBER 25

It is Christmas Day today. We complete exactly six months of detention today. I remark to Madhu: "When we think or speak about our incarceration, we think in terms of months. We had better attune ourselves mentally to thinking in terms of years. We shall feel more settled".

Today is Atalji's birthday. We send him a greetings telegram.

Vinoba Bhave is to break his *maun-vrat* (vow of silence) at 11.00 A.M. today. To all persons approaching him till now and seeking his intervention in the political situation his reply has been: "Wait till December 25". He has written this to Vasant Nargolkar, Sarvodaya leader, who had proposed a fast unto death from November 14 to press the demand for the end of the emergency. Nargolkar agreed to put off his fast till today. A group of women from Nagpur also called on Vinoba and told him that they were wives of detenus. They wanted his advice. Vinoba's written reply to them was: "Trust God; help one another; wait till December 25". So naturally, there is an air of expectancy about what may happen at Paunar.

The first news from Paunar is available from All India Radio at 2.00 P.M. Vinoba is reported as having stressed the need for discipline, deprecated resort to satyagraha and warned against the machination of the big powers. All of us feel let down and bored while we await a fuller report of Vinoba's speech; the All India Radio version at least has made the Baba sound a faithful echo of the Prime Minister.

The taped version of Vinoba's speech played by All India Radio at night conveys a different, and less subservient, flavour than the news report. But it is not quite distinct. It is an edited version and so tends to reinforce the impression conveyed by the earlier radio news reports. Particularly galling is the fact that Vinoba has not said a word about J.P. in his speech.

FRIDAY, DECEMBER 26
Press reports from Paunar are tailored; even so, they do not convey the disgusting impression which the radio version had created about Vinoba's speech. It is noteworthy that nowhere has it been reported that Vinoba ruled out satyagraha. The recorded report on the Paunar conference (second day) relayed by the Nagpur station of All India Radio carried speeches by 'stalwarts' of the Sarvodaya movement like Sitaram Kesari! The Marathi weekly *Sadhana* later reported that when Kesari's name was called out from the dais a veteran Sarvodaya worker blew up in anger. "Have we come here to listen to sermons on Bhoodan from Kesaris?" he asked. To which, another sarcastically replied: "Vinoba is the manifestation of Gyanoba (Gyaneswar); and about Gyanoba it is said that he made even a buffalo recite the Vedas! Why wonder if Vinoba tries to make Kesari perorate on Bhoodan?"

SATURDAY, DECEMBER 27
On the third day of the Paunar Conference, Vinoba Bhave moots the idea of an acharya sammelan (conference of preceptors) to consider and pronounce on the present situation. All India Radio, I notice, omits to report this part of Vinoba's speech. The idea, it seems, is Vinoba's own and does not carry official imprimatur. Subsequent developments showed that Vinoba's low key start on December 25 was deliberate and was consciously intended to lead up to the acharya sammelan denouement without provoking Indira Gandhi to snuff out his moves at the start.

The *Blitz* carries a small news item about J.P.'s letter to the Prime Minister. The report is headlined "J.P. blasts hopes of national reconciliation". The letter is said to be strongly worded, "written in elegant prose", and "oozing anti-Sovietism". The *Blitz* has been obviously misinformed about the date of the letter. The letter was written on July 21 from jail. The *Blitz* correspondent is under the impression that it has been written after J.P.'s release.

Kamala and children arrive from Delhi. It is a joy meeting them after three and a half months.

SUNDAY, DECEMBER 28

There has lately been a welter of statements by Congressmen that the Constitution needs to be changed early and that delay would be disastrous. Indira Gandhi threw cold water on such talk with a statement that changes in the Constitution should be preceded by a thorough-going public debate. As if an electric button has been pressed, the tenor of speeches regarding constitutional amendment changes. Every Congress *chhut-bhaiya* (small fry) now talks of the need for a public discussion on the issue.

Indira Gandhi's statement is a part of an interview she gave to the Souvenir published on the eve of the Congress session at Chandigarh. In the interview, she quotes Thomas Jefferson's well-known dictum about the desirablity of reviewing a country's Constitution every twenty years. She has cited him against the opposition whom she described as being opposed to any change in the Constitution.

For one, none of the opposition parties in the J.P. movement is opposed to desirable changes in the Constitution. Indeed, if one were to go through the election manifestoes of the various political parties for the 1971 and 1972 elections, one would find that they are more committed to constitutional reform than the ruling party. The Jana Sangh has favoured the setting up of a Commission on the Constitution to review its working. The Socialist party has advocated a fresh constituent assembly. So, there is no substance in Indira Gandhi's charge that the opposition parties are for an inflexible Constitution.

We, however, hold that the present Government's annoyance with the Constitution stems not from social or economic factors, as it keeps propagating, but from political considerations. It is the democratic content of the Constitution which the present Establishment regards as a road block to its ambitions. The emergency empowers the Government to suspend any of the fundamental rights. It is significant that Article 31, namely that relating to the right to property, has *not* been suspended. The Articles suspended are Article 14 (right to equality), Article 19 (the seven freedoms of expression, assembly, association, movement, trade etc.) Article 21 (right to life and personal liberty etc). These are the provisions which embody a citizen's democratic rights. The executive can ride rough shod over these rights during an emergency. It is doing so most shamelessly these days. But what the Government would very much desire is to make its present authority perpetual under the Constitution.

The ruling party has the requisite majority also to make the necessary change in the Constitution. But the Keshavananda Bharati judgment which lays down that the basic democratic structure of the Constitution cannot be altered has become an insurmountable hurdle. That is why the Government is so bitter about this judgment.

Incidentally, it is a pleasant surprise to hear Indira Gandhi quote Jefferson. For the past few months, quoting Western Liberal thinkers has become *passe*, if not altogether retrograde and reactionary. However, one wonders how familiar Indira Gandhi is with the political philosophy of Jefferson. His views reek with sedition. "God forbid," he wrote to a friend, "We should ever be twenty years without a revolution".

One of Jefferson's biggest contributions to liberal political thought is his insistence that a citizen has the right to defy an unconstitutional statute. "What country can preserve its liberties if its rulers are not warned from time to time that the people preserve the spirit of resistance?" he asked.

Jefferson abhorred curbs on press freedom even though as President he had personally to suffer considerable mudslinging. "I shall protect them in the right of lying and calumniating", he said. "Censorship of any kind would negate the very spirit of democracy by substituting tyranny over the mind for despotism over the body".

Jefferson was the author of the American Declaration of Independence proclaimed in 1776. There is no doubt that if Jefferson had been living in India in the year of grace 1976, his speeches and writings would have made him one of the greatest threats to the security of the State and landed him behind the bars as a MISA detenu.

Today, Ahmedabad goes to the polls to elect its Corporation. In the last Assembly elections unlike as in Rajkot, Baroda and Surat where the Janata Front made a clean sweep of all the seats, it was a close contest in Ahmedabad. Out of 13 Assembly seats in the city, the Front captured 7 and the Congress 6. Of the six seats won by the Congress five were those which had been allotted to the Majoor Mahajan (the labour wing of the Congress-O).

MONDAY, DECEMBER 29

At Chandigarh, the Law Minister H.R. Gokhale, disowns

having anything to do with the paper on proposed constitutional changes going round the capital, and commented upon adversely by all the leading dailies of the country. The paper was first published by the pro-CPI *Mainstream* of Delhi on November 22. The changes suggested concentrated all powers in the President, virtually did away with fundamental rights, and made the judiciary subordinate to the executive. The preamble offered this rationale for the proposed changes: "The time of the Chief Executive should not be allowed to be frittered away in fruitless debate and discussion and in attending to comparatively less important matters at the expense of major and vital decisions affecting the people as a whole".

Mainstream mentioned that the paper had "the blessings of some of the Congresss luminaries". The journal has the reputation of knowing the mind of official New Delhi quite well. For more than a month after its publication, no one had even hinted that *Mainstream* was wrong. Comments on the document have appeared in a large number of newspapers and journals in the country. Almost all were critical. To top it, the Bar Council of India convened an emergency meeting at Delhi on December 27 and condemned the document. The Bar Council said that if the scheme were adopted, it would lead to the destruction of democracy.

The meeting was held on December 23. On December 28 Indira Gandhi gave her press statement counselling public debate on constitutional changes. Today, the Law Minister tries to wash his hands of the document. The sequence of events does not appear accidental. The paper on constitutional changes was, evidently, a trial balloon. Seeing that it failed to take off, the Government has decided to abandon it, in its present form.

All India Radio relays in the evening an edited version of Indira Gandhi's speech at the Chandigarh session of the Congress. The speech is surprising. In fact, it is hardly a speech, it is one long shriek, angry and bitter. Its sum and substance is: the emergency is not going to be lifted. Why? no reasons. There is a bagful of abuses and invective for the opposition. "The anti-democratic" forces have not been quelled, they are only lying low, she says.

Indira Gandhi's style of speech-making reminds me of the observations made by Hitler in his *Mein Kampf* on political oratory. Hitler says the masses are 'feminine' acting on feeling and sentiment, rather than reasoning, and that whatever you tell them must be addressed to the dullest ignorant among them, in order to reach and convince the broadest possible audience.

The rantings against the opposition parties are not surprising; what is surprising is her bitter outburst against some of her own colleagues, none of whom she complains came to her rescue when she was under attack from the opposition. Some of them, she recalls tartly, even advised her that the late Lalit Narain Mishra should be dropped! She describes such colleagues of hers as 'cowards' and adds: "The country is never going to accept cowards as leaders!"

If Chavan and others are still hoping that Indira Gandhi will one day permit one of them to step into her place, this virulent outburst should help disabuse their minds. Positively, Indira Gandhi has already indicated that she favours Sanjay as her successor; negatively, the speech is a declaration that she would never tolerate any of them howsoever much they may crawl and cringe before her.

TUESDAY, DECEMBER 30

First press reports on the Ahmedabad poll are very heartening. Out of 27 seats declared, the Janata Front has won 22 and the Congress 5 ! All India Radio however has not a word on the subject.

All India Radio relays one more angry speech of Indira Gandhi from Chandigarh. The main target of attack today is the RSS, which she says has taken roots even where it did not exist before. The reference seems to be to Kerala and Karnataka where the response to the satyagraha call given by the Lok Sangharsh Samiti has shocked the authorities.

WEDNESDAY, DECEMBER 31

An important news item reported by the Press relates to a meeting of opposition M.Ps held in Ahmedabad. The meeting decided to form a Janata Front in Parliament. The Congress (O), Socialist Party, B.L.D. and Jana Sangh have agreed to join the Front. N.G. Goray who sponsored the move told newsmen that the DMK and CPI (M) would cooperate with the Front.

The counting of votes in the Ahmedabad civic elections

continues. Out of 59 seats the results of which have been declared, 39 have gone to the Janata Front and 20 to the Congress. The reports indicate that the Muslim-majority areas and the labour constituencies have been voting Congress.

Indira Gandhi's first day's speech at Chandigarh is relayed again. It is full of gall and wormwood. She refers to the detenus and says that while we have only jailed them, if they (the opposition) had been in power, they would have cut our throats.

Arguments can be met by arguments; but how does one answer such malignant hysterics?

1976

THURSDAY, JANUARY 1

The Ahmedabad poll results are complete. The Janata Front has won but the contest has been neck to neck, as it was in the Assembly elections. The Front has won 54 seats and the Congress 51. This is rather disappointing. While we shall have to await a fuller report to assess precisely how and why this has happened, one thing is obvious that even in the case of the urban masses, the impact of purely political issues such as civil liberties and press freedom is marginal. It would be wrong on our part to over-estimate the potential of these factors, insofar as electoral battles go.

The Voice of America reports that the U.S. Government has protested against Indira Gandhi's remarks at Chandigarh suggesting that the U.S. was trying to overthrow the Government in India in the way it had done the Allende Government of Chile. BBC also gives the news. But All India Radio blacks it out! So also we presume will the Indian Press !

FRIDAY, JANUARY 2

As expected, there is nothing in the morning dailies about the U.S. protest against Indira Gandhi's speech. The newspapers carry a summing up of the Chandigarh session of the Congress by the Press Trust of India and the United News of India. They note, inter alia: "A unique feature of the four-day proceedings, first in the Subjects Committee, and later in the plenary, was the absence of any criticism of policies or leader-

ship. Speakers, in fact, vied with one another in extending
support to them".

Lashing out at servile conformity, Mark Twain wrote once:

We are discreet sheep; we wait to see how the drove is going,
and then we go with the drove.

   We have two opinions; one private, which we are afraid to
express; and another one—the one we use—which we force
ourselves to wear to please Mrs. Grundy, until habit makes
us comfortable in it, and the custom of defending it presently
makes us love it, adore it, and forget how pitifully we came
by it.

Mrs. Grundy was a character in Thomas Morton's play
"Speed the Plough", who upheld conventional prudery. The
discreet sheep assembled at Chandigarh said and did all they
did to please their political Mrs. Grundy, Indira Gandhi.

   The Chief Minister of Gujarat, Babubhai Patel, has given to
the Press an overall picture of public opinion in the State as it
has emerged from the electoral support secured by the Janata
Front and the Congress in the recent panchayat and Corporation elections. The votes secured are as follows:

	J.F.	*Congress*
Urban Areas	7.5 lakhs	5 lakhs
Rural Areas	29.75 ,,	29.55 ,,
Total	37.25 ,,	34.55 ,,

   It is noteworthy that in the Assembly elections held in June
1975, the aggregate votes secured by the Janata Front were less
than those secured by the Congress.

SATURDAY, JANUARY 3

Sarojini Mahishi resigns from the Government. The Press
gives no reasons.

   Transistor radios are withdrawn from MISA 'B' category
detenus. They had been earlier permitted singleband transistors.
The order is supposed to apply to all MISA detenus. But it is
not implemented in our case.

It is learnt that Vasant Nargolkar, now detained in Yerawada jail, has been on a fast unto death since December 25. He was arrested on December 24 while he was proceeding to Paunar. Since then he has been on fast.

SUNDAY, JANUARY 4

Ramakrishna Hegde returns from Belgaum. His *habeas corpus* petition is due for consideration by the High Court tomorrow. His visit to Belgaum has been very useful from the point of view of the detenus and satyagrahis there.

All India Radio reports on the deliberations of the Congress Parliamentary Party's eve-of-session meeting. A meeting of the Janata Front M.Ps is also due today. But the radio does not say even a word about it.

MONDAY, JANUARY 5

Parliament session opens today.

All India Radio reports that B.R. Bhagat has been elected Speaker by 344 votes to 58. The Janata Front had put up Jagan-nathrao Joshi (now in detention) for the post. For the opposition to have mustered 58 votes even though 20 of our members are behind the bars is creditable. In her speech felicitating the Speaker, the Prime Minister attacks the opposition, something that is just not done on such occasions. I am sure some one from the opposition must have replied to the Prime Minister's observations. But All India Radio does not report anything.

BBC reports that most opposition members boycotted the President's Address to the joint session of Parliament. All India Radio however, is silent on the subject.

TUESDAY, JANUARY 6

The opposition boycott of the joint session is blacked out by the Press also. Obviously, press reporting even of parliamentary proceedings is going to be regulated hereafter.

More than a century ago, speaking in the House of Commons (26-3-1855), Benjamin Disraeli had defined NEWS "that which comes from North, East, West, and South!" He added: "If it comes from only one point of the compass, then it is a class publication, and not news". The ruling party in India today holds that the country's political compass has only one ne direction that pointing to Indira Gandhi. The be-all and end-all of news dissemination should be to subserve the interests of Indira Gandhi.

Goebbels once wrote in his diary (14-3-1943). "Not every item of news should be published: rather must those who control news policies endeavour to make every item of news serve a certain purpose". The Government's news policy is fully in accordance with the Goebbelsian dictum.

THURSDAY, JANUARY 8

Speaking in the Rajya Sabha during the debate on the Motion of Thanks to the President, Indira Gandhi lashes out furiously at the opposition, and rules out any dialogue with them. She refers derisively to the suggestion for a round-table conference made during the debate by a DMK member (earlier N.G. Goray also had made the suggestion) and declares pompously: "Whether the table is round or square, it is not possible to hold any talks".

FRIDAY, JANUARY 9

Maybe, some one has counselled her that her no-talks-with-the-opposition speech in the Rajya Sabha was indiscreet. Or maybe, on her own, the Prime Minister realised that she has slipped. Anyway, in the Lok Sabha she makes a conscious bid to erase the effect of yesterday's Rajya Sabha speech. She blames the Press for misreporting her (the Press is barred from publishing anything regarding Parliament without clearance from the censors). She says she has never been rigid and has always tried to find ways of conciliation. It is for the opposition, she says, to give up the path of obstruction and violence and to create conditions for a dialogue.

Hackneyed though it is, the old analogy applies. Indira Gandhi's counsel to the opposition is something like "stop beating your wife, and we shall be friends again!"

SATURDAY, JANUARY 10

The morning newspapers carry an important news item, its importance becoming more and more apparent with the passage of time. It is that the proposed "acharya sammelan" will be held at Paunar on January 16 to discuss the current situation in the country. Some 25 acharyas, literally professors unattached to any political section and including Vice-Chancellors, jurists and social workers will attend the conference.

Appa Ghatate, our lawyer, has written to say that his wife
Shiela has offered satyagraha at Nagpur. That makes four
in the Ghatate family who are now behind bars: Appa's father,
Balasaheb Ghatate who is Sangh Chalak of Nagpur RSS,
Appa's sister, Deshpande, her son, and Sheila. Shiela's satya-
graha has an added significance. She is the daughter of Justice
Hajarnavis of the Bombay High Court who has been actively
associated with the officially sponsored lawyers' conference.
The judge is understandably unhappy at the heterodoxy in his
home.

SUNDAY, JANUARY 11

Going through some volumes of Supreme Court judgments,
I have made an interesting discovery—that Justice Krishna Iyer
is a passionate advocate of simplicity of style, both in speech
and writing. He has taken parliamentarians to task for being
abstruse in expression. In one of his judgments (C.J. Vaswani
v. State of West Bengal 10-10-75) he writes:

> The Court has, more than once, pointed out that lack of
> legislative simplicity has led to interpretative complexity.
> The home truth that legislation is for the people and must,
> therefore, be plain enough has hardly been realised by our
> law-makers. Judges, looking at statutes, are forced to play a
> linguistic game guessing at the general legislative purpose
> and straining at semantics. In the present case we have had
> to reach the conclusion against the appellants by broadening
> the dimensions of Hyden's case importing a "context
> purpose" teleological approach.

How lucidly-phrased is this reprimand administered to
legislators! Physician, heal thyself—that's what I am tempted
to say.

But having said this, I must admit that for journalists (as I
am) it is Justice Krishna Iyer's judgments that provide good
copy, and none else's. Notwithstanding the verbosity at places,
they make interesting reading. The judgment which I have
referred to provides a good sample. The opening reads like a
passage from a novel, rather than a judicial pronouncement. It
says: "The scene is the Isias Bar, 15, Free School Street, Calcutta.
A hall of enchantment extends nocturnal invitation to have a
nice time with svelte sylphs. The entrance fee is but a paltry

Rs. 15/- per man, and inside is served animating liquor. Scantily clad female flesh of sweet seventeen or thereabouts flit about or sit on laps, to the heady tune of band music. They solicit carnal custom and the willing male victims pay Rs 30/-, choose whom they fancy, drink together and, taking leave of decencies, indulge in promiscuous sex exercise legally described as operation prostitution. The stage is busy with men and girls moving into rooms, lavatories and chambers. The curtain rises and a raiding party of police and excise officers surprise this erotic company drowned in drink and damsels".

The learned judge then proceeds to deal with the actual issues in dispute in the case which is an appeal against a lower court's order evicting a lessee from certain premises because he has been using them for immoral purposes. The concluding paras of the judgment are no less interesting. Justice Iyer observes:

We are in the International Women's Year—a circumstance meaningful socially, but not relevant legally. Even so, it is time to tighten up this statute (Suppression of Immoral Traffic in Women and Girls Act, 1956) and we may permit ourselves a few concluding observations, hopefully. Maybe, there are other provisions of the Act which have contributed to its dismal failure in the field, and the legislature must, in the International Year of Women, protect the virtue of the weaker sex from the purchasing power of the takers of virginity who sip every flower and change every hour.

No nation, with all its boasts and all its hopes, can ever morally be clean till all its women are really free, free to live without sale of their young flesh to lascivious wealth or commercialising their luscious figures. India, to redeem this 'gender justice' and to prescribe prostitution whereby rich men buy poor women through houses of vice, has salved its social conscience by enacting the Act.

But the law is so ill-drafted and lacunose that few who follow the 'most ancient profession in the world' have been frightened into virtue and the customers of wine-cum-women are catered to respectably in bars, hotels and night clubs in sophisticated and subtle ways, especially in our cities.

MONDAY, JANUARY 12

The Marathi weekly *Sadhana* reproduces an angry letter written by N.G. Goray to Vinoba Bhave. The letter was written

before the conference of December 25. The letter has a sharp,
acerbic tone, and seems to anticipate that Vinoba will not do
anything to annoy Indira Gandhi. The sum and substance of
the letter is: In your speech on December 25, please do not
equivocate. Do not tell us any *neeti kathas* (sermons) speak
your mind in language unambiguous enough to let everyone
know where you stand. Do not delude yourseif that Indira
considers you her guru. She does not deem you even an equal.

Vinoba may not have been as forthright in his December
25 speech as Goray and most of us wanted him to be. But in
that speech Vinoba had certainly not endorsed Government's
policies as the publicity media had tried to project. On January
4, the *Sunday Standard* carried verbatim that part of his speech
which had been interpreted by the Government as an endorse-
ment of the emergency on grounds of discipline. This excerpt
gives quite the contrary impression. Vinoba said: "So the
Acharyas have the discipline and those in power have the
Government. The difference between discipline and Government
should be clearly understood. I shall try to explain it breifly. If
the world fo.lowed the discipline only of the Government, it
would never live in peace and satisfaction. Take Bangladesh. It
was declared that the problem of Bangladesh was solved. . ."

The Socialist weekly *Janata* reports the horrifying treatment
meted out to Mrinal Goray, Socialist leader of Bombay (she
remained underground for six months and successfully organised
a vigorous movement on behalf of the Lok Sangharsh Samiti
in Maharashtra). Mrinal Goray is detained at Akola. She has
been put in solitary confinement. In fact, she is the only political detenue there. Next to her cell is lodged a leper woman
(the two share a common toilet). Opposite her cell is a lunatic
woman who keeps shrieking the whole night. A writ petition has
been filed on behalf of Mrinal Goray in the Bombay High
Court.

President Fakhruddin Ali Ahmed calls on J.P. at the Jaslok
Hospital.

TUESDAY, JANUARY 13

Deve Gowda, leader of the opposition in the Karnataka
State Assembly, is brought to jail. He offered satyagraha yesterday for the second time. The first time he was arrested and let off.

Madhu Dandavate writes an angry letter to the Prime Minister protesting against the conditions of detention of Mrinal Goray. In conclusion, Dandavate tells Indira Gandhi that he is aware the letter would annoy her, and adds challengingly: "I do not care if this prison yard where I have been in detention for the last six months also becomes my graveyard".

WEDNESDAY, JANUARY 14

Today is the last day of the satyagraha in Bangalore. (In some states, the Satyagraha is to last till January 26). We learn that more than 180 satyagrahis offered themselves for arrest at some ten different points in the city. Not all were arrested. About sixty of them were brought to the police stations. Of them about twenty were selected (mostly Vidyarthi Parishad members) and sent to jail under the DIR.

THURSDAY, JANUARY 15

This morning's papers carry the names of 25 acharyas who are to participate in the "acharya sammelan" due to commence at Paunar tomorrow. The list is an impressive one, and at first sight seems to fulfil broadly the three criteria set by Vinoba, that they should be fearless (*nirbhaya*), without bias (*nirvair*) and non-partisan (*nishpaksh*).

I write a letter to the Chairman of the Rajya Sabha, seeking leave of absence from the House for the current session. I avail myself of the opportunity to make a few comments on the subservience shown by presiding officers. After making the formal request for leave of absence, the letter goes on to say: "My absence is not voluntary. The Government of India considers my activities a threat to the security of India. So I am here, detained without trial in the Bangalore Central Jail".

FRIDAY, JANUARY 16

Another batch of satyagrahis arrives. This one is from Dobaballapur, a small taluk town in Bangalore district, which has by now sent more than two hundred satyagrahis.

Kamala and the children meet me. They are to leave for Madras tomorrow en route to Delhi.

All India Radio says nothing about the "acharya sammelan" at Paunar.

SUNDAY, JANUARY 17

The Press carries a brief report of Vinoba Bhave's opening address to the "acharya sammelan". Vinoba stresses the need for unanimity. Suggests that the acharyas should first hammer out a consensus, then meet the Prime Minister and discuss with her the conclusions arrived at by them.

The local newspapers are full of reports about Sanjay Gandhi's scheduled visit to Bangalore tomorrow. Huge banners with his pictures have been put up in the city. In the afternoon pamphlets announcing his programme are airdropped. Some of the pamphlets fall into our prison ward. One of them reads: "If you miss this rally, you will be missing the unfolding of a new chapter in the history of the nation".

MONDAY, JANUARY 19

A letter from Delhi carries the information that Sunder Singh Bhandari has been arrested. Since June 26, he had been looking after the work of the Jana Sangh admirably, and organising underground activity in concert with Ravindra Varma.

A gist of the consensus arrived at in Paunar is released to the Press. The formulation, as it emerges from the summary, appears unexceptionable. If accepted by the Government— which is doubtful—it would certainly provide an opening to end the present impasse! The statement calls for normalisation, which it spells out as removal of curbs on civil liberties and the Press, release of political prisoners, and end of the emergency followed by elections (preceded by electoral reform). It also calls for eschewing of violence from public life. The only point that the Government may have relished is the reference to the "gains accruing from the emergency" and a plea to retain them. The Press reports say that while the text of the statement was being sent to the Prime Minister immediately, Shriman Narayan would be going to New Delhi on January 23 to apprise Indira Gandhi personally of the deliberations of the conference.

TUESDAY, JANUARY 20

Sheikh Abdullah welcomes the Paunar statement. The *Deccan Herald* reports him as saying that he was hopeful about reconciliation prospects. There is a solid basis for my optimism "he is reported as saying." The *Hindu* reports to the effect: "Every time I have met the Prime Minister I have been trying to soften her attitude, but the forces of confrontation are strong so that till now nothing much could be done".

I happen to meet Michael Fernandes in the evening. Michael is the younger brother of George Fernandes and is working in the I.T.I. He is a prominent trade unionist, and General Secretary of the Indian Telephone Industries Union. He has been in detention for about a month.

WEDNESDAY, JANUARY 21

It is Dandavate's birthday today. We have requested the kitchen staff to prepare a special meal. Apart from receiving warm greetings from all his colleagues in the jail, Madhu gets an extra-special surprise—a visit by his 15-year old son Udaya. Udaya is studying at Ahmedabad and has undertaken the long trip with a two-fold purpose—a visit to Yerawada prison, where his mother Pramila is detained, and a trip to Bangalore where his father is held. For Madhu, this is the first interview in seven months.

BBC reports Indira Gandhi's interview with Agence France Press, the French news agency. She makes three main points: (a) that the presidential system will not solve India's problems and that the parliamentary system, with some changes is best suited to the country; (b) that the main problem today is how to reform the mentality of some opposition parties who think that everything should happen as they want it to happen; and (c) as far as she knows Sanjay is not interested in politics. He felt that it was a time of crisis for the country and so wanted to contribute his bit. She also stresses that he has been elected to the Youth Congress and not nominated.

All India Radio reports the interview, but mentions only the first of the three points.

Dandavate receives a letter from S.M. Joshi mentioning, inter alia, that J.P. has written to Indira Gandhi indicating his willingness to try to break the impasse if he is enabled to consult his colleagues now in prison. Earlier N.G. Goray and H.M. Patel, Janata Front leaders in the two Houses of Parliament addressed a joint letter to the Prime Minister refuting her charges of violence and obstructionism and urging her to follow up her Lok Sabha statement about dialogue. J.P.'s letter endorses their joint statement.

THURSDAY, JANUARY 22

Press reports about the Prime Minister's interview with the AFP mention the first two points reported by BBC, namely the suitability of the parliamentary system and the need to reform the opposition, but nothing about Sanjay Gandhi.

We chance to meet Banarasi Das, M.P. He says that J.P. is much better now. The information in Delhi is that J.P. was treated at Chandigarh for cancer instead of his kidney trouble! He also mentions that P.K. Deo, Loknath Mishra and other BLD members from Orissa have not joined the Janata Front. Another item of news provided by him is that Biju Patnaik has been released on parole to enable him to attend the obsequies of his father-in-law.

SATURDAY, JANUARY 24

In the afternoon, three of our co-detenus are told to pack and get ready to leave by the evening. They have been transferred. They are Malikarjunaiah to Belgaum, Subbaiah to Gulbarga and Anand Rao to Bellary. The transfer orders are surprising. They would cause considerable inconvenience to their families. There is no paucity of space. In our ward at least one guess is that the Inspector General of Prisons has suggested the transfers. The information gathered subsequently, however, suggests that the Government regards them as the nucleus of the team organising the satyagraha in the State. The decision is intended to disperse the nucleus. To us it appears that the transfers might help organise resistance in the other jails. Even so, it is decided that all the three should file writs against the transfer and aver that the transfers make the detention punitive, instead of merely preventive as it is purported to be.

Discussions with the jail authorities later make them postpone the transfer to Sunday morning. So far as Anand Rao is concerned, his health does not permit him to undertake a journey, and so his transfer is deferred indefinitely.

SUNDAY, JANUARY 25

Subbaiah and Malikarjunaiah leave for their respective destinations.

In its night bulletin, BBC reports that 1,500 Indians residing in Britain organised a demonstration on the eve of India's Republic Day to protest against the continued detention of political workers and curbs on civil liberties. The demonstrators marched to 10, Downing Street and submitted a memorandum to the British Prime Minister urging that the U.K. should recall its High Commissioner in New Delhi to register its protest against the conditions in India. Among those who addressed the demonstrators was Mary Tyler who said that conditions in India were far worse than anyone in the U.K. could imagine.

MONDAY, JANUARY 26

We had celebrated Independence Day last year behind bars. Today, we observe the nation's Republic Day too in gaol. We have a formal function in the 'B' ward, where sports competitions are followed by brief speeches appropriate to the occasion. The atmosphere exudes enthusiasm, confidence and a determination to triumph over all odds. Incidentally, this is the first time we are allowed to enter the 'B' ward.

Today's *Indian Express* carries an article by Acharya J.B. Kripalani reminiscing about the 1942 movement. Without saying a single word about the current political situation he draws a striking parallel between the two, which no reader can miss. In part the article reads:

What were the charges against us? Not that we were Fascists or Nazis? The charge was that we were the friends of the Fascist and Nazi powers, who had unleashed World War II. We were also the friends of the Japanese and would help them to occupy India as soon as they invaded the country. We were thus enemies of democracy and wanted the triumph of totalitarian regimes. We were the enemies of our country, whose interests our foreign masters knew better than those who were fighting for its liberty at great sacrifice and personal peril; no language was strong enough to denounce the leaders of the movement. Men like Gandhiji, Jawaharlal, Patel, Rajen Babu and others were the enemies of the civilised world, represented by the Allies.

War emergency was declared in the country and there was strict censorship of the Press. The judiciary could not inter-

vene to safeguard the liberty of the individual against executive fiats. The country was silenced by leonine violence and
cruelty.

However, a time came when things changed. Gandhiji was
released on grounds of health unconditionally, after his historic fast. The members of the Working Committee and the
rank and file of the Congress were also later released
unconditionally. We were not asked to repudiate the Quit
India resolution. We were not asked to renounce our belief
in non-violence and satyagraha as a civilised substitute for
war to redress political wrongs and injustice.

If any such conditions were imposed, the British knew that
we would, in Jawaharlal's language, tell them *jehnum main
jao* (go to hell). We would in that case have preferred to
remain in confinement rather than accept such humiliating
conditions for our release.

A sustained campaign has been going on against the Janata
Front Government of Gujarat, that it has been encouraging
lawlessness in the State, that it has been indifferent to the drive
against economic offenders, that satyagrahis were not being
arrested, etc. Today's *Hindu* publishes the figure of arrests
and detentions released by the Gujarat Government to nail the
lie effectively. The note is prefaced by a forthright declaration
that it has been the State Government's pronounced policy not
to use MISA for political purposes. And it has stuck to it. Even
so anti-social elements have been detained under MISA. Such
detenus number 407. Besides, 2,187 arrests have been made
under the DIR. The news report gives the partywise breakdown
of DIR arrests as follows:

Congress-O 793, BJS 446, RSS 141, SP 25, BLD 19, Anand
Marg, 11, Jamaat-e-Islami 8, CPI (M) 7, KMLP 4, RPI 2,
Lok Sangharsh Samiti (bulk presumably may be RSS) 731.

Out of these, 1,059 were convicted while the others were under
trial.

TUESDAY, JANUARY 27

A report is received from Bombay about activity outside.
Along with the report are sent three important letters written
recently by those guiding the movement. The first letter, dated

January 16, is that written jointly by N.G. Goray and H.M.
Patel to the Prime Minister, the substance of which was given
in S.M. Joshi's letter to Dandavate. The second letter dated
January 18, was the one addressed to Indira Gandhi by J.P.,
also mentioned in Joshi's letter. The wording of the letter makes
Shyam Nandan Mishra very unhappy. Mishra thinks the letter
is out of character. He feels it has been drafted by some one else
and that J.P. has only signed it.

J.P. should not have requested the release of party leaders
as he had done in the letter, Mishra feels. It is not becoming to
do so. Continuing detentions are a problem for Indira Gandhi,
not for us. Why give her an opening by making a prayer of
this kind, he says. Dandavate and I do not agree with his
criticism. The wording of the letter, I think, could have been
better. But there is nothing in it that can be said to be humiliating for us.

THURSDAY, JANUARY 29

There is a disturbing report obtained from convicts that earlier in the week there was a severe lathi-charge on satyagrahis
in Bellary jail. Discreet enquiries made in the jail office reveal
that the Inspector-General of Prisons, Mallaya, has gone to
Bellary on an unscheduled visit.

FRIDAY, JANUARY 30

Mallaya returns from Bellary. He admits to Deve Gowda and
Hegde that the Bellary incident was really ugly, that he had
suspended the superintendent of the jail and several lieutenants
of his, and also personally attended to the numerous grievances
of the detenus and DIR undertrials there. Their grievances are
justified, he says.

SATURDAY, JANUARY 31

All India Radio announces the imposition of President's rule
in Tamil Nadu.

MONDAY, FEBRUARY 2

The Tamil Nadu Governor's Report to the President recom-
mending imposition of President's rule in the State is placed
before Parliament. The All India Radio news bulletin at 2.00
P.M. devotes 8 out of its 10 minutes to an indictment of the
D.M.K. Government through an elaborate account of the report

as well as anti-D.M.K. speeches made in Parliament. On the other hand, it takes the news reader barely five seconds to present the other side of the picture thus: "Some opposition members made statements opposing President's rule".

In the evening BBC reports the arrest of some 700 D.M.K. activists in the State—about a hundred in Madras city and 600 in the rest of the State. Voice of America says that among those arrested are several legislators.

TUESDAY, FEBRUARY 3

A letter from Nagpur jail written by the Nagpur Jana Sangh President, Ahuja, conveys the sad news of the death of the veteran political leader V.G. Deshpande, a former member of Parliament. He had been detained under MISA but released when his condition became serious.

The Government announces in Parliament the setting up of a one-man commission to inquire into charges of corruption against the ousted D.M.K. Government. Also, a Bill is introduced in Parliament seeking to extend the life of the present Lok Sabha by one year.

BBC reports a press conference addressed by the former Tamil Nadu Chief Minister, Karunanidhi. Neither All India Radio nor the Indian Press carries a word about it. Karunanidhi makes the following four points at his press conference: (*i*) D.M.K. members will defend democracy with their lives; (*ii*) they will remain peaceful whatever the provocation; (*iii*) the corruption charges against him and his Government are baseless; also, why has there been a departure from the past practice of appointing commissions of enquiry while the Government remains in office and calling for its resignation only if and when the commission finds it guilty, and (*iv*) the charge of secessionist activities by the D.M.K. is totally without foundation. The D.M.K. had given up the secession demand years ago; all that it stressed now was greater autonomy.

FRIDAY, FEBRUARY 6

Yet another bit of sad news, this time from Tihar Jail, Delhi. The death has occurred of Baijnath Kapil, a prominent worker of the Jana Sangh in Delhi. He was in detention since June. He was not released even when he was seriously ill. He was merely shifted to the hospital where he died.

I address a condolence telegram to his son, Ashok. The jail authorities tell me that the rules do not permit my communicating with any one who is not a relation of mine, or a MISA detenu elsewhere. I point out that the telegram is a condolence message on the death of a detenu. If they do not permit me to send it to his son I shall have to send it to a co-detenu of the deceased in Delhi, who will later send it on to his son. Is it not absurd that I should have to resort to such a roundabout method of conveying my grief to the bereaved son of a friend? Ultimately, the authorities relent and send my telegram.

BBC reports about an article published by the *Guardian* comparing Bhutto with Indira Gandhi. The article is written by a *Washington Post* correspondent, Lewis Simmons, who has been expelled from New Delhi and is now based in Lahore. Simmons writes that both Indira Gandhi and Bhutto have taken to the totalitarian path; in both India and Pakistan, the Constitution is undergoing basic changes, civil liberties have been curbed, political opponents of the Government jailed, and federal units (Tamil Nadu and Baluchistan) have come under Central rule. Simmons, however, takes note of one difference between Indira Gandhi and Bhutto. Unlike the former, Bhutto he says, treats foreign correspondents well, even those who criticise him. The article is indeed proof of Simmon's last observation.

WEDNESDAY, FEBRUARY 11

Madhavrao Muley writes that Yadavrao Joshi, RSS organiser for south India, was arrested in Bombay on February 3. Muley's letter also conveys a message from Vajpayee that I should contest for the Rajya Sabha from Gujarat and that necessary formalities in that regard should be completed. Enclosed with the letter are blank application forms for enrolment as a voter.

I am now enrolled as a voter in New Delhi. But that does not come in the way of my registering myself as a voter in Gujarat. My permanent home address is Adipur where my father lives. The letter stresses the urgency of the matter and says that a messenger is in Bangalore and will be personally taking the registration forms the next day. I send the forms duly filled in, applying for registration as a voter at Adipur, and requesting that my name be struck off from the Delhi rolls.

FRIDAY, FEBRUARY 13

Yadavrao Joshi is brought to Bangalore jail. He had first been arrested in Bombay under the DIR. Later it seems the authorities discovered that a MISA order issued by the Karnataka State Government was pending against him. So they have executed the order and detained him under MISA.

A.K. Subbaiah, who had been earlier transferred to Gulbarga, returns to Bangalore. He is brought here because of a writ petition filed on his behalf in the High Court. In fact, his transfer to Gulbarga has been very helpful to the detenus there. He has helped almost everyone there to file writ petitions in the High Court. As a result of the petitions all of them have to be brought to Bangalore.

BBC reports that a spokesman of the Pakistan High Commission in London has written a letter to the *Guardian* replying to Lewis Simmon's article comparing Bhutto with Indira Gandhi and affirming that both are behaving like dictators. The letter denies the charge so far as Bhutto is concerned. Referring specifically to the Baluchistan–Tamil Nadu analogy, the letter says that it is totally misleading. In Tamil Nadu, the Government dislodged by Indira Gandhi was being run by a party opposed to her whereas in Baluchistan the party in office is Bhutto's own party.

SATURDAY, FEBRUARY 14

The Prime Minister after a short visit to Bangalore (February 13) and Mysore (February 14) reaches Madras to attend the so-called merger conference of the two Congress parties. At Mysore, the Chief Minister tries to impress her by arranging a showy reception for her. She is taken through the city in an open car. Of course, thousands of security men, in uniform as well as in plain clothes, have been posted all along the route. But three students penetrate the elaborate security net-work, manage to reach her car and shove into her lap a number of pamphlets condemning her authoritarian rule.

We received this report in the evening, along with the news that the three young men had been arrested and taken to some unknown place for interrogation.

Yadavrao Joshi confirms the press report that Rajmata Vijaya Raje Scindia of Gwalior has quit active politics. Joshi said she had been subjected to immense pressure and harassment by Government.

Malikarjunaiah returns from Bellary jail in connection with the hearing of his habeas corpus petition.

SUNDAY, FEBRUARY 15

The Press carries a report that Indira Gandhi will be going to Poona on February 24 to meet Vinoba Bhave. The news touches off a fresh wave of speculation about the purpose and likely outcome of the meeting between the two. The meeting is being held against the background of the acharya sammelan, whose decisions Indira Gandhi has positively resented. Her refusal to meet Shriman Narayan who went to Delhi specifically to meet her on behalf of Vinoba was a deliberate demonstration of her resentment.

BBC reports the Government of India's decision to withdraw the accreditation of about fifty Indian journalists.

MONDAY, FEBRUARY 16

Press reports of the so-called 'merger' conference in Madras, attended by Indira Gandhi, make fantastic reading. The *Indian Express* says that the rally addressed by Indira Gandhi was 2.5 million strong! And it wants its readers to believe it. In her speeches Indira Gandhi said that the D.M.K. was planning to launch an agitation from February 1 and, therefore, the Central Government had to intervene. It is noteworthy that the State Governor's report to the President which was the basis for clamping President's rule on Tamil Nadu made no mention of the D.M.K. plan which the Prime Minister now talks about.

An interesting portion of her speech, quoted by the *Indian Express*, reads thus: "In my fifty years of public life, I have been ridiculed, I have been abused, I have been beaten, I have been imprisoned, I have been shot at. . . . But I have not been deterred from my path".

Ridiculed and abused yes: very few in public life who have risen to high positions have ever been spared ridicule and criticism. But 'beaten' and 'shot at'? It is the masochistic streak in her that makes her indulge in such baseless statements so glibly. The statement is certainly indicative of a waspish angry mood. One wonders whether it has anything to do with the pamphlet hurling incident at Mysore two days ago.

TUESDAY, FEBRUARY 17

The morning papers have a shock for me. Vasant Gajend-ragadkar, Secretary of the Gujarat Jana Sangh, and one of the chief architects of the Janata Front victory in the State Assembly elections last year is no more. The *Indian Express* carries a report datelined Ahmedabad saying that Gajendra-gadkar passed away in Bombay on February 16, after being in hospital for seven days It's a grave loss to the party and to public life in Gujarat. I can imagine what a great a blow it is going to be for Vidyabehn, Vasantbhai's wife. I hasten to send a condolence message to her. Shortly, thereafter, a telegram arrives from Ahmedabad informing us officially of Vasantbhai's demise.

Satyavrat Gundachar, a prominent Sarvodaya worker of Karnataka, is brought to jail under MISA. We are surprised to see him. He had been earlier arrested under the DIR but was discharged by the magistrate before whom he was charged. His account of his re-arrest surprised us even more. It is a distressing commentary on how the police are misusing their extraordinary powers. On February 11, two days before Indira Gandhi came to Bangalore hundreds of persons were rounded up; only a handful of those arrested were formally charged, the others were taken to a police station and kept there for two, three or more days depending on the police assessment of the person's potential for causing trouble. In Gundachar's case, he was taken to the police station nearly a week prior to the Prime Minister's visit and told specifically that he would be let off after Indira Gandhi's departure. On February 15, however, when he enquired when he was going to be free there was no reply. He kept asking the police officials on the spot but to no avail. So yesterday morning he announced that unless he was told why he was being kept in custody or released, he would undertake a fast. This morning he began the fast. The upshot: a MISA detention order was prepared post haste, and Gunda-char brought here to give us company.

In the Supreme Court the arguments on behalf of the detenus are concluded. BBC gives this evening a summary of the arguments advanced. A galaxy of legal luminaries led by Shanti Bhushan has appeared on our behalf. Among those who pleaded the case of the detenus towards the concluding stage of the arguments was Ram Jethmalani, President of the All India Bar Council. According to a report published by the *Evening View*[16] (15-2-76), a Delhi weekly, Jethmalani wound up his arguments with a stirring appeal to the judges. "Democracy in India lies in a coffin today, but the lid is still open. Let not Your Lordships slam the lid shut. The decision by the court alone would stand between democracy and totalitarianism. This is the last chance before Your Lordships to save democracy through your judgment".

WEDNESDAY, FEBRUARY 18
It is Jayant's tenth birthday today. I send a greetings telegram to him.

Lokavani, the local Kannada daily controlled by Virendra Patil and projecting the Congress(O) point of view carries an editorial which disturbs everyone of us here, our Congress(O) friends particularly. The editorial welcomes the merger of the two Congress parties in Tamil Nadu. It also hails the dismissal of the D.M.K. Government there. Linge Gowda, a Congress(O) leader, is the first to draw attention to this editorial and transcribe it for us, the three non-Kannada-knowing detenus here. Linge Gowda, of course, is very angry and bitter about the writeup. Nagappa Alva describes it as disgraceful. Hegde and Deve Gowda also are upset and decide to contact Patil and get his explanation. Most of the Congress(O) friends here express doubts about Patil's intentions. The general feeling is that the editorial could not have been written without his consent.

THURSDAY, FEBRUARY 19
Information is received from Bombay that Ravindra Varma who has been very ably organising all activities of the Lok Sangharsh Samiti as its General Secretary after Nana Deshmukh was arrested on February 12. Dattopant Thengadi, M.P. and General Secretary of the Bharatiya Mazdoor Sangh, who also has been underground for all these months was with Varma at the time but he escaped arrest.

In a note written by him before his arrest Ravindra Varma

---

[16] Edited by P.L. Lakhanpal. After it was stopped from publishing from Delhi the editor moved to London and resumed publishing it from there.

commented on the consensus of the acharyas and made a very
pointed reference to attempts to divide our ranks. He takes
note of the fact that the acharya sammelan has spoken about
"the detention of social and political workers who believe in
ahimsa (non-violence) and sarva dharma sama bhava (impartiality
towards all religions)" and observes: "Whatever may have
been the considerations that prompted the acharyas to arrive at
this formulation, the Government may find in it an excuse for
discriminating against detenus belonging to the RSS, some
leaders of the Jana Sangh and a few of the Socialist Party. We
will have to resist this discrimination not only because it is
meant to divide our ranks, but also because it is based on an
accusation that is untrue and unfair. The Socialist Party does
not believe in violence. Nor do the Jana Sangh and the RSS.
It will be totally wrong to accuse them of having harboured any
plans or intentions for violent action in the struggle. We will,
therefore, have to resist the Government's efforts to make us
acquiesce in their accusations against the Jana Sangh and the
RSS by reiterating our repudiation of the charge and taking the
stand that the Government's accusation can be entertained only
if they produce evidence that can satisfy a judicial authority".

Loksatta a Marathi daily of Bombay, reports that on
17-2-76, N.G. Goray called on Vinoba Bhave and had discussions with him for an hour.

FRIDAY, FEBRUARY 20

Newspapers report Indira Gandhi as telling a group of French
writers who called on her that the emergency had already been
relaxed, and that "many detenus" had been set free. After all,
she added very condescendingly, "we have no intention of keeping them in prison indefinitely". The French writers were led
by Lapierre, co-author of "Freedom at Midnight".

Four days hence Indira Gandhi is to go to Paunar to meet
Vinoba Bhave. One question which Bhave is bound to ask her is
about detenus. So the lie that was hitherto being voiced by
Brahmananda Reddy, Om Mehta and other lesser fry is sought
to be given a measure of authenticity by being pronounced by
the leader herself. Since no one knows how many persons are in
detention and who is kept where, and since the Press is not
allowed to report detentions and even the health of any detenu,
it is possible for official spokesmen to get away with fibs of this

kind. If Karnataka can be regarded as a sample, I can say
without fear of contradiction that till today not a single detenu
has been released!

BBC gives excerpts from a scathing *Guardian* article dated
February 19 about the emergency in India. The article
entitled "Paranoia and Paradox" is by David Selbourne who
was in India on an Aneurin Bevan Fellowship and has had a
long session with Indira Gandhi. Introducing the article the
Guardian writes: "On this page we publish an article that
Indira Gandhi will absolutely loathe. . . . In Delhi the argument
from high Indian officials is taking a fresh turn. Why, they
inquire, does India get such a lousy press whilst China gets
such a fulsome one? Because China keeps the Western Press at
bay, and firmly corrals those few it allows in. . . . It is a fascinat-
ing but bizarre line, because even its staunchest proponents
skid to a halt when asked to examine the reality of Indira
Gandhi's new ideology, a patchwork of pseudo-democracy
and covert intimidation. She says she has launched a revolution.
A bumper crop has helped. Corruption is under carpet. The
opposition is too enfeebled to offer much resistance. Sanjay
Gandhi may indeed be a comely leadership acquisition for the
future. But is this China at the start of the Long March? Or
is it India begining the long slide towards rickety dictatorship?. . . No one who cares about human life wished India anything but immense success. Yet even her friends now lie
bleeding."

SATURDAY, FEBRUARY 21

There is yet another report in the Press identical with
yesterday's meeting of the Prime Minister with French writers.
On Friday she met an American delegation and repeated that
emergency had been relaxed, and that "lots of detenus" had
been released.

All India Radio reports that the Central Government had
addressed a letter to all the States urging speedy implementa-
tion of the 12-point prohibition programme. This programme
was announced on October 2 last year. Nothing has been done
in that respect till date. And nothing is likely to be done in
the future also. Like the Prime Minister's statement about
detentions this announcement also appears to be a bid to

soften Paunar before Indira Gandhi goes there. Those who
know Vinoba Bhave say that he is unlikely to be taken in by
such gimmicks.

SUNDAY, FEBRUARY 22

Information is received from Hyderabad that the Andhra
High Court has quashed the detention of 15 MISA detenus
belonging to the RSS, the Jana Sangh, the Socialist Party and
the C.P.I. (M-L). The fifteen detenus were ordered to be
released by the High Court. Two of them, Gowd, the RSS
Sangh Chalak of Mahboobnagar and Murli Manohar, advocate
and Secretary of Vijayawada RSS, went away from the court
itself. The others returned to jail to collect their baggage. The
moment they reached the jail they found fresh detention orders
awaiting them! So the High Court release order proved to be
of no avail, and back they were inside the jail.

MONDAY, FEBRUARY 23

I address a letter to Ram Jethmalani warmly complimenting
him on his arguments in the Supreme Court. "Judging even by
the snatches published in the *Evening View*, it (your address)
was excellent. All friends here wish to convey to you our
immense appreciation, gratitude and regards. Keep the flag
flying".

The morning papers carry a report of the Defence Minister,
Bansi Lal's speech at Jhajhar in which he talks about detenus
being kept in 'luxury and comfort'. In the case of one detenu
he said, the Government was spending Rs. 70/- per day on his
food alone. The detenu is in an air-conditioned bungalow.

Bansi Lal's reference is obviously to Morarji Desai who is
the only detenu in the country now (earlier J.P. also was in
the same category) who is not kept in a jail, but is detained in
a separate house. Desai is detained in a P.W.D. rest house near
Gurgaon. I do not know if Bansi Lal has ever known jail life.
Perhaps not. Anyway he should know that living comforts can
never be a substitute for freedom. Even more relevant in this
context would be the knowledge that the worst torture a
prisoner can be subjected to is solitary confinement. Ever
since his imprisonment in June 1975 Morarji Desai has been
all alone. We who have been detained in jails are far better.
Having subjected this octogenarian leader to such harassment

to talk about spending Rs. 70/- per day on him is adding insult to injury. The British kept Gandhiji in the Aga Khan Palace. But they knew that for Gandhiji that palatial mansion, with all its comforts, could never be a substitute for his own austere Sabarmati Ashram. The British, as far as I recall, never bragged about the money they were spending on Gandhiji. Bansi Lal, however, could not contain his own pettiness. As they say, a man cannot behave better than what he is.

TUESDAY, FEBRUARY 24

Today Indira Gandhi is going to Paunar to meet Vinoba Bhave. Ever since the acharya conference last month, many hopes regarding resolving the present impasse have been hinged on Vinoba. In the jail too, there is an air of expectancy. I feel that the present over-optimism about what Vinoba can achieve (in our ward Shyambabu is particularly hopeful) is an unconscious reaction to the cynicism about Vinoba harboured earlier in most quarters. Indira Gandhi would like to keep Vinoba on her side but she would not hesitate to ignore him altogether, and even to suppress him if he decides to project himself as her opponent. The acharya conference and its decisions have annoyed her and she demonstrated it by refusing to meet Shriman Narayan.

WEDNESDAY, FEBRUARY 25

It happens to be our wedding anniversary. I send a happy remembrance telegram to Kamala. She is bearing the burden of the present situation. I feel proud that she has borne it well so far.

Press reports about Paunar say that the Prime Minister was with Vinoba for an hour. She said later that they had discussed several matters. She declined to say what had been discussed. Vinoba told newsmen later: "Have patience; you'll get the news gradually. We may meet again". He also said that after a month they might expect "something *pucca*".

Arguments in the habeas corpus case before the Supreme Court are concluded and the judgment is reserved.

THURSDAY, FEBRUARY 26

BBC gives a resume of the arguments advanced by both sides in the Supreme Court case relating to MISA detenus.

FRIDAY, FEBRUARY 27

Mallayya, Inspector-General of Prisons, mentions that a story making the rounds "in the northern States" (he specifically mentioned Delhi, Rajasthan, M.P. & U.P.) is that we three M.Ps have been deliberately kept at Bangalore, and that Indira Gandhi has instructed the Inspector General of Prisons to harass us! Mallaya feels aggrieved that his name should have been dragged into the story.

"I think this is the price Government has to pay for clogging the normal channels of information," I tell him. I try to explain how a story of this kind might have originated. We three had come to Bangalore for a parliamentary committee meeting and found ourselves in the Bangalore jail. But this fact is not allowed to be published. For quite some time our friends and supporters might have been unaware of our whereabouts; their normal assumption would be that if at all we had been arrested we must be in Delhi, or in some jail nearabout. When after a few months people come to know that we are in Bangalore, it must have baffled them. With no means of ascertaining or checking up, they must have drawn their own conclusions. This story is born out of this. Indira Gandhi keeps complaining about rumours. She must know that rumour is a child of censorship.

SATURDAY, FEBRUARY 28

I gather that some letters addressed to me have been intercepted at the post office and sent to the Home Secretary. I wonder whose letters they are. I enquire from the jail authorities but they plead ignorance about any such intervention. Later in the evening I learn from Mallaya, editor of the weekly *Vikrama*, that he had received a letter from Jhamat Wadhwani, President of the Bombay City Jana Sangh (presently a MISA detenu kept at the St. George's Hospital, Bombay) saying, inter alia, that he had written several letters to me but had not got any reply. This solves the riddle of the missing letters, at least partially. On my part, I was feeling surprised why Jhamat had not replied to me. The last letter I received from him was dated January 19. It reached me on January 27. I had replied to him that very day.

MONDAY, MARCH 1

Two Congress(O) MLA's who meet Deve Gowda discuss with him the issue of forming one united Opposition party.

They say that unification seems unlikely; even Advani, they understand, is opposed to the idea. Deve Gowda tells them that I am all in favour of the proposal.

THURSDAY, MARCH 4
Shyambabu asks me what has happened about my nomination to the Rajya Sabha. The last date for filing nominations is March 10, less than a week from now. I tell him that I am not aware. Since signing the papers for inclusion of my name in the electoral roll of Gujarat about three weeks ago, I had had no information.

FRIDAY, MARCH 5
In an interview with *Blitz*, reproduced extensively by the daily Press Indira Gandhi has a sharp dig at the acharyas. *Blitz* asked her about her reaction to the decisions of the acharya conference. She tartly replied: "I do not know how representative they are, or how closely in touch with what happened before the emergency, or what the situation is today". So, the very credentials of the acharyas no less than their understanding of problems are in question. That a remark of this kind has come so soon after her visit to Paunar suggests that the Vinoba-Indira talks could not have been very smooth.

In reply to another question, she says: "What had happened was not really a constitutional crisis or constitutional failure. It was a pure and simple political challenge to the Government and it has been met well within the provisions of the Constitution". This above reply fully substantiates our charge against Government that the emergency is politically motivated, and has no constitutional justification. No one denies that on the eve of the emergency, the Opposition, by successfully closing ranks, did pose a powerful political challenge to the ruling party. How real the challenge was put to test in Gujarat. The outcome upset Indira Gandhi. Simultaneously came a severe blow to her personal political standing in the shape of the Allahabad judgment. Instead of facing the challenge politically, she clamped down a ruthless emergency on the people, jailed political opponents, muzzled the Press and paralysed all political activity.

In the afternoon, on my way to the jail superintendent's office I find Hegde returning from there. Hegde tells me that a

Congress(O) leader of Belgaum, Gaonkar, had come to the jail and that Hegde had sent a message through him to Virendra Patil asking him to ring up Babubhai Patel, Chief Minister of Gujarat and find out what has happened about my nomination to the Rajya Sabha. Hegde, it seems, sent the message after discussing the matter with Shyambabu.

I appreciate their concern but I feel it is not proper. So I request Hegde to send another message to Virendra Patil asking him *not* to contact Ahmedabad. It happens that Gaonkar is still in the jail office. We go ahead to him and Hegde asks him to drop the matter.

Just an hour later the detenus who had gone to the High Court for the hearing of their petitions bring me a message that a Gujarat Minister, Makarand Desai, had arrived from Ahmedabad to have my nomination paper filled. He was having trouble in getting an interview with me. So he filed a writ in the High Court in support of which Santosh Hegde was arguing.

Around 5.30 P.M. I am summoned to the office to find Makarand Desai and Santosh Hegde awaiting me. They have secured a court order to interview me and secure my signatures on my nomination paper to the Rajya Sabha. The Government counsel, I am told, tried his utmost to have the hearing deferred. Advani is a Central Government detenu; permission to interview him can be granted only by the Government of India; instructions have been sought from the Central Government, and so the matter may be postponed to Monday. This was the line of his argument. It seems that even when its counsel was saying so the State Government had the necessary permission sent from New Delhi in its pocket. Immediately after his arrival here, Makarand Desai sought the Home Secretary's permission to meet me and when he found him reluctant, he rang up the Gujarat Chief Minister who in turn contacted the Union Home Minister and made him send the necessary instructions to Bangalore. Even so, the Government counsel tried to see that the matter was put off. The High Court does not meet on Saturdays. So, he thought a postponement would mean adjournment to Monday. The High Court perhaps sensed this intention and with a view to thwarting the delaying tactics said it was willing to defer the matter but would meet on Saturday morning to decide the issue. By then the Government must have received the necessary instructions from New Delhi. It was when the Court thus made its mind clear that the Government counsel abruptly announced that instructions had been received from the Central Government and so the petitioner, Makarand Desai, could meet Advani. The Court then made out a formal order directing that Desai and Santosh Hegde be permitted to meet me that very evening for the purpose of securing my signatures on the nomination papers.

Santosh Hegde told me that yet another writ had been filed on my behalf seeking a week's parole in order to enable me to go to Gandhinagar (capital of Gujarat), take the necessary oath before the returning officer, attend the scrutiny of my nomination papers and complete all other formalities with regard to my nomination. Hegde said he was not very hopeful about the outcome of that petition partly because there is a specific provision that in the case of a person in detention, the superintendent of the jail is empowered to administer the oath. The right to attend the scrutiny is, however, important. Also, the tight time schedule that will have to be observed for a proper nomination is another factor which may make the Court decide in our favour.

My own reaction is that I will not go on parole. Instead, care should be taken to see that even without my actual presence, the nomination formalities are properly gone through. Makarand Desai assures us that it has been ensured. He himself would be returning to Gandhinagar immediately with the nomination papers already signed. Another colleague, Jariwala, would be staying on to take my oath certificate (which would be provided by the jail superintendent after I had taken the oath). The rules provide that the oath is to be administered after the nomination has been filed.

Even as Makarand Desai and Santosh Hegde are discussing with me the nomination procedures there is a phone call for the superintendent. He lifts the receiver, listens for a while (with an expression of uneasiness and disquiet slowly appearing on his face), and then observes in a protesting voice: "But they have already met him! I should have been told earlier".

We learn later that the phone call was from the State authorities asking the superintendent not to let Desai and Hegde meet me, and to take the nomination papers from them and have them signed by me. That, the State authorities felt, would meet the requirements of the court order!

MONDAY, MARCH 8

The writ petition filed on my behalf is taken up for hearing by the High Court. The transport that took me to the High Court is delayed and so when I reach the High Court I find Santosh Hegde already on his feet arguing the case. The application as originally filed was for parole. On reaching the Court I told Hegde that I would not accept parole. The plea may be amended to seek directions for my transfer to Ahmedabad so as to enable me to file my nomination, take the oath, and attend the scrutiny of the papers.

The Advocate-General seems to have come prepared with a long list of precedents when parole was not allowed to a MISA detenu. The amended plea found him without a basis for rebuttal. Justice Chandrashekhar kept on asking the Advocate-General what objection Government could have to the transfer of the detenu to Ahmedabad. The Court held that it was my right to be present at the scrutiny of my nomination papers in order to be able to meet any objections that might be raised against them and to enable me to raise objections, if possible, to the nomination papers of my adversaries.

In its order that day the Court directed the Government of India to take me to Gandhinagar in time to take the oath, file my nomination and appear at the scrutiny. The Advocate-General was seemingly upset with the order. We could see him rushing here and there seeking instructions as to what to do, but one reverse after another was in store for Government that day.

First, it filed an application for stay of the transfer orders. The Court rejected it. It filed another application seeking leave to eppeal to the Supreme Court. That application, too, was rejected. Then I filed an application asking the Court to direct the superintendent to administer the oath that very evening as a matter of abundant caution. The Advocate-General opposed my application but the High Court granted it!

At 5.45 that evening the superintendent, Chablani, administered the oath to me in his office. The certificate of oath-taking was handed over to Jariwala who later that evening flew to Bombay en route to Gandhinagar.

TUESDAY, MARCH 9

The most important news item of the day is about the release of Chaudhri Charan Singh. The reports are bald, and say nothing about the why and the wherefore of his release.

Early in the morning, I am informed by the superintendent that I am to be taken to Bombay by the afternoon flight and that the Assistant Commissioner of Police, Nayak, who is to accompany me would be coming to meet me after a short while. Nayak arrives some time later and meets me at the superintendent's office. He tells me that according to instructions from New Delhi he is not only to accompany me to Gandhinagar but is to be in charge of my custody even while I am in Gujarat. The Government of India is not willing to entrust me to the custody of the Gujarat Government. He further informs me that he as well as the other police official accompanying him would not be in uniform but would be in plain clothes throughout the journey and so would request me not to communicate with other passengers on the plane. I told Nayak that this was not possible. If the officials escorting me were in uniform it would be obvious that I was still a prisoner and so passengers on board the plane would themselves be hesitant to talk to me but if, as proposed, they were to be in civilian clothes no one would be aware of my prisoner status. If anyone spoke to me or if I ran into an acquaintance it would be discourteous on my part not to talk. Nayak appreciated the point but kept on pleading with me that his position would be seriously compromised if there was to be any overt communication between me and others.

Our co-detenu, Malikarjunaiah, maintains a very active communication link with those outside. Within minutes of my being informed as to which flight I would be taking he had sent a message about my itinerary, and had it conveyed to my family in Delhi, my brother-in-law in Bombay, my sister in Baroda and to party workers in Bombay and Ahmedabad. The flight from Bangalore to Bombay was at 12.55 P.M. I am taken to the airport police station. Looking out of the window I see Gopi Nath hovering around. Along with Vithal Nayak, the Assistant Commissioner of Police, there is a sub inspector, Kishan Singh, who is to accompany me. As I proceed to the plane Gopi Nath wearing dark glasses comes to my side and whispers, "All have been informed. Is there any further message?" By a nod I indicate that nothing more need be done.

At Bombay also, Nayak escorts me to the airport police station. The airport police station is in a corner of the main

waiting hall and so is open to public gaze. I look round to see
if anyone is there and I locate Vasant Kumar Pandit, MLC,
Chhatrasal, an old party colleague, Kanta Goel, a prominent
Jana Sangh worker, and my brother-in-law, Santosh, at some
distance hesitating whether to meet me or not. Kanta Goel
boldly strides forward and seeks to enter the police sub-station.
Kishan Singh stops her but Nayak asks him to let her in. And
I tell Nayak my brother-in-law is there, he may be called inside.
Thereupon Santosh is allowed entry into the police station.
Pandit and Chhatrasal, however, are not allowed to meet me
despite some sharp exchanges between Pandit and Kishan Singh.
Pandit then shouts from a distance "Do you need any reading
material, Advaniji?" "Get me the latest *Illustrated Weekly of
India*" I replied. Pandit fetches an issue of the weekly from the
news stand and gives it to Kishan Singh. Kishan Singh meti-
culously leaves through every page of the *Weekly* lest there
should be any paper inserted inside, and after assuring himself
that the journal is innocent hands it over to me. Kanta Goel
gives me some information about the goings on in Bombay and
tells me that the Bombay branch has done very well in the
satyagraha. Santosh apprises me about the welfare of relations.

After an hour's halt at Bombay we leave for Ahmedabad.

At the Ahmedabad airport a police van picks us from the
airfield itself denying me any opportunity of passing through
the airport. Vithal Nayak who had perhaps apprehended a
crowd at the airport organised under official auspices feels
pleasantly surprised and remarks: "The authorities here seem
more loyal than the queen". The Gujarat Government has very
rightly chosen to remain absolutely correct in this regard and
has made no attempt to extract any political dividend out of
my transfer. As the police van comes off the airfield I see
Nathabhai Jhagda, the Jana Sangh organising secretary for the
State, and several other workers standing near the airport gate.
They can only wave to me. I wave back in return. The police
van drives straight to Gandhi Nagar and there to the V.I.P.
Guest House.

After reaching the V.I.P. Guest House the State police official
informs Nayak that arrangements for my custody can be made
either in the V.I.P. Guest House or at the Central Jail. It
would be for Nayak to make the choice. It is also communicated
to him that if I am lodged in the V.I.P. Guest House, Nayak

would be in direct charge of my custody. The Gujarat Government would only place at his disposal a few policemen. But if
I am taken to the Central Jail of Ahmedabad the immediate
responsibility for my custody will naturally vest in the superintendent of the jail.

Nayak had a look round the guest house and then told the
State police authorities that he would prefer to have me kept
there. One obvious consideration that made him take the
decision was that here he was in a position to regulate the
meetings that anyone might have with me. The Gujarat Government at the time was passing through a very precarious phase
with defection of legislators very much in the air. Nayak
seemed to have had strict instructions not to allow anyone
except my relations to meet me. Actually Makarand Desai and
some other Ministers who came to the Guest House later in
the evening and wanted to meet me were turned away by him.
Nayak tells me about it but says that the Chief Minister,
Babubhai Patel, wanted to call on me and that he had asked him
to do so early next morning.

The main room in the guest house has been allotted to me.
Nayak and Kishan Singh have their luggage in a different room
but as I am about to retire for the night Kishan Singh enters
my room and apologetically asks, "May I sleep in here?" "Why
not", I replied immediately without realizing that the idea is
to keep a watch on me during the night also. Kishan Singh then
mentions that he is the son of Anant Singh, a veteran freedom
fighter of Karnataka. He says that he felt ashamed of doing
this kind of job because those in detention at the moment are
also freedom fighters.

WEDNESDAY, MARCH 10

Babubhai Patel is to come to meet me at 8.30 A.M. However,
early in the morning I am informed that the Chief Minister
would be coming one hour earlier as he has a Cabinet meeting
to attend at 8 o'clock. Patel comes punctually at 7.30 A.M.
Nayak quietly slips out of the room to enable us to talk freely.
We are closeted for nearly half-an-hour, and I have a first hand
glimpse of what is going on outside. I find the Chief Minister
worried about the discovery of some sticks of dynamite in
Baroda. I guess that perhaps the Cabinet meeting also is in that
connection. The Chief Minister tells me that he would be coming
to the returning officer's room at 11 A.M. to propose my

nomination personally. Patel says that Morarjibhai has been keeping perfect health and that on his birthday, on February 29, he received more than 60,000 letters.

At about 10.55 A.M. I reached the office of the returning officer to find a large number of party workers awaiting my arrival. Among them is Vidyabehn Gajendragadkar. I meet her for a brief while and offer my condolences personally. Inside the room where I am to file my nomination papers a limited number of journalists and colleagues are allowed. Among these I discern J.P. Mathur who has been underground since the very beginning. We exchange a few words. He tells me that he had been to Adipur to meet my father.

Babubhai Patel also arrives to file my nominations. Nominations filed, I take my oath before the returning officer.

Both Vithal Nayak and Kishan Singh have come to Ahmedabad for the first time and so seem keen to go out sightseeing. But their problem is that they cannot hand me over to the Gujarat police as per orders. So they ask me if I am willing to accompany them. In the meanwhile, however, Nayak receives an angry communication from Bangalore. This is in response to his message the previous evening that he had opted for the V.I.P. Guest House for my custody. A wireless message from Bangalore said, "Detenu Advani is to be lodged in Central Jail, nowhere else".

When Nayak told me about the message I said to him that that would suit me better because I would be able to meet my colleagues in the jail. The number of detenus in Ahmedabad jail at that time was not very large but there were quite a few, mostly belonging to the RSS. Nayak said that he proposed to phone to Bangalore and to explain the position to them. They perhaps did not realise that if I was kept in the Central Jail the kind of restrictions he had been able to put on senior party leaders in Government wanting to meet me could not be made effective. Late that night Nayak came to my room once again to tell me that he had spoken to Bangalore, and that Bangalore appreciated his stand. So I continued to be at the V.I.P. Guest House, comfortably bored.

THURSDAY, MARCH 11

Welcome guests arrive early morning. Kamala, Jayant and

Pratibha from Delhi, my sister Sheela and aunt Jamuni from Baroda. It is a happy get-together for all.

Scrutiny of the nomination papers takes place at 1 P.M. Sitting members and Congress candidates Makwana and Kumud-behn are present in the chamber. So also are Capt. Golandaz, Janata's other nominee for this election and Chamanbhai Shukla (my covering candidate). Scrutiny takes just a few minutes. All papers are declared in order. Chamanbhai withdraws right there and then; Makwana, Kumudbehn, Golandaz and I remain the only four candidates for the four seats to be filled.

By evening, it is apparent that the Government is facing a serious crisis. The Congress party has been indulging in all kinds of tactics to seduce Janata Front MLAs. Janata Front MLAs are called for an urgent meeting that evening and I learn that right below where I was lodged they will be having their dinner. I can hear the hustle-bustle but I can meet no one.

FRIDAY, MARCH 12
I am to leave today back for Bangalore. The first thing that Kishan Singh does in the morning on getting up is to touch my feet and crave pardon for having to work as my guard.

Kamala and others come at 12.30 P.M. We spend another happy half hour talking about many things, and at 1 P.M. I leave for the airport.

At the Bombay airport I am taken to the V.I.P. lounge this time. Evidently the police sub-station is too open. Kanta Goel and Kanta Jhamatmal Wadhwani come to meet me. Back in Bangalore by the evening I go around the various wards of the jail sharing with our co-detenus the tid-bits of information I had collected during the brief visit to Gujarat.

TUESDAY, MARCH 16
The surprising news item from abroad in the Press today is the British Prime Minister, Harold Wilson's resignation. Of pertinent relevance to us in India are Wilson's observations after his resignation. If any one person is considered indispensable, he says, that is a real threat to democracy. The concept of indispensability is anti-democratic, he reaffirms and adds: "I do not

believe in the dynastic system of succession. I believe in selec-
tion by election, not by nomination".

THURSDAY, MARCH 18

The Congress(O) leader, Deve Gowda who had been held
under the DIR is discharged by the Court. We give him a hearty
send-off in the evening. But at 12.30 A.M. he is back re-arrested
under MISA.

SATURDAY, MARCH 20

I receive the Certificate of Election to the Rajya Sabha from
the returning officer. Immediately thereafter, I send this telegram to the Secretary, Home Affairs, Government of India,
New Delhi:

My term as Rajya Sabha Member expires on second April.
Having been re-elected I wish to take oath as required under
Article 99 of Constitution. Kindly arrange temporary transfer
Delhi jail and facility to take oath on third April last day of
current session.

L.K. Advani, MISA detenu

SUNDAY, MARCH 21

A note from outside sent by Seshadri, in charge of the RSS
underground movement in Karnataka, carries a few important
points. First that an all-party meeting is taking place at Jayaprakash Narayan's instance in Bombay on March 21 and 22 to
plan the formation of a single party; second, after his release
Chaudhri Charan Singh met Atalji and discussed with him plans
for the Rajya Sabha elections. Seshadri wrote that Chaudhri
Charan Singh seemed firm and determined in his resolve to
carry on the fight against the present establishment.

MONDAY, MARCH 22

BBC reports that Madhu Limaye has resigned from the Lok
Sabha as a protest against the extension of its term. All India
Radio also reports it in its 9 P.M. bulletin but gives no reasons.

TUESDAY, MARCH 23

All political prisoners in this jail are heartened to get a report
from outside about the Bombay meeting. The meeting lends
support to the acharya sammelan statement. It demands the

release of all political prisoners and further decides to form a single unified democratic opposition party. A steering committee headed by N.G. Goray and comprising, H.M. Patel, Shanti Bhushan and O.P. Tyagi is set up to draw up a policy and programme for the new party. The participants in the Bombay meeting are, apart from J.P., Acharya Kripalani, Chaudhri Charan Singh, N.G. Goray, H.M. Patel, Shanti Bhushan, O.P. Tyagi, Tridib Chaudhry, Narain Desai, S.M. Joshi, Uma Shankar Joshi, Krishan Kant, Mavalankar, Nijalingappa, Babubhai Patel, Uttamrao Patil, Era Sezhian, Sequeira, Digvijay Narain Singh and Yadu Nath Thatte. It is indeed a fully representative gathering. All those who matter, and who are outside are there.

WEDNESDAY, MARCH 24

The Gujarati weekly, *Sadhana*, reports that its editor Vishnu Pandya has been arrested.

The High Court has been regularly summoning detenus on whose behalf habeas corpus petitions are filed. We learn today that Government counsel objected to it and said that production of detenus day after day was causing a lot of harassment to the Government. The Government's objection evoked from Justice Chandrashekhar a sharp retort. He said the harassment caused to Government was certainly not more than the harassment caused to the detenus by their detention. Santosh Hegde meets me in the evening and we prepare a writ to be filed in connection with my oath taking.

FRIDAY, MARCH 26

The writ regarding oath is admitted. The hearing is fixed for March 30.

There is one more resignation from the Lok Sabha. Sharad Yadav's resignation is announced in Parliament by the Speaker. When H.M. Patel stood up to ask the reason why, the Speaker is reported to have said: "Reason need not be told. I can assure the House he has not resigned under pressure".

SATURDAY, MARCH 27

Polling for biennial elections to the Rajya Sabha takes place in various States. As a result of the defection of MLAs from

our side to the Congress we suffer some major setbacks. Ram
Hit loses in Madhya Pradesh and T.N. Singh in Uttar Pradesh.
However, Sunder Singh Bhandari is elected from U.P.

SUNDAY, MARCH 28

Occasionally I get copies of *Evening View* from the capital.
Today's *Evening View* carries the report of an important judgment delivered on March 23 by the Gujarat High Court,
which has been blacked out by the daily Press. A division
bench of the High Court comprising Justice J.B. Mehta and
Justice S.H. Sheth struck down three clauses of the Central
Government order of June 26 relating to press censorship.

The Judges said "Censor is not above the Court. The law
which we have declared must hold good until a superior Court
takes a different view. The censor cannot sit in judgment upon
our decision, and decide which law should be allowed to be
made known to the people and which not. It is impossible for
us to imagine that a court proceeding or judgment of the Court
can ever amount to a prejudicial report".

Allowing a prayer by Chunibhai Vaidya, editor *Bhumi Putra*
(a Sarvodaya journal), the Bench said "we cannot permit the
liberty of the people to be under the weight of censorship".

The High Court examined rule 48 of the Defence of India
Rules and found that it empowers the Government of India to
issue pre-censorship orders only for certain purposes, specified
in the rule viz. maintenance of public order, among others.
But clauses (c), (d) and (e), the Court observed, went beyond
these purposes. These clauses require that any news or comments regarding the Proclamation of Emergency, Presidential
Order suspending Fundamental Rights and regarding detention
orders made under MISA should be submitted to the censors.

The right of the people to make comments . . . form the
requirement of a democratic Government to know its errors so
that it could correct them and harmonise its policies with the
will of the people. Infallibility and democracy go ill together.
Infallibility and dictatorship go hand in hand. The founda-
tions of dictatorship lie in the strong desire on the part of an
individual or a group of individuals to entrench itself in
power for ever regardless of what the people want or desire.
The desire of a would-be dictator can be achieved by him only
if he is able to sell the idea, either by press censorship or

otherwise by fully controlling the mass media of communications, that what he does is always correct and admits no error. Right of dissent and free Press are two out of three elements which constitute the essence of a democratic setup. The third is an independent judiciary acting as a watchdog and discharging the duty of protecting the freedom of the people against executive and legislative inroads on it. Public comments or criticism which do not lead to violence cannot be forbidden in a democratic society.

The High Court examined the speech of M.C. Chagla the publication of which brought the *Bhoomi Putra* into a clash with the censor. The Court said that the speech emphasised Mahatma Gandhi's principle that the end does not justify the means. It no doubt criticised the emergency and suspension of fundamental rights, and also stated that in a democratic society everyone had a right to demand the change of the Prime Minister. No doubt, the language was strong and charged with emotion. But no person could think that the speech would lead the readers of *Bhoomi Putra* to violence or public disorder.

The Court dealt with the contentions advanced on behalf of the Government of India that though Chagla ostensibly advocated non-violence it was only a cloak for preaching violence in a veiled manner. The Court rejected the contention as without substance and held that having regard to the high judicial office which he had held in the past and his whole career and having regard to the fact that the *Bhoomi Putra* believed in the Sarvodaya ideology it was not at all likely that the readers would imagine Chagla advocating violence under the cloak of non-violence.

TUESDAY, MARCH 30

My interim application regarding taking of oath in the Rajya Sabha is taken up for hearing by the High Court today. I argued the case myself. My arguments are essentially two-fold i.e. constitutional and practical. Dealing with the constitutional aspects I pointed out to the Court that a person elected to the Rajya Sabha is under obligation to take the oath of allegiance to the Constitution under Article 99. The process set in motion on March 3 when the Election Commission issued notification to fill the seats of retiring members of the Rajya Sabha concludes not with the declaration of election results but with the elected members taking their seats in the House after taking oath.

As to the practical aspect of the question I pointed out that as a sitting member of the Rajya Sabha, certain privileges and amenities accrue not only to me but to my family as well. Thus, my family is entitled to residential accommodation in Delhi on a subsidised basis. My family is also entitled to avail itself of the medical facilities provided by the Central Government Health Scheme. My wife is entitled to a free railway pass from Delhi to my usual place of residence. I myself am entitled to various other facilities like the use of the Research & Reference Section of Parliament, the use of the library etc. All these amenities and facilities have continued to be enjoyed by my family and me notwithstanding my detention. As has been laid down in several earlier cases relating to detentions under MISA, a MISA detention is a *preventive* detention. Government cannot convert it into a *punitive* detention. If I am not allowed to take my oath, the facilities I have indicated will be taken away from me and my family and this detention would have been converted into a punitive detention.

Justice Chandrashekhar thereupon wanted to see the law that governs salaries and emoluments of Members of Parliament. A copy of the Act was procured from the High Court library and I read out to the Court the relevant provisions.

Justice Chandrashekhar was pleased to observe that in order to be entitled to all these facilities, it is not enough for an MP merely to take the oath. He would also have to take his seat in Parliament. The prayer made by me, he pointed out, sought the facility only to take the oath. Even if the Court were to grant this relief and direct the Government to administer the oath to me while in detention, the purpose would not be served. I tried to argue that the phrase "taking seat", like vacating seat, was not a physical act and the moment a person elected to Parliament takes his oath he is supposed to "take seat". The Court seemed unconvinced by this approach and so I requested adjournment to study further the implications of taking seat in the House. The hearing was then adjourned till April 1.

THURSDAY, APRIL 1

I spent the intervening day doing a lot of home work on my writ petition and felt confident that I would be able to convince the Court even on the line of argument I had initiated the day before. But as a matter of abundant caution I decided to modify my application and instead of seeking directions from the Court that merely an oath be administered to me I prayed that I be enabled to take my seat in the Rajya Sabha also.

The Government of India's counsel, Narain Rao, strongly opposed my application but after prolonged discussion the High Court ruled in my favour. It directed the Government to take me to Delhi and to the Rajya Sabha on April 3 to enable me to take my oath.

The Government counsel immediately applied for stay of order and also for leave to appeal to the Supreme Court. The High Court declined to grant stay on the ground that it would frustrate the objective of the order, but granted leave to appeal.

FRIDAY, APRIL 2

The superintendent informs me that I would have to leave around 4 P.M. and that the Assistant Commissioner of Police, Nayak would be accompanying me again on my flight to New Delhi. In the afternoon, however, Nagappa Alva returned from the Court with the information that the Government of India had moved the Supreme Court in my case. He also said that the Karnataka High Court orders had issued a few days earlier permitting two student detenus to appear for their examinations had been stayed by the Supreme Court. This latter piece of information made me feel that in my case also the Supreme Court may stay the High Court order. And that is exactly what has happened. Around 3.30 P.M. a message came from the superintendent's office that I do not have to go to Delhi as the Supreme Court had stayed the High Court's orders.

SATURDAY, APRIL 3

Going through Press reports about the Lok Sabha debate on the Ministry of Home Affairs demands for grants (April 2) I find that the Home Minister, Brahmananda Reddy, unwittingly perhaps, makes a confession. The situation in the jails is not happy, he said and added, "It is true also that because of the heavy pressure of the political situation there has been over-crowding in many jails and this has led to some undesirable results".

MONDAY, APRIL 5

I am invited to MISA 'B' ward for the first in a series of

four talks on political developments, and the decline of democracy in the last one decade.

In my first talk I deal with the period commencing from
February 1966 with the induction of Indira Gandhi into the office
of Prime Minister to the end of 1973 when mounting discontent
among all sections of the people erupted sharply in the form
of a student agitation in Gujarat. It is during this period that
Indira Gandhi engineered the split in the Congress party for
purely personal reasons, but succeeded in covering it up by an
ideological veil. The abuse of governmental machinery and
mass media for party ends that took place in the 1971 elections
brought about a qualitative change in political style and functioning. It was during this period that serious erosion of democratic
values and norms really began.

TUESDAY, APRIL 6

In my second talk in the series I dealt with the years 1974
and 1975 up to the proclamation of the emergency on June
25, 1975. I tried to analyse at some length the implications of
the J.P. movement in Bihar, the formation of the Janata Morcha
in Gujarat and of the Allahabad High Court judgment in Indira
Gandhi's case. The J.P. movement and the coming together of
opposition parties had no doubt a very invigorating effect on
the debilitated democratic institutions in the country. The
victory of the Janata Morcha in Gujarat coming simultaneously
as it did with the Allahabad verdict became a clear threat to
the political future of Indira Gandhi.

WEDNESDAY, APRIL 7

In my third talk I tried to analyse the legal as well as the
political implications of the proclamation of emergency and the
steps taken thereafter to destroy democracy in the country
altogether even while preserving the trappings of democracy.
There was a disturbing similarity between the steps taken by
Indira Gandhi during this period and the steps taken by Adolf
Hitler to convert Republican Germany into a dictatorship.

THURSDAY, APRIL 8

In my last talk in the series I attempt to deal with the possibilities for the future. Despite reports of hesitation among some
colleagues outside, a unified political party of the democratic
opposition would certainly come about. But in the ultimate

analysis, the future would depend not only upon the unity but also upon the stamina of those waging a battle against authoritarianism.

SATURDAY, APRIL 10

Today's *Indian Express* carries a news report from Ahmedabad which quotes the Congress President D.K. Borooah as telling a meeting of Gujarat Congressmen (9-4-76) that the RSS and Anand Marg people had to be put into jail because they could not be "thrown away into the sea or externed from the country".

Mainstream, April 10, carries an editorial on the issue of constitutional reforms which shows very clearly that either Communist enthusiasm for curbs on judicial review has ebbed or Nikhil Chakravarty, the editor of this journal, is not in tune with C.P.I. thinking. The editorial entitled "Where is the national debate?" asks Government to seek an electoral mandate for whatever it wants to do with the Constitution before going ahead.

The journal cautions the authorities that "the need for the judiciary to act as a watchdog on the executive cannot be minimised". It adds : "Whatever may be the constriction that the emergency has placed on the powers of the judiciary vis-a-vis the executive, any discussion on the normal functioning of our democratic system has to keep in view the need for ensuring necessary checks on the powers of the executive not only by the elected legislatures but by the judiciary as well; otherwise there is also the danger of the executive making serious inroads into the accepted freedom under a democratic system".

The editorial also refers to a paper circulated by some Congressmen (this was first published by *Mainstream* in November 1975) urging a presidential system. It says: "Although it is widely known that certain important Congressmen in their individual capacities were associated with the framing of the document, the uproar that followed its circulation led them to repudiate their own brainchild".

Concluding, the journal disputes the right of the present Lok Sabha to take upon itself "the responsibility of making any radical changes in the present Constitution". It has to be remembered, it says, that the present Lok Sabha was elected on a different mandate when Indira Gandhi commanded the confidence of the nation in her struggle against the 'syndicate.' A

fresh mandate for constitutional change must be secured from
the electorate, it urges.

The same issue of *Mainstream* carries a breezy article by the
veteran writer, C.L.R. Shastri, "On saying 'no' ". One does
not come across many articles of this kind nowadays. Both the
author and the publisher have to have guts for such writings.
The article bemoans the proliferation of yes-men in the country and puts in a powerful plea for no-men. Shastri writes:
"Freedom of expression is the first of the celebrated four freedoms, and one ought in my considered opinion to be appreciated
as much for saying 'no' as for saying 'yes'. I should like to go
further and affirm that one ought to be appreciated more for
saying 'no' than for saying 'yes'. To me, 'no' is as musical as
Apollo's lute".

He adds: "A democracy properly so called connotes the
existence of an opposition; and an opposition, I need hardly
stress, is a collection, a conglomeration, a condominium of
no-men".

WEDNESDAY, APRIL 14

Today's papers publish the recommendations made by the
Congress Committee (headed by Swaran Singh) on amendments
to the Constitution. Most of the amendments are aimed at
limiting the scope of judicial review. The present ruling party
obviously considers the judiciary as a stumbling block in the
way of its aims. Of course, the executive has always been trying
to project its own hostility to the judiciary as if it were a clash
between the legislature and the judiciary. Many parliamentarians too have been taken in by this ruse. The trend of debates
in Parliament often reveals this. In this context I recall a recent
article by A.G. Noorani in which he has recounted an interesting episode which took place once in the U.S. Senate early this
century.

Senator Spooner of Wisconsin was speaking warmly about
the Supreme Court and its views when he was interrupted by
the Senator from South Carolina Tillman: "I am tired of
hearing what the Supreme Court says. What I want to get at is
the commonsense of the matter".

Rejoined Spooner: "I too am seeking the commonsense of
the matter. But as for me, I prefer the commonsense of the
Supreme Court to that of the Senator from South Carolina".

THURSDAY, APRIL 15

The morning papers carry one more diatribe by Indira Gandhi against opposition parties. Speaking to a group of trainees from the Indian Institute of Mass Communication (April 14) she said the opposition parties have not changed their objectives or methods. She claimed that the attitudes and activities of several opposition leaders who have been released continued to be the same.

One wonders if the remark is a general one or whether it refers specifically to Chaudhri Charan Singh who was released last month !

SATURDAY, APRIL 17

Among the cyclostyled papers received from outside there is an interesting one containing a conversation between Ganesh Shukla of the *New Wave* (once supposed to be very close to Indira Gandhi) and Subramaniam of the *Indian Review*. The conversation is a sequel to a raid on the *New Wave* office by income-tax authorities. Shukla tells Subramaniam that the raid had been prompted by an article published by the journal severely criticising demolition activities in Delhi. An even more interesting tidbit revealed by the paper is that the income-tax authorities, while going through the accounts saw a credit entry of Rs. 50,000/- in the firm's books with no particulars mentioned. The publishers were asked to reveal the source. At first they refused to answer. Later under pressure, they admitted that the amount had been received by them from Indira Gandhi to launch the paper!

SUNDAY, APRIL 18

One of the proposals made by the Swaran Singh Committee in regard to constitutional changes is that Article 226 be amended and its scope restricted. Today's *Hindu* quotes Justice V.R. Krishna Iyer as saying that if the people were conscious of their rights today, it was due to Article 226. Addressing a Conference of Electricity Board Engineers of Southern States here at Bangalore, Justice Iyer said that while on the one hand this Article had created a national awareness among citizens about their rights, it had, on the other, created "a haunting fear of natural justice" among the administrative and political bosses. Justice Iyer said that there was now a talk of amending the Constitution and jettisoning the Article. The Courts and the politicians would not suffer because of it. In fact, the Courts would have less work and would relax. "You will be the potential victims", he said, pointing to the participants.

TUESDAY, APRIL 20

Yet another eminent jurist has spoken against the proposed constitutional changes. Today's *Hindu* carries a news report of a meeting at Bangalore in which K. Subbarao, former Chief Justice of the Supreme Court said: "The Parliament-is-supreme slogan is contrary to the elementary principles of a written Constitution. It is an elementary principle of constitutional law that the Constitution is supreme and not any institution created by it. In the ultimate, supremacy lies with the people".

WEDNESDAY, APRIL 21

Voice of America reports that there has been a major firing incident in the Jama Masjid area of Delhi. It quotes official sources in New Delhi as admitting that five persons have been killed, but adds that unofficial sources put the toll much higher. All India Radio, however, says nothing about any such incident.

THURSDAY, APRIL 22

We scan the daily newspapers carefully to see whether there is any report on the Delhi firing but there is none.

FRIDAY, APRIL 23

A letter from Madhavrao Muley informs me that progress towards the formation of a single party has been very slow and halting. The Congress(O), he says, has been having strong reservations. J.P. is very upset about it. Muley also informs us that Subramaniam Swamy is in London busy organising a Friends of India Society Conference which is scheduled to take place on April 24 and 25. I share the contents of the letter with colleagues in the ward. Deve Gowda feels extremely depressed about the report that Congess(O) is opposing formation of a single party of democratic opposition.

Meanwhile, we receive a report from Kerala that Congress (O) General Secretary, Mahindar Kaur has disbanded the party unit in Kerala and formed an ad hoc committee. It is known that even though the Congress(O) unit in Kerala is

formally with the movement many of its leaders may cross over
to the other side.

SUNDAY, APRIL 25

All India Radio reports that the Kerala Congress(O) has
decided to merge with the ruling Congress party; obviously, the
erstwhile President of the Congress(O) has walked over. Of
course, the radio cannot be expected to mention that the unit
has been reconstituted.

MONDAY, APRIL 26

BBC reports that a save-democracy conference was held in
London in which 300 delegates from various parts of the world
participated. The conference was presided over by Subramaniam
Swamy. Messages were received from, among others, J.P.,
Charan Singh, T.N. Singh, N.G. Goray and E.M.S. Namboo-
diripad.

In response to a call from the Lok Sangharsh Samiti all
detenus and DIR prisoners in the jail observed a one-day fast to
protest against conditions of detention in various jails in the
country.

TUESDAY, APRIL 27

For the first time, the Press carries a report that there was
police firing in Delhi some time back. The date is not mentioned
but the Deputy Minister of Home Affairs is reported to have
told Parliament that six persons had died as a result of the firing.

Detenus who have been to the Court in connection with their
habeas corpus petitions bring the news that the Supreme Court
judgment in the habeas corpus case is going to be announced
tomorrow.

WEDNESDAY, APRIL 28

Today the Supreme Court is to announce its verdict on the
habeas corpus issue. There is an air of expectancy in the jail
from early morning. Reports from outside sent by those who had
been watching the proceedings of the case seem to suggest that
the decision would be four to one or three to two in favour
of the High Courts' stand that even though fundamental rights
have been suspended, a habeas corpus petition cannot be shut
out at the threshhold and that the Courts are required to examine

whether the detention is under the law. It is generally felt that H.R. Khanna, Chandrachud and Bhagwati would be firmly in favour of the detenus while M.H. Beg may be as firmly endorsing the Government stand. The Chief Justice may go one way or another.

Every news bulletin of All India Radio, BBC, VOA is being followed carefully. But the first report heard is from BBC which in its 4.30 bulletin reports that the Supreme Court has held four to one that habeas corpus petitions by MISA detenus are not maintainable. The BBC report mentions no names but everyone thinks that the dissenting judge must be Khanna.

The report shocks everybody. By the judgment the Supreme Court has reversed the verdict of nine High Courts. All India Radio does not report the case even in its 6 P.M. bulletin. The first report that we hear from the radio is in the 7.45 P.M. Kannada bulletin.

Voice of America's night bulletin, besides reporting at some length the Supreme Court judgment, also informs us that Subramaniam Swamy's passport has been impounded.

THURSDAY, APRIL 29

I am invited to MISA 'B' ward to address the detenus there on the implications of the Supreme Court judgment.

SUNDAY, MAY 2

The Law Minister, H.R. Gokhale is reported as having said in Washington (May 1) that the number of political prisoners in India was not in thousands as stated by the Western Press, but only in hundreds! Gokhale said this while addressing the Federal Bar Association. He said that there were three categories of prisoners; firstly, political prisoners who believed in violence or had affiliation with communal bodies. Their number was in hundreds. The second category was of anti-social elements. Their number had gone down because crime had gone down. The third category was of economic offenders. This was a large number because Government had come down heavily on them!

MONDAY, MAY 3

Michael Fernandes, the youngest brother of George Fernandes, informs us that his elder brother, Lawrence has been picked up from home presumably for interrogation.

WEDNESDAY, MAY 5

Lawrence has still not returned home nor has he been brought to jail. This naturally causes a lot of anxiety here. The Supreme Court judgment has obviously emboldened the police authorities.

FRIDAY, MAY 7

Snehlata Reddi, the famous film star who played the key role of Chandri in the award-winning Kannada film, "Samskar" is brought to jail charged with conspiracy to commit acts of sabotage. None of us is able to meet her. Though I happened to meet her husband, Pattabhirama Reddi, she is taken straight to the women's ward and locked up there. George Fernandes whom the police have been frantically trying to locate is believed to have stayed with the Reddis in Bangalore.

THURSDAY, MAY 6

The afternoon bulletin of All India Radio has a sad announcement. K. Subbarao, retired Chief Justice of India, is dead. Friends outside have planned a seminar on the proposed constitutional amendments on May 15 in Bangalore over which Subbarao was to preside.

WEDNESDAY, MAY 12

Voice of America reports a meeting of the International Press Institute at Philadelphia where a resolution was adopted condemning several countries for their onslaught on press freedom. Prominent in the list of countries is India.

I inquire from Michael whether these has been any news about Lawrence. He says none.

THURSDAY, MAY 13

Virendra Patil sends a report on the deliberations of the Conress(O) Working Committee held last week. The report shows that there is sizeable opposition in the committee to the one-party idea. Those reported to be opposed to the proposal are Dinesh Shah, P.C. Chunder, Sadiq Ali, Niaz Hussain and Banarasi Dass.

SATURDAY, MAY 15

News is received from friends outside that Asoka Mehta has been released.

SUNDAY, MAY 16

The morning papers carry a report on Asoka Mehta's release but give no details.

Voice of America, however, mentions that he was kept in detention in Rohtak and adds that Government gave no reasons for his release. A report received from party circles outside says that Mehta has not been keeping good health for some time and that his release is on health grounds.

THURSDAY, MAY 20

Lawrence Fernandes, picked up from his house on May 1, is brought to the jail today and taken straight to a solitary cell. He has been badly tortured. Those who have seen him arrive say that he is unable to walk and seems a physical wreck. Warders in the jail confirm that Lawrence has been badly tortured. The atmosphere in the jail becomes very tense.

SATURDAY, MAY 22

All detenus and DIR prisoners in our jail undertake a one-day fast as a protest against the tortures inflicted on Lawrence Fernandes. That leads to retaliatory action by the authorities. They shut us up in our wards and completely ban the inter-mingling of inmates of different wards.

WEDNESDAY, MAY 26

The newspapers carry a brief report about J.P.'s press conference in Bombay in which he announced the launching of a new party. Another news item is about Indira Gandhi's speech at Malerkotla in which she reacts furiously to J.P.'s announcement saying, "People have not forgotten the destructive activities of some of the parties which now propose to join as one party". She added that some of these parties have not hesitated to receive money from abroad. This violent reaction would only show how jittery she feels about the impending unification of democratic forces.

THURSDAY, MAY 27

The Indian Express reports Brahmananda Reddi as having told the Lok Sabha that the families of 2,348 detenus are receiving family allowances. The allowance, he said, varied from case to case and was decided on merit with due regard to the financial circumstances of the family.

We know that in Karnataka today there are over 250 MISA detenus in various jails. Information compiled about detenus who have been receiving family allowance shows that only eight of the 250 are being paid a monthly allowance of Rs. 100. If the ratio of the number of detenus being paid family allowance to the total is the same in the rest of the country also, one can guess the total number in detention. .

FRIDAY, MAY 28

BBC quotes a *New Statesman* despatch from Patna that on the eve of Indira Gandhi's visit there some 8,000 people were arrested. The despatch refers to J.P.'s call for a protest day on June 26 and mentions a New Delhi official as saying that large scale arrests may be made before that date. It further states that the Government of India is extremely unhappy over the police failure to apprehend a large number of persons still underground. BBC also quotes a leading article carried by the London *Economist* affirming that it is now clear that while one of the objects of Indira Gandhi's emergency is to protect her own self another is to ensure that Sanjay becomes her successor. The editorial is headlined, "the Son also Rises".

Further, BBC has an interesting item from the House of Commons. On Thursday night (May 27) the House had to be adjourned after a shouting match and fisticuffs among members. The occasion was the adoption of a Government motion to speed up nationalisation of 43 ship building and aircraft firms. The ruling party won by just one vote. As Socialist members sang the anthem 'The Red Flag', a Conservative opposition industry spokesman snatched the symbol of Parliament, the golden mace of the Speaker, and brandishing it over his head advanced towards the treasury benches. Indira Gandhi never tires of condemning opposition members of Parliament for obstructive and "indecorous" behaviour. She has also mentioned it as one of the reasons for the imposition of the emergency. But I do not know if in the entire history of the Indian Parliament anything of this kind has ever happened.

SATURDAY, MAY 29

We receive information from High Court sources in Bangalore that there have been numerous punitive transfers of High

Court judges. We sit down to consolidate the information received. The tally is really formidable.

(1) Chief Justice S. Obul Reddi of Andhra transferred to Gujarat.
(2) Justice B.J. Diwan of Punjab transferred to Andhra.
(3) Justice O. Chinappa Reddi of Andhra to Punjab.
(4) Justice Chinna Kondaiya of Andhra to Madhya Pradesh.
(5) Justice S.M. Sheth of Gujarat to Andhra.
(6) Justice Virenda Lal of Bombay to Andhra.
(7) Justice S. Rangarajan of Delhi to Assam.
(8) Justice S. Sadanand Swami of Karnataka to Assam.
(9) Justice B.M. Chandrashekhar of Karnataka to Allahabad. (Justices Swami and Chandrashekhar were the judges who heard and disposed of my case).
(10) Justice Tiwatia of Punjab to Karnataka.
(11) Justice P. Biharilal of Himachal Pradesh to Karnataka.
(12) Justice A.P. Sen of Madhya Pradesh to Rajasthan.
(13) Justice T.U. Mehta of Gujarat to Himachal.
(14) Justice P.N. Mukhi of Bombay to Calcutta.
(15) Justice C. Lodha of Rajasthan to Madhya Pradesh.
(16) Justice A.B. Kaushal of Punjab to Madras.
(17) Chief Justice Sachar of Sikkim to Rajasthan as a puisne judge.
(18) Justice Grewal of Punjab to Sikkim.

MONDAY, MAY 31

We appear in the High Court today perhaps for the last time. Following the Supreme Court judgment in the habeas corpus case the Karnataka High Court has to dismiss formally our writ petitions. Despite Government protestations the High Court has summoned all detenus who filed such petitions and before formally dismissing the petitions allowed the petitioners to have their say. Every one of us spoke briefly but sharply. The emergency comes in for condemnation, the High Court receives rich encomiums while sore disappointment is expressed at the Supreme Court decision.

THURSDAY, JUNE 3

Voice of America reports that the International League of Human Rights has submitted to the U.N. a 73-page memorandum urging it to investigate suppression of human rights in India. It says that some 35,000 to 70,000 political activists have been jailed by the Indian Government. The memorandum has also documented cases of torture. The gagging of the Press has been referred to.

The *Statesman,* New Delhi, has not reported the contents of the memorandum but mentions that a spokesman of the Indian Embassy in Washington has denied the charges. In Sydney, Australia, the Minister of State for Home, Om Mehta, is reported to have said that the figure of 100,000 political detenus given by the Australian Press is grossly exaggerated. Not even one fourth of this number has been detained, he says.

So, on Om Mehta's own admission MISA detenus in the country number 25,000. The Law Minister has said only a few days ago that the number runs only into hundreds.

TUESDAY, JUNE 8

A letter from Madhavrao Muley addressed to Yadavrao Joshi mentions that J.P.'s health has improved remarkably. When he went out for a stroll to Nariman Point in Bombay the people were thrilled to see him and kept following him for some distance. May God bless J.P. with many more years of life.

In 1944, the Viceroy, Lord Wavell, had released Gandhiji only when doctors said he was at death's door. Wavell was in Sikkim at that time. Gandhiji's condition became serious. Major General R.H. Candy, Surgeon-General of Bombay who was attending on the Mahatma, sent a telegram to the Viceroy saying, "He might die at any moment". On May 6, 1944, Gandhiji was set free. Wavell's own reaction as recorded by him in his "The Viceroy's Journal" reads: "Personally, I cannot see that we gained much credit by releasing him at the point of death, and if he was not at the point of death there was no need of such a hurry. I did not entirely trust the medical information".

Wavell sounds almost disappointed that the doctors were proved wrong. He has recorded in his diary that a few days after Gandhiji's release Wavell received a telegram from Churchill asking "why Gandhi had not died yet".

New Delhi must be experiencing the same disappointment about J.P. Who knows whether the rest of history is also not going to be repeated? Gandhi lived to see the Britishers quit. Pray God J.P. too lives to see the ouster of the present dictatorship.

THURSDAY, JUNE 10

Satyavrat Gundachar, Sarvodaya worker detained along with us, shows us a pamphlet announcing Vinoba's decision to undertake a fast unto death from September 11 in case the Maharashtra Government does not ban cow slaughter by then. All of us are intrigued by Vinoba's announcement. At the present juncture when every thinking person should be concerned only with the question of human liberties it baffles us why Vinoba has picked upon the issue of cow slaughter to embark on a fast. Some of the co-detenus who have never concealed their cynicism towards Vinoba's activities go to the length of saying that this may be a diversionary tactic undertaken in collusion with the Government. This, I feel, is totally unfair. Shyam Nandan Mishra who is an ardent admirer of Vinoba feels that though Vinoba has ostensibly chosen the cow protection issue for his proposed fast in reality he intends heading towards a confrontation with the Government on the emergency and related issues.

FRIDAY, JUNE 11

BBC reports that George Fernandes was arrested in Calcutta on Thursday (yesterday) afternoon.

SATURDAY, JUNE 12

The Press also reports Fernandes's arrest but there are no details.

SUNDAY, JUNE 13

There is a meeting of the Karnataka Congress(O) State Executive in Bangalore today, to discuss the subject of forming a single party of democratic opposition. We receive a report by the evening which shows that a majority of the members present are in favour of unification. Two who strongly opposed the move are Poonacha a former Central Minister and Raj Sekhara Moorthy. Virendra Patil who presided did not commit himself.

TUESDAY, JUNE 15

We receive a cyclostyled copy of *Opinion* (June 8) edited by A.D. Gorwala. He has been putting up a valiant fight against Government repression. This issue recounts at length the tribulations the journal has undergone because of its journalistic uprightness. On March 28 it was served with a notice by Government to show cause why 10 specific issues of *Opinion* should be not banned and the press where they were printed should not be forfeited. The next day, the press (which had been printing *Opinion* for 16 years) told Gorwala that it could not print the journal any longer. Gorwala shifted to another press which after publishing three issues asked the editor to find another printer. Gorwala then shifted to a still smaller press which too said 'no' after publishing two more issues. Yet another press printed one more issue and gave it up.

On April 30 the Commissioner of Police, Bombay, served a notice on the journal requiring it to deposit a security of Rs. 25,000, within 15 days, as the 10 issues earlier indicated and the three issues published since, contained prejudicial reports which sought to promote feelings of enmity and hatred between different classes of India "and are likely to cause fear or alarm to the public".

Gorwala promptly filed a petition in the High Court. The High Court readily issued a stay order. But from May 18 the postal authorities refused to transmit *Opinion* unless the issue was first cleared by the censor. Early in June, however, the order was suddenly and surprisingly rescinded. Then *Opinion* resumed publication as a cyclostyled journal.

THURSDAY, JUNE 17

The *Indian Express* today carries a brief report on the deliberations of the Congress(O) Working Committee meeting. Asoka Mehta told the Press later that Congress(O) favoured formation of a single democratic party but felt that it should be done after normalcy was restored.

FRIDAY, JUNE 18

A letter received from Madan Lal Khurana from Tihar jail informs us that George Fernandes has been brought to Delhi. I convey the information to Michael and Lawrence.

Voice of America features a press conference addressed by Leila Fernandes at the National Press Club in Washington. Leila expresses concern about the health of her husband. She also refers to the brutual torture Lawrence has been subjected to.

TUESDAY, JUNE 22

The *Times of India* reports the victory of two Jana Sangh

candidates in the elections to the Maharashtra Legislative
Council from the Graduates' constituencies. The victors, G.B.
Kanitkar and V.K. Pandit, had thumping majorities over their
Congress-backed C.P.I. and Shiv Sena rivals.

FRIDAY, JUNE 25

In an article "Legalising Ethics" the editor of the *Indian
Express*, V.K. Narasimhan, severely criticises the code of
ethics for editors now sought to be given legal sanction.
Narasimhan writes: "It is interesting to note that one of the
major items which the Press Commission had suggested as a
moral imperative of the journalistic profession does not figure
in the editors' code of ethics. The Press Commission had
suggested that freedom in the honest collection and publication of news and facts and the right of fair comment and
criticism are principles which every journalist should always
defend. It is an accident that nowhere in the code of ethics
prepared by the All-India Newspaper Editors Conference does
the word freedom appear".

SATURDAY, JUNE 26

Today is the first anniversary of the emergency. At the small
Shiva temple in the jail all the detenus assemble in the evening.
Homage is paid to the martyrs in the struggle.

THURSDAY, JULY 1

Deve Gowda has news that all COFEPOSA detainees are
likely to be released shortly. Yesterday's newspapers had
headlined a report that all smuggling gangs had been liquidated.
A story current in the jail is that negotiations are going on
between representatives of the smugglers in the jail and the State
Government and that a deal is in the offing.

FRIDAY, JULY 2

BBC reports the Indian High Commissioner, B.K. Nehru's
interview with a press panel. Nehru is severely grilled over
the question of detentions. Asked how many political prisoners there are, he replies, "I do not know". Asked why the
number is not being revealed, he says again "I do not know".
Nehru has severely criticised Subramaniam Swamy. Most of
the pressmen defended Swamy equally vehemently.

MONDAY, JULY 5

Sixteen COFEPOSA detainees are released but a short while later they are re-arrested and brought back.

My wife Kamala mentions a meeting with Roxna Subramaniam Swamy[17] in Bangalore when she wanted me to be informed that Swamy is planning to return to India to attend the Parliament session and if possible to get away again. I tell Kamala that it would be wonderful if it could be done.

WEDNESDAY, JULY 14

Scindia, a Vidyarthi Parishad leader in detention is informally interrogated by a couple of State Intelligence men in the jail office itself. They came to know him personally while he was an in-patient in the local hospital. Scindia later reported the entire conversation to me. The four questions that they posed to him in a seemingly casual manner may be listed thus:

(1) Generally speaking, how is the morale of the detenus?
(2) How are the RSS detenus getting along with the rest? Are there differences among them?
(3) Whether S.N. Misra, Hegde, and J.H. Patel have been strongly critical of the RSS?
(4) Whether the RSS Chief here (meaning Yadavrao Joshi) is being given special treatment by the jail authorities?

The authorities obviously have an obsessive fear of the RSS. Considering the spectacular contribution the RSS has made towards this struggle this is hardly surprising.

THURSDAY, JULY 15

There is a new arrival in the jail today—Bhaurao Deshpande, Organising Secretary of the Karnataka Jana Sangh, who has been successfully evading arrest for over a year and organising the resistance movement outside. He has been doing remarkable work. When I meet him, I am shocked to see his pale and emaciated appearance. He seems to need rest badly.

---

[17] Wife of Subramaniam Swamy

FRIDAY, JULY 16

The morning papers report that the Cow Protection Committee formed in 1967 is likely to submit its interim report in a few days. It seems a settlement with Vinoba Bhave is round the corner.

Whispers are again going around that COFEPOSA detainees are to be released and that negotiations are on for a fresh deal.

Voice of America reports that the monthly journal *Seminar* has been closed down. Its editor, Romesh Thapar, told *Reuters* that he had been served with an order from the censor subjecting him to pre-censorship. Obviously, he said, Government is angry with his July issue in which he had criticised the emergency. He saw no point in continuing the journal with pre-censorship on.

TUESDAY, JULY 20

Opinion also has decided to close down. In a letter to readers editor Gorwala says it has become impossible to continue the journal even in a cyclostyled form.

WEDNESDAY, JULY 21

In a letter received from outside, it is mentioned that a new controversy has arisen over the question of RSS membership of the proposed single party of democratic opposition. Some senior leaders are reported to have objected to RSS members joining the new party while retaining their original membership.

THURSDAY, JULY 22

Yesterday's *Patriot* reports the AITUC (All-India Trade Union Congress) Secretary, Y.D. Sharma, as saying that during the emergency the process of collective bargaining had suffered a setback. One wonders whether he has been following what his more senior leaders have been saying about the wonders wrought by the emergency. The *Hindustan Times* of July 17 carried the following news item: "Mr. C. Rajeshwara Rao, General Secretary of the C.P.I., told Soviet leaders today that reaction's bid to seize power had been thwarted, thanks to the unity of the Indian National Congress, the Communist Party and other democratic forces. He said: 'Thanks to firm measures, ranging from the proclamation of the emergency to the arrest of a few active leaders of the conspiracy, the forces of reaction were defeated' ".

FRIDAY, JULY 23

Subscribers of the *Seminar* receive a letter from editor Thapar which says, inter-alia, "I am afraid it is not going to be possible to print any more issues of *Seminar*. On the morning of July 16 a precensorship order was imposed on *Seminar*. This means that the censors claim the right to alter by deletion the analysis and opinion of the intellectuals and academicians who have been contributing to the pages of *Seminar* for the past 17 years. Obviously, a responsible journal like ours devoted to thoughtful debate cannot surrender the integrity and right of free expression in this way".

The letter also says that the journal had examined whether it had any legal remedies open to it. It came to the conclusion that exerting in that direction would be "an exercise in futility". The editor adds: "It may be asked why we cannot do as others are doing. Mahatma Gandhi's advice was that he 'would rather see the complete stoppage of a newspaper if the editor cannot without fear of the consequences freely express his sentiments or publish those which he approves'. Gandhiji remains an infallible guide".

SATURDAY, JULY 24

The morning papers report that Ram Jethmalani has been declared an absconder and asked to surrender himself within 45 days.

In the afternoon Shyam Nandan Misra receives a telegram that his mother is seriously ill. A message is then conveyed to Virendra Patil who speaks to the Union Home Minister, Brahmananda Reddi, on the phone. The jail authorities are told that evening that Shyambabu has been granted parole for a week.

SUNDAY, JULY 25

Shyambabu leaves for Patna.

TUESDAY, JULY 27

BBC reports the arrest of Japan's former Prime Minister

Tanaka for suspected involvement in the Lockheed scandal. In any country which subscribes to the rule of law there can be no immunity from law for any one, not even an ex-Prime Minister.

An All India Radio news bulletin quotes the Law Minister, Gokhale, as saying that in the matter of Constitutional amendments the Government proposes to consult the opposition. Talks with the opposition would be held from August 7 onwards.

FRIDAY, JULY 30

BBC quotes Subramaniam Swamy in London that when J.P. reached Patna on July 20, section 144 Cr.P.C. was promulgated in the city and the airport cordoned off to prevent people from receiving him.

SATURDAY, JULY 31

The jail authorities have received a communication that Shyambabu's parole has been extended up to August 9.

MONDAY, AUGUST 2

BBC reports that on July 20, the directors of the *Statesman* New Delhi and Calcutta, received notices from Government asking them to show cause why their New Delhi press should not be confiscated. The BBC report mentions that the July issue of *Seminar* which has roused the ire of the Government was printed at the *Statesman* press. The report also mentions that unlike other English dailies the *Statesman* has been resisting inclusion of a Government nominee on its board of directors. It has also succeeded in getting a stay order from Calcutta High Court in the matter.

THURSDAY, AUGUST 5

BBC announces the winding up of its office in New Delhi. It said it is being done against its wishes.

SATURDAY, AUGUST 7

Both Voice of America and BBC report that the principal opposition parties have declined Government invitation for discussions on Constitution amendments. Their stand is that the present Lok Sabha on an extended term by virtue of the emergency has no right to make any basic changes in the Constitution.

Also most leaders of the opposition are behind bars. Thirdly, the ruling party must first get an electoral mandate for the proposed changes.

The two media also say that the opposition parties will be staying away from the Parliament session due to commence on August 10.

SUNDAY, AUGUST 8

The daily Press reports that the C.P.I., the Muslim League and the A.D.M.K. have accepted the Government's invitation for talks on constitutional amendments. Meanwhile, however, Government has abandoned the idea of a joint meeting between Government and the opposition. These three parties have been asked to meet the Law Minister individually.

MONDAY, AUGUST 9

A communication is received by the jail authorities that Shyambabu's parole has been further extended till August 16.

TUESDAY, AUGUST 10

Under a heading, "When Parliament Meets", editor V.K. Narasimhan of the *Indian Express* has written one of the boldest articles to be published these days by any daily paper. Narasimhan pleads for the release of political detenus, respect for opposing views in the matter of constitutional amendments and freedom to report Parliament proceedings. He recalls an exhortation for bravery made by Mahatma Gandhi in 1931: "In this country of suppression and cowardice, we cannot have too much bravery, too much self-sacrifice. I want the greater bravery of the meek, the gentle and the non-violent, the bravery that will mount the gallows without injuring or harbouring any thought of injury to a single soul!" Narasimhan appeals to Members of Parliament, irrespective of party, to "act as the conscience of the nation and trustees for generations to come".

Making an impassioned plea to the Government to forge a consensus with the opposition, the *Indian Express* editor writes: "In the Indian context, such generosity and consideration are all the more necessary because an opposition of even 150 members including those under detention represents a population of nearly 150 million. When one witnesses the extreme courtesy and regard with which visiting dignitaries from even small countries like Fiji or Lesoto, or Mauritius are received in New Delhi because they represent sovereign States, though each of them has a population of less than a million, it seems both undemocratic and unfair that opposition members of Parliament representing a much larger population should be denied the consideration due to them".

Narasimhan particularly urges the immediate release of detenus "against whom there are no serious charges", and a quick review of all other cases. All detenus, he says, must be released or put up for trial. The present atmosphere of "fear and uncertainty" must be transformed into that of "trust and hope".

Voice of America and BBC report today that four major opposition parties have boycotted Parliament's monsoon session which commenced today.

Voice of America also reports that the International Commission of Jurists has sent a cable to Indira Gandhi urging her to grant amnesty to all political prisoners on the coming August 15, our Independence Day.

As expected, All India Radio blacks out the news about opposition boycott of the Parliament session.

WEDNESDAY, AUGUST 11

The Press also blacks out the news. It is reported, however, that the C.P.I. and C.P.M. members opposed the proposed amendment of MISA at the introduction stage. This indicates that the C.P.M. has not boycotted the session. It has, however, declined the Government's invitation for discussions on constitutional amendments.

Voice of America reports that on August 9 Babubhai Patel, former Chief Minister of Gujarat along with "dozens of others" had courted arrest. It said Patel was arrested while paying homage to martyrs at the martyrs' memorial, Ahmedabad.

THURSDAY, AUGUST 12

The Minister of State for Home Affairs Om Mehta is reported to have told the Rajya Sabha that the Enforcement Directorate was proceeding against members of the Birla family involved in the United Commercial Bank case relating to foreign exchange conversion. He denied opposition charges that any attempt was being made to hush up the case. It is noteworthy that according to yesterday's *Times of India* (August 11) K.K. Birla has waxed eloquent in London about the boons of the emergency. Birla told British businessmen and bankers, "The emergency has created a remarkable transformation in India, generated a sense of national discipline, a feeling of national involvement, and accelerated economic growth".

SUNDAY, AUGUST 15

Today's *Sunday Standard* quotes from an interview given by Indira Gandhi to *Socialist India*. According to it, she says she has gone much farther than either her father or Lal Bahadur Shastri in trying to meet opposition leaders and accommodate their point of view.

She said, "I think that if there is that kind of co-operation we should try to find it and cooperate in that area".

But at the ceremonial Red Fort function today, she speaks in a different tone. She said that while there are queries as to when the emergency would end, nobody refers to its relaxation in the past many months. She added: "It is not in our hands as to what will happen. It is in the hands of those who are bent on disintegrating the country, spreading indiscipline and encouraging those groups and individuals who never had any belief in democracy, secular approach or nonalignment".

Sunday Standard's editorial today titled "Facing the Future" has as its concluding note this observation: "If we cannot learn to work together, we face a grim future. Co-operation, no less than discipline, must be our watchword".

MONDAY, AUGUST 16

A report comes from outside about Subramaniam Swamy's sensational arrival in Parliament and his even more sensational disappearance. All detenus here feel thrilled. "It is another Entebbe", says Dandavate. "Swamy came to Parliament, slapped Indira Gandhi and went away—that is what it adds up to", remarks Hegde. "It is really fantastic", says Deve Gowda.

We gather from the jail office that Shyambabu's parole has again been extended by two weeks.

TUESDAY, AUGUST 17

The Home Minister, Brahmananda Reddi, has spoken in the Lok Sabha about detenus. He has said (August 16) that the total number of detenus in the country was just 2 per 100,000 population! It was 'premature' to set any date for ending the emergency. "Everything is quite on the surface. What may be quiet on the surface may not be quiet underneath", he adds. He also referred to 'a grouping or regrouping of the forces' whose activities led to the proclamation of the emergency.

There should be something radically wrong with a Government which gives statistics about detentions in terms of "per one lakh population". Even so, one discerns one more official admission that the number of detenus in the country is in thousands and not in hundreds as the Law Minister said the other day. It seems however that mutually contradictory statements by ministers no longer worry the Government. Only a few days ago Om Mehta put the number of detenus at 25,000 and now Brahmananda Reddi suggests it is only 12,000. Who is telling the truth, if at all?

Indira Gandhi who has gone to Sri Lanka is reported as telling a gathering of Indians there that the emergency in India has been considerably relaxed. "Most" of the detenus have been released. "Only a few" remain in jail.

FRIDAY, AUGUST 20

Sunder Singh Bhandari who is in Tihar Jail has written me a letter from there, dated July 26, it reaches me here only today. It mentions that in Delhi jail there are no MISA rules. MISA detenus are treated as undertrial prisoners.

WEDNESDAY, AUGUST 25

A *Hindu* write-up by G.K. Reddy suggests that the normal terms of the Lok Sabha and the State legislatures are to be extended from five to six or seven years. This is one of the new constitutional amendments contemplated. "The five-year term", writes Reddy, "is not considered long enough for ushering any wide-ranging socio economic reforms without the distractions of another general election". A longer life span, Reddy argues, will "free legislatures from the vagaries of frequent elections which have an unsettling effect in a parliamentary system".

How long a term is long enough? In the U.K., a four-year term is deemed long enough. So also in Japan and Switzerland. Even the Supreme Soviet of the U.S.S.R. and the National People's Congress in China have a life span of just four years. In Australia, the Lower House of Parliament has a term of only three years. And the U.S. elections to the House of Representatives are held every two years. The proposal to extend the term of the Lok Sabha and the rationale given reminds one of the Gospel of the Brothers Barnabas propounded in Bernard Shaw's "Back to Methuselah". The two brothers think that the term of human life must be extended to at least three centuries! Argues Conrad Barnabas: "Can't you see that three-score-and-ten, though it may be long enough for a very crude sort of village life, is not long enough for a complicated civilisation like ours? Flinders Petrie has counted nine attempts at civilization made by people exactly like us; and every one of them failed just as ours is failing. They failed because the citizens and statesmen died of old age or over-eating before they had grown out of schoolboy games and savage sports and cigars and champagne".

FRIDAY, AUGUST 27

The Minister for Parliamentary Affairs, Raghuramaiah, announces in the Lok Sabha that Government would be introducing next week a Bill to provide for pension for M.Ps. The Lok Sabha and Rajya Sabha sessions have been extended for the purpose. Rules would be suspended to enable consideration and passing of the Pensions Bill without due notice. For several years now a powerful section in the ruling party has been lobbying for pensions for M.Ps but the opposition, generally speaking, has not favoured the proposal. So there was no official Bill on the subject till now. Now, of course, there would hardly be any resistance. The ruling party M.Ps may well regard this as one of the real gains of the emergency!

SATURDAY, AUGUST 28

Ganapati Utsav is celebrated in the jail with a lot of gaiety and festivity. Week-long celebrations commence from today in the MISA 'B' ward.

SUNDAY, AUGUST 29

Even the ultra-conformist *Illustrated Weekly* pleads for normalcy in a clever editorial entitled "Independent Thoughts on Independence Day". In it, the editor, Khushwant Singh, talks longingly about every anniversary arousing in him hopes that Indira Gandhi will now "transform herself into a Santa Claus and give the country a sackful of presents", release of

political prisoners, freedom to the Press and fixing of a poll
time-table. Describing such optimism as "his second childhood",
Khushwant Singh says, he "first detected these symptoms in
October 1975". He goes on: "They recurred on Nehru's birthday
on November 14 and were very pronounced on Indira Gandhi's
birthday on November 19. On the last Republic Day I was
like a spoilt Christian brat on Christmas-eve. And on August
15, I was in a festive mood expecting Indiraji to flood my
apartment with gifts". But his expectations have been belied
every time. He notes, "I may be wrong in my conjecture, I may
be jaundiced in my observation, but on Independence Day I
noticed less enthusiasm in Bombay that I had seen earlier,
including last year. This may be due to the non-fulfilment of
hopes of the kind I had nurtured in my bosom".

With unconcealed sarcasm Khushwant Singh concludes:
"Being an incorrigible optimist, I look forward to Bapu's
next birthday anniversary, failing that Nehru's, Indira Gandhi's
and the next Republic Day. I will keep my fingers crossed".

Khushwant Singh's is an outsiders' view. Here inside jail I
can see for myself the intense strain many detenus are put to
whenever the talk of release becomes loud.

In Solzhenitsyn's "Cancer Ward" there is a touching passage
about the feelings of political prisoners perennially looking
forward to amnesty. It bears reproduction at this point. "Only a
prisoner in his first year of sentence believes, every time he is
summoned from his cell and told to collect his belongings, that
he is being called to freedom. To him every whisper of an
amnesty sounds like the trumpets of archangels. But they call
him out of his cell, read him some loathsome documents and
shut him into another cell on the floor below even darker from
the previous one but with the same stale, used-up air. The
amnesty is always postponed—from the anniversary of victory
to the anniversary of Revolution, from the anniversary of the
Revolution to the Supreme Soviet session. Then it bursts like
a bubble, or is applied only to thieves, crooks and deserters
instead of those who fought in the war and suffered".

The Lok Sabha has passed the M.P. Pensions Bill.

WEDNESDAY, SEPTEMBER 1
The Constitution (44th Amendment) Bill is introduced in the
Lok Sabha. After adoption it would become the 42nd Amend-

ment. Apart from providing for a six-year term for the Lok Sabha and the State Assemblies, the Bill seeks to make changes in the Constitution which will alter its basic structure.

BBC and Voice of America report that most opposition members resisted the introduction of the Bill and walked out in protest. All India Radio, however, has blacked out the news of the walkout.

THURSDAY, SEPTEMBER 2
All India Radio reports that the Rajya Sabha has appointed a committee to investigate "the conduct and activities" of Subramaniam Swamy. The House has also passed the M.P. Pensions Bill.

Shyambabu's parole has been further extended.

FRIDAY, SEPTEMBER 3
Today is the concluding function of the Ganapati festival week. There are games and sports. An idol of Ganesh is taken out in procession and immersed in a small tank we have inside the jail compound.

SATURDAY, SEPTEMBER 4
Voice of America announces the U.S. Government's decision to grant political asylum to Ram Jethmalani. A U.S. Government spokesman said that the decision is in accordance with established U.S. policy. Whenever a foreign national seeks asylum because in his home country he is being subjected to oppression or harassment solely because of his political beliefs, asylum is granted.

WEDNESDAY, SEPTEMBER 8
Vinoba Bhave announces that he has given up his plans of fasting. His demand has been conceded, he says. What he adds is even more significant. Credit for the ban on cow slaughter, he says, goes first to God; second, his mother; third, Mahatma Gandhi and fourth, Indira Gandhi. The first three are in heaven. Indira Gandhi is here. I thank her, he says. As things have been shaping no one had any hope of an initiative from Vinoba, none among the detenus here. But this is an incredible let down. Sarvodaya workers in jail feel particularly bitter and disappointed.

THURSDAY, SEPTEMBER 9
Mao Tse-tung is dead. A great leader of a great country is
no more.

FRIDAY, SEPTEMBER 10
The 1 o'clock bulletin of All India Radio announces that an
Indian airlines plane flying from Delhi to Bombay via Jaipur
and Aurangabad has been hijacked to Lahore. The plane took
off from Delhi at 7 A.M. and landed at Lahore around 8.45
A.M. but Pakistan's first announcement in this regard came only
at 6.30 P.M.

SATURDAY, SEPTEMBER 11
Pakistan claims to have rescued the hijacked passengers and
captured the hijackers. The passengers return to India.

Shyambabu's parole is extended up to October 6.

MONDAY, SEPTEMBER 13

Occasionally, it has been possible for me to meet relations
of other detenus who came to visit them. Today, 1 chance to
run into one such visitor who makes no attempt to conceal his
intense indignation not only with the current situation, but also
with the Lok Sangharsh Samiti's response to it.
This visitor who had come to jail along with his wife takes
me to a corner and says: "The proposed amendments to the
Constitution, if allowed to be 'enacted, will destroy the last
vestiges of democracy in our country. This must not be
permitted".
"What do you have in mind?", I enquired.
"Peaceful methods won't do. Before Parliament meets for its
next session, she should not be there".
Then he went on to speak about himself: that he was an
aged man, that his children were well settled in life, that he
had nothing to worry about at all, that he had a licensed revol-
ver, and that he was willing to pay the price for what he wanted
to do. All that he needed was some guidance in Delhi so as to
reach the object of his wrath.
The person speaking to me was an educated, mature, old
man. The intensity with which he argued was moving. He was

not a fanatic. But he was honestly convinced that what he was suggesting was the only way to save Indian democracy. I could see his wife anxiously watching us from a distance. It took me quite some time to impress upon him that his line of thinking was totally perverse and that the course of action he had in mind would irreparably damage the cause which he wanted to serve. Whatever else may emerge out of such a plan, it certainly wouldn't be democracy, I told him.

A few moments later I saw him speaking agitatedly to his wife, who came to me later and said: "I feel relieved that you have advised him as you have".

Today's episode fully corroborates the thesis propounded by Ashish Nandi in the course of an article he wrote for *Quest*[18] some time back. I wonder if the censor had seen that article. Perhaps not. If they had seen it, the journal would have been banned and the publisher and the author of the article put behind bars.

The article is real dynamite. It warns Indira Gandhi almost in so many words that if you persist in what you are doing you will be assassinated! This issue of *Quest* (Nov-Dec., 1975) was among the books and journals sent by friends outside for our reading. It would be worthwhile reproducing at some length excerpts from the article. Unambiguously titled "Invitation to a beheading: A psychologist's guide to assassinations in the third world", the article says:

> The relationship between an assassin and his victim is deep and enduring. Death only openly and finally brings them together. Of course, there are tyrants who turn virtually everyone in a country into a prospective assassin and leaders who build bastions against their assassination in the minds of men, thereby reducing the circle of prospective assassins to the microscopic group of hired psycho-paths and the mentally ill.
>
> Emperor Nero belonged to the first category and Martin Luther King to the second.
>
> There is also the special case of rulers who by the consent of the majority are tyrannical within the country

---

[18] Quarterly journal published from Bombay

and, to the extent they get the chance, in the world outside. Their pathology leads to collective suicides rather than individual assassinations. Adolf Hitler is the hackneyed but glaring example of the species.

But such leaders are hardly typical. There is a much broader range of situations where the ruler is popular and charismatic but propelled by his inner drives, prepares the ground for his assassination. In such cases there is a close fit among the motivational imperatives of such a man, his attempts to remould the polity after his own psychological needs, and the type of invitation he extends to his potential assassins.

The first characteristic of such a ruler is an inability to trust deeply and wholly. Though his flamboyant style may hide it for a long time, he lives in an inner world peopled by untrustworthy men. Even when he trusts some, it is transient. A chain of lieutenants comes in and goes out of his favour in a fashion reminiscent of people getting in and out of a railway compartment.

The ruler suspends this suspiciousness only in the case of his family members, men recruited from outside politics to act as 'commissars', and politicians who have no independent bases and are fully dependent on him. . . .

Power, thus, continues to be concentrated in the ruler's hand. Worse, he is seen as all powerful. As a result, all grievances gradually begin to be directed at him. After a while, there remain no intermediate shock-absorbers whom he can fob off as subverters or reactionaries within the ruling circle . . . .

The regime which Richard Nixon built must have nurtured many political assassins and those who hooted him out might have, for all we know, saved his life. Sheikh Mujib's Bangladesh, too, was an instance of such a polity.

Not merely may the ruler become too deeply identified with the regime, the regime may seem closed to internal competition to large numbers of people.

Yet no regime is psychologically closed. It could be so only normatively. Even the most rigidly closed regime is open to one whose values permit him to include in the available means of political competition—revolution, rebellion, *coup* and assassination.

Of these, revolutions require immense planning, massive organisation, first-rate mobilisational skills, and a developed ability to feel the pulse of a large section of the population ....

To some extent, the pre-conditions of revolutions apply to rebellions and *coups*, too.

On the other hand, an assassination is the cheapest of the four means mentioned, requires the least planning and organisation, and does not need the assent of any section of the population. Understandably, it is a premium in the Third World. In some part of it, such killings have, in fact, become a standard means of deciding political succession. In Latin America, for instance the popularity of political assassinations is exceeded at the moment only by bull fights ....

The tragedy of the assassinated ruler is that though he can avoid the fate towards which he often moves blindly and inexorably, he is in effect a driven man. Like his killer, he rebels against a part of himself which seeks self-preservation, rationality and contact with the real world of people.

TUESDAY, SEPTEMBER 14

Voice of America relays a brief report on the proceedings of a Congressional sub-committee enquiring into the condition of human rights in India. Among those who gave evidence before the sub-committee are Leila Fernandes and Poddar, Chairman of Indians for Democracy. Leila Fernandes said that one by one all the lights of liberty are being extinguished in India. She refers to an article recently published in the Western Press severely criticising the emergency and says it was written by a close relation of Indira Gandhi. Poddar said that Indians in the U.S. who are cooperating with Indians for Democracy are being threatened by the Embassy. Nevertheless, they will continue to exert themselves for restoration of civil liberties in India.

WEDNESDAY SEPTEMBER, 15

It is announced that the next session of the Lok Sabha will be held from October 25 to November 3.

THURSDAY, SEPTEMBER 16

An interesting Voice of America report relates to a CBS newsman who published a confidential intelligence report but refused to divulge the source of his information to a Senate

committee. Some members of the committee wanted to arraign
the journalist for contempt. But the majority did not agree.
Winding up the discussion on the issue the committee chairman
said: "Though it is within the rights of the committee to get all
information it needs for the proper performance of its duties,
the role of the Press must be kept in mind. The role of the Press
is to monitor the activities of the Government".

SATURDAY, SEPTEMBER 18

Both the *Hindu* and *Indian Express* publish vitriolic write-
ups against Siddhartha Shankar Ray, Chief Minister of West
Bengal. I have no doubt that other newspapers must also have
carried similar attacks on Ray. It all appears to be a command
performance. Ray seems to be on the way out.

A very sad piece of news is received in the afternoon. Syed
Abdul Salaam, a MISA detenu belonging to the Jamaat-e-
Islami passes away. Some days ago he was taken to the
hospital. Detenus who have been visiting the hospital during
the last few days say that Salaam's is a case of gross negligence.
All detenus are naturally very upset about it. A *dharna* is
staged in front of the superintendent's office demanding an
inquiry into this tragic happening. Even while the *dharna* is
on a messenger arrives from the State Government Secretariat
and delivers a communication to the superintendent. The
communication says that Salaam was released on Friday, September 17, that is yesterday. Obviously there are no limits to
Government's callousness and shamelessness.

SUNDAY, SEPTEMBER 19

BBC reports a Government of India announcement that
censorship on despatches of foreign journalists is being lifted.
The announcement is made at a dinner for foreign correspondents hosted by the I and B Minister, Vidya Charan Shukla.
All India Radio has nothing to say on the subject.

MONDAY, SEPTEMBER 20

There is still no report in our Indian newspapers about withdrawal of restrictions on foreign journalists. Even so, the BBC
announcement of the lifting of censorship on news despatches
by foreign correspondents is hardly in doubt. One wonders
whether this is a pointer to possible elections.

A political report put out by BBC indicates that Siddhartha Ray who was nearly pushed out of political life has got a fresh lease of life. The political analyst ascribes Ray's decline to his failure to assess correctly Sanjay Gandhi's position in Indian politics.

TUESDAY, SEPTEMBER 21

This afternoon we heard that there has been a severe clash in Bangalore city between the police and the Indian Telephone Industries employees agitating for bonus. There has been a lathi charge and use of teargas. By the evening 67 I.T.I. employees are brought to the jail arrested under the DIR.

Hanumantha Gowda, a MISA detenu belonging to the Congress(O) is released. He has had a paralytic stroke and was on parole for three months. But he was put back in custody three weeks ago. Another ailing detenu Putte Gowda of Mysore is also released. News is also received from Belgaum that Gudadini, a Congress(O) member of the Legislative Council has been released. From Gulbarga there is a report that Gundu Rao of the Jana Sangh is free. Gundu Rao has had three heart attacks in detention. All these releases seem to have been prompted by Salaam's death in detention. Government is not concerned about the health of detenus. It is not worried even if they die because of detention. It is, however, interested in seeing that they do not die in detention. This explains the heartless cynicism displayed in Salaam's case.

In Solzhenitsyn's "Cancer Ward," doctors used to be very particular about seeing that patients who are doomed are discharged before their death. According to Solzhenitsyn, they felt that this would increase the turnover of beds; it would also be less depressing for those who remain, and would help improve the statistical picture because the patients discharged would be listed not as "deaths" but as "deteriorations".

WEDNESDAY, SEPTEMBER 22

All India Radio news bulletin says that the President has entrusted the Fertilisers and Chemicals portfolio to K.D. Malaviya in addition to his present duties. The report does not explain the reason why P.C. Sethi, the incumbent, has been divested of his portfolio. Is he ill? In the past even when ministers

suffered heart attacks (one recalls the case of C. Subramaniam)
they have never been stripped of their portfolios. Visitors from
outside have been lately bringing all kinds of stories about
Sethi's condition. One wonders if they are true.

FRIDAY, SEPTEMBER 24

The Ford Government's Aid Administrator, Arthur Gardener,
has been subjected to severe grilling by a Congressional sub-
committee inquiring into the state of human rights in India.
Reporting on it, Voice of America quotes the sub-committee
chairman Donald Fraser that since the clamping of the emergency, thousands of political opponents of the Prime Minister
have been jailed.

Gardener said that arms aid to India had been discontinued
since the Indo-Pakistan war in 1971 but food aid was being
given for humanitarian considerations. He said that the Ford
Administration had been circumspect in expressing itself on
the political situation in India but it appreciated Congress
concern about violation of civil liberties in India. In any future
bilateral talks with India, Gardener said, the Government
would keep the question in mind.

SATURDAY, SEPTEMBER 25

The *Daily Telegraph* of London quotes Indira Gandhi as
having told its correspondent, Ann Morrow, that she did not
know about the total number of detenus in the country because it is the State Governments that detained people and
not the Central Government! What an explanation!

SUNDAY, SEPTEMBER 26

Today's *Sunday Standard* carries a brief report of Indira
Gandhi's interview with Independent Television, London. In
the interview she says that release of detenus is continuing
and barring five or six opposition leaders, all others have been
released. She also says that she has no intention of putting off
elections but she is not going to disclose to a foreign media the
date of a future election before announcing it at home. Asked
if she had any intention of retiring she said she could not quit
in times of difficulty.

Detenus in both 'A' and 'B' wards join to celebrate Id-ul-Fitr.

TUESDAY, SEPTFMBER 28

I have just completed reading an interesting book on Hitler recently published which I managed to procure some time back. Titled "The Mind of Adolf Hitler", the book is actually a top-secret study written in 1943 for the U.S. Government's Office of Strategic Studies by a group of psycho-analysts headed by Walter C. Langer.

In the study, Langer has identified a number of factors pertaining to group psychology which enabled Hitler to win the support of large sections of the people. Three of the more important factors listed have been explained thus :

1. Hitler's ability to repudiate his own conscience in arriving at political decisions has eliminated the force that usually checks and complicates the forward-going thoughts and resolutions of most socially responsible statesmen. He has, therefore, been able to take that course of action that appeals to him as most effective without pulling his punches. The result has been that he has frequently outwitted his adversaries and attained ends that would not have been attained by a normal course. Nevertheless, it has helped to build up the myth of his infallibility and invincibility.
2. He is a master of the art of propaganda. His primary rules were : never allow the public to cool off; never admit a fault or wrong; never leave room for alternatives; never accept blame; concentrate on one enemy at a time and blame him for everything that goes wrong; people will believe a big lie sooner that a little one; and if you repeat it frequently enough people will sooner or later believe it.
3. Ability to surround himself with and maintain the allegiance of a group of devoted aides whose talents complement his own.

Indira Gandhi possesses the first and second attributes in full measure. Her unmitigated failure in the matter of the third attribute, I am sure, is going to prove her Achilles heel.

SATURDAY, OCTOBER 2

People outside may be prevented from observing Gandhi Jayanti but here inside we suffer from no such constraints. All detenus assemble in MISA Ward 'B' to celebrate the birth anniversay of Gandhiji. Sarvodaya leader Venkoba Rao and Madhu Dandavate address the gathering.

BBC and Voice of America have an important news item today. It is that the Delhi edition of the *Indian Express* could not be published on October 1 and 2 because its electricity was cut off. The *Indian Express* filed a writ in the Delhi High Court which has ordered restoration of the power supply.

A few days ago BBC had quoted from a circular letter issued by the Directorate of Advertising and Visual Publicity in August to all Government departments and public undertakings that the *Statesman, Junior Statesman*, the *Indian Express* group of newspapers and the *Tribune* of Chandigarh should not be given any advertisements.

MONDAY, OCTOBER 4

Radio Australia reports that the *Indian Express* Office in New Delhi had been sealed, allegedly because it failed to pay municipal dues.

BBC and Voice of America report that George Fernandes and 22 other accused in the Baroda Dynamite Case are brought to the Court today in handcuffs and fetters. While lawyers argued, George Fernandes addressed an impromptu press conference saying that their fetters symbolise the chains clapped on the whole country. He said that the case against them was cooked up and that they would stoutly defend themselves against the charges.

TUESDAY, OCTOBER 5

An *Indian Express* spokesman is reported by Voice of America as saying that they would be moving the Delhi High Court against the sealing of their press. He said that this was only the latest in a series of steps taken by the authorities to compel the *Indian Express* to follow a policy favourable to Indira Gandhi.

WEDNESDAY, OCTOBER 6

Voice of America says that the Delhi High Court has ordered the restoration of its press to the *Indian Express*, New Delhi.

The release of an important opposition personality is announced not by All India Radio but Radio Australia. According to the late night bulletin of Radio Australia, Piloo Modi has been released. Immediately after his release, Piloo told the Associated Press of America that his first task would be to work for the merger of the opposition parties.

THURSDAY, OCTOBER 7
Jail authorities receive a telegram informing them that Shyambabu's parole is again extended, this time up to October 24. It strikes us that the Lok Sabha is due to commence on October 25. I hope Shyambabu will be released before the session.

FRIDAY, OCTOBER 8
The Indian Press reports only today the release of Piloo Modi, Biju Patnaik and Babubhai Patel.

It is *Sharad Poornima* today. Detenus assemble in the MISA 'B' Ward and participate in various kinds of sports.

SUNDAY, OCTOBER 10
A seminar on the constitutional amendments is organised in Bangalore. Among those who addressed the seminar were Shanti Bhushan and Virendra Patil. The meeting took place at Gandhi Hall but the authorities refused to permit the use of a microphone in the hall.

MONDAY, OCTOBER 11
It is J.P's birthday today. A function is organised in the MISA 'B' Ward and tributes are paid to the great leader.

By the evening the jail office receives six release orders. All the released detenus belong to Coorg district.

THURSDAY, OCTOBER 14
Venkat Ram of the Socialist party who had gone on parole a fortnight ago returns to the jail. He reports about his meeting with Surender Mohan who apprised him of the goings-on in Delhi. The merger issue has been finalised, Surender Mohan told him.

FRIDAY, OCTOBER 15
The latest *Blitz* has a front-page story by R.K. Karanjia

saying that elections will be held in 1978 and not in 1977.

SATURDAY, OCTOBER 16

On his arrival in Bhubaneswar, Biju Patnaik is reported as saying that the gains of the emergency should be strengthened "not through fear but by the awakening of the national consciousness". He said that the first flush of enforced discipline was eroding. It needed to be replaced by voluntary discipline.

While this part of Biju's statement is unexceptionable the complimentary references reportedly made to Sanjay Gandhi provoked very angry reactions here.

WEDNESDAY, OCTOBER 20

Vishwanath, a Jana Sangh worker of Puttur (Mangalore district), is brought to the jail today. He had undergone harrowing torture for 15 days in a Mangalore police station. Vishwanath's arms still bear marks of the torture. The right half of his back is paralysed. This 22-year-old young man is one of the scores of workers picked up in his district for torture following what has now come to be known as the Kalhadka episode. A Congress worker of Kalhadka was killed in the course of what was presumably an internecine fight inside the Congress party. The authorities are using it as an excuse to wreak vengeance on RSS and Jana Sangh cadres in the district. Mangalore district has sent over 5,000 satyagrahis to jail, perhaps a record for the whole country. Puttur is one of the talukas of the district; Puttur town with a population of only 22,000 has sent as many as 790 satyagrahis.

THURSDAY, OCTOBER 21

For us in the Jana Sangh it is a significant day today. Founded by Syama Prasad Mookerjee on October 21, 1951 the Bharatiya Jana Sangh completes 25 years of its existence today. The party can be proud of its performance during this period.

A letter from Madan Lal Khurana received from Tihar jail refers to the possibilities of a unified opposition party emerging in the near future and says that Jana Sangh members who have been exerting themselves in this direction would have a feeling of satisfaction, not unmixed with sorrow, when this actually comes about. It would be the feeling a Hindu household has on the occasion of a daughter's marriage, Khurana writes—happy that a duty has been discharged, but sad over the parting.

The morning papers carry a curious report today. The U.P. and Punjab Pradesh Congress Committees have demanded convening of a constituent assembly to draw up a "people's constitution". They want more time for discussion on constitutional amendments. Indira Gandhi, it may be noted, is in U.P. these days.

FRIDAY, OCTOBER 22

The constituent assembly proposal gets top play in the Press. Bihar and Haryana Pradesh Congress Committees also have voiced the same demand. It is interesting to note that four other Pradesh Congress bodies which met on October 19— Maharashtra, Madhya Pradesh, Gujarat and West Bengal—and passed long resolutions hailing the 44th Amendment Bill, said not a word about a constituent assembly. And another four which met on October 20—U.P., Bihar, Haryana and Punjab— have made the demand in chorus. For those who know Sanjay's relations with these four bodies the meaning should be clear.

SATURDAY, OCTOBER 23

Addressing the Congress Parliamentary Party, Indira Gandhi affirms that Parliament is fully empowered to change the Constitution. I think her address should be taken as rejection of the constituent assembly proposal.

Shyambabu's parole has again been extended up to November 15.

MONDAY, OCTOBER 25

The Lok Sabha session begins. The four main opposition parties—the Jana Sangh, the Congress(O), the B.L D. and the Socialists—have decided to boycott the session. The C.P.M. and the R.S.P. stage a walkout.

Today's good news is about the release of Deve Gowda. We are sure his presence outside will help accelerate the process of unification of democratic parties.

TUESDAY, OCTOBER 26

A small news item in the Press says that the Andhra Pradesh Congress Committee has urged postponement of elections to 1978.

WEDNESDAY, OCTOBER 27

I receive a message from outside that Atalji is coming to Bangalore to meet me. The news is surprising because ordinarily, except for family members and legal counsel, nobody is allowed to meet detenus. In the afternoon, however, the Inspector-General of Prisons also confirms it and says that though he has not received any formal communication yet he has heard that Atalji has been permitted by the Government to meet me.

Voice of America reports the arrest of K.R. Sundar Rajan, Assistant Editor of the *Times of India*, Bombay. The arrest has followed publication of a couple of critical articles by him in the *Christian Science Monitor*.

THURSDAY, OCTOBER 28

BBC reports that firing has taken place in Muzaffarnagar in U.P. In the course of her speech in Parliament on the 44th Amendment yesterday Indira Gandhi admitted the firing in Muzaffarnagar but said that the opposition statement about 40 deaths was exaggerated. The BBC report says that the police have now admitted 13 deaths. The incident occurred in the wake of a demonstration against forcible sterilization. Earlier when an Associated Press correspondent visited Muzaffarnagar he was told by the District Magistrate that there was no police firing and that no one was killed.

A letter from Punjab gives an interesting account of the happenings there. During the last few weeks hectic efforts are being made by the Central Government to win over the Akali Dal. Government-inspired rumours kept circulating both inside and outside the jail about a Congress-Akali understanding.

Gurucharan Singh Tohra, President of the Shiromani Gurdwara Prabandhak Committee, was brought from Ferozepur to Ludhiana to join Prakash Singh Badal. Government representatives spoke to them jointly. Sardar Santokh Singh of Delhi, former Akali now with the Congress, was sent to Amritsar to negotiate with Sant Harcharan Singh, Chief of the Akali Dal.

The Sant first refused to see him. But Santokh Singh persisted in his efforts and the Sant ultimately relented and agreed to meet him. Meanwhile the police had information from intelligence that some persons threatened to tar Santokh Singh's face and pour ash on his head.[19] So they advised Santokh Singh not to meet the Sant. Former Secretary of the Akali Dal Gurmeet Singh, was then sent to meet the Sant. But the Sant refused to see him. He asked the Akali leaders in Ludhiana jail not to succumb to Government overtures. The Government of India is believed to be prepared to concede all the regional demands of the Akali Dal and is also willing to give the Chief Ministership of Punjab to an Akali in a future coalition government with the Congress. The Akali leaders, however, have spurned the offer and declared that their agitation would continue so long as the emergency lasted, civil liberties were not restored and elections were not announced.

The Akali satyagraha continues to gather momentum. Recently Mohan Singh Tur offered satyagraha along with 500 others. Some five to six thousand persons gave them a hearty send-off. Garlands of currency notes valued at Rs. 16,000/- were offered to them on the occasion.

FRIDAY, OCTOBER 29

Atalji has arrived in Bangalore but only a letter of his reached me in the jail. The letter says that before leaving Delhi by train on Wednesday he had been told that he could see me and that the Government of India was sending necessary instructions to Bangalore. But that on arrival here he is informed that permission to see me has not been granted. According to Atalji the Government seems to have been annoyed by the large number of persons who met him at the wayside stations on his train journey. In Bangalore too, Atalji had a warm reception at the station. I shared the contents of Atalji's letter with other colleagues. I drafted a reply at night and sent it out early in the morning.

SATURDAY, OCTOBER 30

Dandavate and I have a date with our dentist today. Both of us go to the superintendent's office in time to find that our

---

[19] Much more than the physical hurt involved, it is a gesture of humiliation.

escort has not turned up. We waited and waited but the escort never arrived. The jail authorities first tried to explain it away but later kept mum.

The reason for the non-arrival of the escort is obvious; Atalji is in town.

All India Radio reports in its afternoon bulletin that Gokhale has announced in the Lok Sabha that the life of the Lok Sabha is being extended by one year. Gokhale said that disruptive elements which forced the proclamation of the emergency were still active.

From Bangalore jail there is one more release today. The only B.L.D. detenu in the State, 74-year-old Ganappaiah, is released.

TUESDAY, NOVEMBER, 2

Cherian, one of our co-detenus has been trying hard for parole because his mother is ill. But it is not being granted to him. Word came today that Cherian's mother had passed away. Some months ago his father had passed away without his being present at the parent's bedside. Now also instead of being able to meet his ailing mother, Cherian will be going out on parole today for her funeral!

The United States will be going to the polls today to elect a new President. Jimmy Carter's pronouncements on human rights have naturally endeared him to most people in India who have been watching the campaign.

WEDNESDAY, NOVEMBER 3

Jimmy Carter is elected President of the U.S. Addressing a cheering crowd at Atlanta he pays rich tributes to President Ford whom he describes as not only a "formidable opponent but also a good and decent man". Ford sends a telegram congratulating the President-elect and assuring him of full support in the coming months.

A note from outside mentions that on October 29 Atalji met Satya Sai Baba at White Field. A Madhya Pradesh Minister was also present at the time. In the presence of everyone Sai Baba said that there was no democracy in the country today, no freedom of expression. He later took Atalji to his chamber and said that the fight for democracy must continue; ultimately *dharma** will triumph.

MONDAY, NOVEMBER 8

Ramakrishna Hegde is the first to greet me early morning today on my second birthday inside the jail. Several telegrams are received, one of them from home and another from Shakuntala Hegde and her children—Bharat, Mamta and Samta. Shakuntala Hegde has also sent flowers and a basketful of fruit.

WEDNESDAY, NOVEMBER 10

Early during the emergency period the *National Herald* had espoused one-party democracy. Now a "political commentator" writing in the *Economic Times* (November 10) has commended the same idea. The article says: "Politically, Arunachal Pradesh has the distinction among the States and the Union Territories of being the only unit with just one party, the Congress. Experience so far has been quite encouraging. The party has been functioning smoothly and all its energies are directed towards progress and prosperity. Indeed it might fortuitously prove to be the crucible for an experiment in one-party democracy in view of a significant proposal currently going the rounds in political circles".

THURSDAY, NOVEMBER 11

A note from Delhi mentions that Roxna Swamy has been subjected to a lot of harassment by the police. Her car, refrigerator, television and other articles have been taken away.

FRIDAY, NOVEMBER 12

The Rajya Sabha Committee constituted to investigate the activities of Subramaniam Swamy has submitted its report. It has recommended that Swamy be expelled from the House.

SATURDAY, NOVEMBER 13

A letter from Khurana in Tihar jail informs us that a Sarvodaya worker, Prabhakar Sharma, has committed self-immolation.

---

* Righteousness

MONDAY, NOVEMBER 15
Despite protests by the opposition members present, the Rajya Sabha adopts a resolution expelling Subramaniam Swamy.

Under a headline, "Is opposition irrelevant?" the *Indian Express* writes a scathing editorial on D.K. Borooah's reported statement in the Rajya Sabha (during the discussion on Constitutional amendments) that "the country can do without the opposition; they are irrelevant to the history of India". It is wrong to suggest, says the *Indian Express*, that any of the released opposition leaders had advocated subversive politics, even if they are unreconciled to the continuance of the emergency and the curbing of civil liberties. Advising Borooah to realise the distinction between legitimate opposition in a democratic system and the politics of subversive groups, the editorial approvingly quotes Walter Lippman who observed, "Under a strategy of obstruction the opposition seeks to stop the Government and to force it to go another way; under a strategy of criticism it forces the Government to hear complaints, and to account for itself, but it does not seek to deprive it of power or responsibility". The editorial adds, "The more powerful a Government is, the more it needs", as Lippman warned, "protection from its own courtiers, from the delusion of its own un-examined premises, from the conceit that sooner or later afflicts every human animal when everybody around him says yes".

TUESDAY, NOVEMBER 16
Copies are received in jail of letters exchanged between Asoka Mehta and Om Mehta.

Om Mehta's letter is somewhat significant; it is on behalf of the Prime Minister to whom Asoka Mehta had written urging normalisation and free and fair elections; it is the first letter written on behalf of the Government to an opposition leader commenting on the current situation. Earlier letters, even from J.P., Goray, Vajpayee and Patel have remained unreplied, in fact unacknowledged. Om Mehta's letter dated November 8 says inter alia, "As the Prime Minister has declared time and again, we would not like to continue the present emergency for a moment longer than it is necessary. However, it is a matter of regret that the attitude of the opposition has not undergone any significant change and they persist in a negative and agitational approach which is coming in the way of normalisation of the situation. As soon as there is evidence of some change, the response from our side will not be wanting".

Asoka Mehta's reply, dated November 11, says, "You assert that the attitude of the opposition has not undergone any significant change and they persist in negative and agitational approach which is coming in the way of normalisation of the situation. I am sure you are aware that we are not allowed to hold public meetings; in many places, even hall meetings are not permitted and when permitted, loudspeaker facilities are often denied. Recently when information about firing and killing of a number of innocent persons in Muzaffarnagar was received, a group of opposition M.P.s sought to visit the place to ascertain facts for themselves. They were prevented from meeting the affected people and were unceremoniously bundled out of the district. Under the restrictions imposed on the Press it is virtually impossible to convey to the people our reactions to various developments in the country. I would be interested to know from you as to the Government's conception of legitimate functioning of the opposition in the circumstances now prevailing.

"Anyway, we are naturally anxious for a normalisation of the situation. We would welcome a meaningful dialogue, if the Prime Minister is prepared for it. Both the sides would then appreciate each other's difficulties and strive to find a solution".

WEDNESDAY, NOVEMBER 17

The four-monthly memo from the Home Ministry has arrived. It says that "the detention of the said Lal K. Advani continues to be necessary for effectively dealing with the emergency". I have to acknowledge on the memo and retain a copy with myself. I acknowledge it thus: "Received a copy of this memorandum. November eight, the date on this memo, happens to be my birthday. I regard this therefore as a birthday gift. Thanks".[20]

THURSDAY, NOVEMBER 18

On his way to Gauhati for the Youth Congress session Sanjay Gandhi tells newsmen at Calcutta airport that "the C.P.I. has been interfering in our work. It has been confusing the people. It has no programme and does no work".

[20] See Appendix 3.

FRIDAY, NOVEMBER 19

The *Hindu* of Madras reports Sanjay Gandhi's reception at Gauhati under a five-column banner headline. Immediately below on the same page there is a brief news item with a single column heading reading "P.M. arrives".

SATURDAY, NOVEMBER 20

At the Youth Congress session at Gauhati Indira Gandhi says that many Chief Ministers have been treating their States as if they were their *jagirs*. She specifically names West Bengal, Orissa and Karnataka in this context.

SUNDAY, NOVEMBER 21

At the AICC session Indira Gandhi says that she is not going to yield to foreign pressure. Opposition members now in detention would have been released earlier she says had it not been for the foreign propaganda that is going on. This is really like Vorster of South Africa saying that on his own he would have ended apartheid but because outside elements are trying to pressurise him he is determined to continue his policies. Can Indira Gandhi explain why the pressure of world opinion on Rhodesia or South Africa is right and doing the same in support of civil liberties in India is wrong?

A copy of a letter from Asoka Mehta to Virendra Patil is received. In it Asoka gives a report of his discussions in Patna with J.P. and other leaders regarding unification. Asoka Mehta's stand is that all other parties should merge in the Congress (O).

SATURDAY, NOVEMBER 27

Today's *Indian Express* says that Parliament is likely to skip its winter session this year. It will be for the first time in parliamentary history if it happens.

FRIDAY, DECEMBER 10

A function is organised in the jail to observe Human Rights Day. Dandavate addresses the detenus.

SUNDAY, DECEMBER 12

A communication from outside informs us that Atalji has written to the Home Ministry asking that either the restrictions imposed on his movement under the parole order be removed or he be sent back to jail.

MONDAY, DECEMBER 13

The 6 P.M. bulletin of All India Radio announces the unconditional release of Atalji.

TUESDAY, DECEMBER 14

Gopinath conveys from outside that he has spoken to Atalji on the phone early in the morning. Atalji says he has had no official communication about his release. He learnt about it yesterday when the Press was told about it.

According to newspaper reports Rajeshwar Rao of the C.P.I. has voiced the support of his party to Sanjay's five-point programme. The C.P.I. General Secretary said his party would be campaigning for it.

Snehlata Reddi who has been ailing for some time is released on parole.

THURSDAY, DECEMBER 16

Rajeshwar Rao denies that he has supported Sanjay Gandhi's five-point programme. What is more surprising is that All India Radio has reported the denial.

Nandini Satpathi resigns as Chief Minister of Orissa. Within minutes, the Centre announces suspension of the State Assembly and imposition of President's rule. C.P. Majhi, Deputy Minister at the centre who is the main instrument employed by Sanjay for Nandini's ouster hails the decision and says that "a catastrophe has been averted".

FRIDAY, DECEMBER 17

Abuses and epithets are freely traded by the pro- and anti-Ray factions in West Bengal. All India Radio and the Press give full publicity to the anti-Ray campaign.

MONDAY, DECEMBER 20

The radio and Press campaign against the West Bengal Chief Minister Siddhartha Shankar Ray has stopped abruptly. Not a single item in the Press, not a word on the radio. The campaign had been going on for over a fortnight now and following

Satpathi's removal had reached a crescendo. It seems Ray is going to get another lease of life.

TUESDAY, DECEMBER 21

The Chief Censor in New Delhi has instructed all news-papers not to publish anything regarding the internal squabbles of the ruling party. This bit of information is reported by BBC which also says that when instructions were given on phone some papers requested that they be sent in writing. The BBC report added that the directive seems to be aimed at stopping criticism of Sanjay Gandhi.

THURSDAY, DECEMBER 23

Indira Gandhi lashes out at C.P.I. Addressing a Congress workers' training class at Delhi she says that the C.P.I. is criticis-ing Sanjay Gandhi, Bansi Lal and others because they dare not attack her directly. On the issue of a dialogue with the opposition she says the opposition is still unrepentant. She again claims that almost all detenus have been released.

FRIDAY, DECEMBER 24

All India Radio and Samachar report a "spontaneous" rally of 50,000 people at the round about in front of the Prime Minister's residence in New Delhi "to express their support for her speech against the C.P.I. yesterday".

SUNDAY, DECEMBER 26

It is reported in the newspapers that yesterday Vinoba Bhave announced "Karma Mukti" (renunciation of interest in worldly affairs).

I remember having read Voltaire's *Candide* in which there is a Greek philosopher by the name of Pangloss (in Greek Pang-loss means a wind bag) who keeps prattling all the while that "this is the best of all possible worlds" even while his friends are being tortured.

MONDAY, DECEMBER 27

In its lead editorial the *Indian Express* makes a pungent comment on Vinoba's "Karma Mukti" declaration. The edito-rial commends his advice to Sarvodaya workers to shun power or party politics but adds, "no citizen, let alone a worker who is deeply concerned with welfare of the poor and underprivileged can possibly isolate himself from political and governmental decisions that affect them. He cannot condone corruption, fail to counter injustice or be silent when truth is misinterpreted, even if this involves opposing the false propaganda of a political party or standing up to administrative misbehaviour. If he looks the other way in such circumstances he is no follower of Mahatma Gandhi".

THURSDAY, DECEMBER 30

The 2 P.M. All India Radio bulletin announces the release of Ram Dhan. Ram Dhan is described as an M.P. from Azamgarh. No mention is made of the fact that he was Secretary of the Congress Parliamentary Party when he was jailed.

FRIDAY, DECEMBER 31

The closing day of the year brings particularly happy tidings for our jail. Dandavate's detention is revoked. He is given a warm and affectionate send-off.

The evening bulletin announces two more names of persons released, those of Rabi Ray and Balraj Madhok.

1977

WEDNESDAY, JANUARY 5, 1977

The *Indian Express* publishes the text of a letter written to Asoka Mehta by Indira Gandhi and also Mehta's reply. Indira Gandhi says in her letter: "My party and Government have always been committed to parliamentary democracy in which I believe as an ideal as well as a practical necessity". She refers to the changes that have taken place in the last few months and adds "once there is a genuine acceptance of the changes that have taken place, a clear disawoval of communal and separatist policies, repudiation of the politics of violence and extra-constitutional action, and also a constructive approach to social change then it would not be impossible to find solutions to the problems between the opposition and the Government".

Asoka Mehta's reply is brief. He says he has shared the Prime Minister's letter with leaders of the B.L.D., Jana Sangh and the Socialist Party and they reiterate the desirability of having direct discussions between Government and the opposition so that the points raised by her and the points he had raised in his earlier letters can be discussed. When Indira Gandhi insists on acceptance of the changes that have taken place she wants us to reconcile ourselves to the authoritarianism that has now been built into the Indian polity. When she calls for a repudiation of extra-constitutional action etc. she wants all those who have been in the J.P. movement virtually to abandon their position. It is futile for her to expect this to happen.

THURSDAY, JANUARY 6

Early this morning the assistant superintendent, Desai comes with the message that the detention order on Nagappa Alva has been revoked. At the function held to give a send-off to Alva, I expressed the hope and desire that the MISA 'B' Ward also starts getting depleted at the same pace as the 'A' Ward. Later in the evening my wishes are partly fulfilled when two inmates are released from the 'B' ward: P.G.R. Scindia of the Vidyarthi Parishad and Shiva Nand of the Congress (O). All India Radio announces the release of Kanwar Lal Gupta.

FRIDAY, JANUARY 7

The Press reports Indira Gandhi's interview with the American fashion magazine, *Vogue*, in which she repeats her Gauhati statement about "outside interference" being responsible for thwarting Government's moves towards liberalisation. Asked about political activists arrested without charges and detained without trial, Indira Gandhi said "we have released almost all of them. There are very few still in detention; just a handful of leaders".

The letters from various jails I have received recently (I have been in communication with more than 40 jails in the country) indicate that in Maharashtra there are 2000 detenus, in Madhya Pradesh more than 2000, in U.P. and in Bihar 1000 each. The number of detenus, released during October and November throughout the country is about 100.

I learn that a telegram from Delhi has arrived for me. The telegram is not delivered to me but I manage to get its contents verbatim. The contents make it obvious why it has been held back from me. It reads: "Met prominent members of joint family about new house to be set up. Proceeding to Patna to see grandfather today.

Madhu Bala Advani"[21]

---

[21] Madhu Dandavate sent the telegram under an assumed name.

BBC reports Kedar Nath Sahni's visit to London and a forthright interview with the *Times*, London. The *Guardian* carries
a strong editorial criticising Labour leader, Michael Foot, for
the praise he has bestowed on the emergency in India.

WEDNESDAY, JANUARY 12

All India Radio announces the release of Chandra Shekhar.
Dharia is also released but the radio somehow does not mention
his name.

THURSDAY, JANUARY 13

A large batch is released today—10 MISA detenus, seven
of them from Bangalore and three from other jails in the State.
The seven released from here are Ramkrishna Hegde and Ibrahim
of the Congress(O), J.H. Patel, Appa Rao and Snehlata
Reddi of the Socialist Party and Venkoba Rao and Satya Vrat,
Sarvodaya workers. Most RSS and Jana Sangh detenus are
still kept behind.

This morning's papers carry a Samachar report saying that
at a secret meeting held in Bangalore the CPI has decided to
oppose the 20-point programme as well as the five point
programme while publicly voicing support for them. I have
not the slightest doubt that this news item has been cooked up
at the Samachar desk. I have never known a news agency
putting out a patently mischievous report of this kind.

SATURDAY, JANUARY 15

Five more detenus are released from Bangalore jail. They
are Chandra Sekhar, Lakshmi Narsaiah and Some Gowda
(Congress-O), Raju (Socialist party) and Cherian (Jana Sangh).
With this, all Congress(O) detenus in this jail are released.

SUNDAY, JANUARY 16

The *Indian Express* carries a lead story saying that the Lok
Sabha poll is likely by March-end or April beginning and that
a formal announcement to this effect may be made on the
opening day of Parliament's next session i.e. February 9.

TUESDAY, JANUARY 18

It is around 1.30 in the afternoon when the superintendent,
Chablani, comes to my room and says that a wireless message

has arrived from New Delhi revoking my detention order. He says that the State Government would like me to leave at the earliest, say within an hour. The superintendent indicates that the State Government does not want a crowd to collect outside. I tell Chablani that it is just not possible for me to leave the jail in such a short time. I have to meet the colleagues in other wards and that would take time.

As it happens, I spent two or three hours in the other wards. There is the usual send-off function as well. Somehow the release news has not made me happy. From the pattern of releases so far it is becoming obvious that the Government has no intention of releasing the R.S.S. detenus who form the bulk of those inside and even from among the Jana Sangh activists they are releasing only the leaders or legislators to gain publicity. In fact, as head of the organisation, I feel oppressed by a sense of guilt that while I am being released junior colleagues of mine are being held back. Judging from the emerging scheme of things I am not sure that they will all be released soon. (As it happened many of them were released only after the elections).

When at 5.30 or so I returned to my room I found a heap of letters lying on my table. They are more than 600, all of them from abroad, sent by members or associates of Amnesty International. Most of them are Christmas or New Year greeting cards, but there is a line or two inscribed on each, which gave strength, confidence and hope to all of us engaged in the struggle. Here is a sample—a Christmas greeting card from one Laurie Hendricks from Amsterdam in Holland. She wrote:

Freedom and hope don't go hand in hand. They can steal your freedom but can't take your hope.

Yes, they stole the freedom of 600 millions, but they just could not destroy their hope!

PART TWO

Underground Literature

In the following pages are presented five of the pamphlets written by the author while in detention for distribution as Lok Sangharsh Samiti literature.

A Tale of Two Emergencies

by

A Detenu

(October, 1975)

Autocratic power everywhere entrenches itself and tends to perpetuate itself in the name of public good; history records that abuse of constitutional despotism inevitably leads to absolute despotism.

K. SUBBA RAO
Former Chief Justice of India
(*At a New Delhi Seminar on*
March 15-16, 1975.)

William Shirer's "The Rise and Fall of the Third Reich" is regarded as a monumental, definitive work on the history of Nazi Germany. Going through it a second time these days, I have been greatly struck by the remarkable, but disturbing similarity between the methodology of Adolf Hitler to make himself an absolute dictator and the steps being taken by Indira Gandhi here to decimate and destroy Indian democracy.

When the Weimar Constitution was adopted in 1919, it was hailed as the "most liberal and democratic document of its kind the twentieth century had seen". Shirer describes it as "mechanically well-nigh perfect, full of ingenious and admirable devices which seemed to guarantee the working of an almost flawless democracy".

But the Weimar Constitution, like our own, had its emergency provisions, incorporated into it in good faith by the Founding Fathers with the confidence that they would be used only in times of grave crises, such as war.

Hitler became Chancellor (Prime Minister) of Germany on January 30, 1933; on February 28, he made President Hindenberg invoke Article 48 (Emergency Powers) and sign a decree "for the protection of the people and the State". Among other things the decree proclaimed:

> Restriction on personal liberty, on the right of free expression of opinion, including freedom of the Press; on the rights of assembly and association; and violations of privacy of postal, telegraphic and telephone communication; and warrants for home searches, orders for confiscations as well as restrictions on property, are also permissible beyond the legal limits otherwise prescribed.

The decree also authorised the Reich to take over complete power in the constituent states of the union, and prescribed harsh penalties for a number of crimes including "serious disturbance of the peace".

The excuse for this emergency was a fire in the Reichstag (German Parliament House) on February 27, just one day before the proclamation of the emergency. In India too, the emergency was proclaimed on June 25, the avowed provocation being an opposition resolution of June 24. In both cases, obviously the decision had been taken earlier, and any pretext was deemed handy.

After the Reichstag fire, Hitler's Government issued a statement that they had unearthed "a Communist conspiracy to burn down Government buildings, museums, mansions and essential plants" and that the burning of the Reichstag was to be a signal for a bloody insurrection and civil war.

Thirteen years later, in the historic Nuremberg trials it was substantially established that the Reichstag fire was the handiwork of the Nazis themselves; Goebbels had conceived the idea and had executed it under Goering's instructions.

Every other day, Indira Gandhi and her cohorts keep asserting that whatever they have done during these past months is "within the four corners of the Constitution". The charge being levelled against them by the opposition and by the Western Press that they have subverted democracy is therefore untenable, it is argued.

The history of Nazi Germany conclusively shows that doing anything constitutionally is not necessarily the same thing as doing it in a democratic manner. Hitler always used to boast that he had done nothing illegal or unconstitutional. Indeed, he made a democratic constitution an instrument of dictatorship. Shirer has noted:

Though the Weimar Republic was destroyed the Weimar Constitution was never formally abrogated by Hitler. Indeed and ironically, Hitler based the legality of his rule on the despised republican Constitution.

A vigorous opposition, a free Press and an independent judiciary are the three essential features of democracy. These are the institutional checks which a democratic polity possesses to restrain not only the executive from going the authoritarian way, but also the legislature from becoming a handmaid of an arbitrary tyrannical majority.

A myth assiduously propagated these days is that parliamentary imprimatur justifies everything, sanctifies even sin. With the German experience in mind, noted American columnist Walter Lippman had pertinently observed:

> Where the will of a majority of a people is held to be sovereign and supreme, that majority is bound by no laws because it makes the laws, that it is itself the final judge from which there is no appeal of what is right and wrong. This doctrine has led logically and in practice to the totalitarian state—to that modern form of despotism which does not rest upon hereditary titles of military conquest but springs directly from the mass of the people. This is the supreme heresy of our time, it masquerades as democracy.

Hitler had no use for the opposition: nor has Indira Gandhi, who never tires of referring to opposition parties as "a minority seeking to subvert the wishes of the majority". She conveniently forgets that even when her personal popularity was at its peak, as in 1971, her party could secure the support of only a minority of the electorate of 43 per cent (comparisons are odious, but it is interesting to note that Hitler was at the peak of popularity in 1933 and in the elections held that year his Nazi party polled 44 per cent votes).

On the eve of the emergency, however, Indira Gandhi was at the nadir of her popularity graph. A gallup poll published around May had established this very clearly. With her popularity as a leader already at a low ebb the Allahabad verdict of June 12 suddenly stripped her of her legitimacy as a leader and as Prime Minister.

The opposition, on the other hand, successfully closed ranks, and under the inspiring leadership of Jayaprakash Narayan, formed themselves into a solid phalanx of alternative political power. The genesis of the emergency lay in this situation. The so-called conspiracy " to create internal disturbance" was even more phoney than the supposed conspiracy behind the Reichstag fire.

Shortly after the 1933 elections in Germany, Hitler decided so to amend the Constitution as to convert his forty-four per cent power into cent per cent power. He proposed an Enabling Act that would confer on Hitler's Cabinet exclusive legislative powers for four years.

A two thirds majority in Parliament was required to carry out his amendment. The Nazis, together with the Nationalists who were supporting Hitler's Government, had a majority of only 16 in the Reichstag, and this was far short of the two-thirds needed.

So, at the very first meeting of Hitler's Cabinet held on March 15, 1933 the main item of business was how to procure this two thirds majority. A plan was drawn up, and effectively put through. Some opposition parties, like the Catholic Centre, were 'managed', while others like the Social Democrats and the Communists were 'tamed'. Quite a few socialist members and almost all the 91 communists were put behind bars; they called it *Shutzaft*, or 'protective custody'.

The German Parliament met on March 23. Hitler had no difficulties in having it adopt the Enabling Act. The voting was 441 for, 84 against. Hitler proudly observed that it was Parliament, the representative body of the nation, which had by an overwhelming majority reposed such confidence in him. Shirer has commented:

> Thus was parliamentary democracy finally interred in Germany. Except for the arrests of the Communists and some of the Social Democratic Deputies, it was all done quite legally, though accompanied by terror. Parliament had turned over its constitutional authority to Hitler, and thereby committed suicide, though its body lingered in an embalmed state to the very end of the third Reich, serving infrequently as a sounding board for some of Hitler's thunderous pronouncements.

The stratagem resorted to by Indira Gandhi to secure parliamentary approval for the emergency proclamation, and for the series of constitutional amendments designed to place Indira Gandhi above the law provides a remarkable parallel. But there are some notable differences also.

Essentially the strategy was the same: manage some parties; tame the others. However, to force the Reichstag into submission Hitler had to jail only opposition Deputies; he did not have to put any Nazis behind bars.

Here, Indira Gandhi has had to imprison not only a host of opposition MPs but also two senior members of her own party's central executive. One of them, Ram Dhan, had been elected the Secretary of the Congress Parliamentary Party only in May last.

Hitler is not known to have stopped the publication of parliamentary proceedings. Here, however, even the fact of the opposition expressing its strong disapproval of the emergency, by staging a walkout and boycotting the rest of the session, was blacked out.

Incidentally, it is saddening to reflect that the presiding officers of the two Houses should have meekly acquiesced in this shameful, unheard of censorship of parliamentary proceedings. The Indian Parliament had seen a Speaker like Vithalbhai Patel who forced even the British Viceroy to acknowledge that within the precincts of Parliament, only one writ could run—that of the Speaker. It is blasphemy to compare present day presiding officers to Vithalbhai, let alone expect them to act like him.

The day the Reichstag passed the Enabling Act, abdicating its authority in favour of Hitler, Goebbels wrote in his diary: "The German revolution has begun". Shortly after the proclamation of emergency in India, India's Ambassador in Washington told American newsmen that India was passing through "something of a revolution".

After having subverted the Parliament and subordinated the opposition, Hitler's revolution turned its attention towards the Press and the judiciary, two other institutional road-blocks on his path to despotism. Censorship was, of course, peremptorily introduced. Goebbels was appointed Minister of Propaganda. On October 4, 1933 the subservience of the German Press to the wishes of the Government was formalised by enacting the Reich Press Law. Journalism was declared thereunder 'a public vocation'. Section 14 of the law ordered editors, to keep out of the newspapers anything which tends "to weaken the strength of the German Reich, or the Common Will of the people".

If one were to make a compilation of all the speeches made by Indira Gandhi ever since the emergency with regard to the Press, the cardinal sin of the Indian Press, according to her, has been precisely this one over which Hitler had imposed an embargo under the Reich Press Law, namely, publishing material which tended to weaken the strength of the state, or the common will of the people.

Is the will of the people, or the strength of the state, weakened by criticism, or by exposure of its failings, or even condemnation of the follies of its high-ups? A totalitarian's answer to this poser would be an unhesitating "Yes". A democrat's reply would be an emphatic "No".

In the late thirties Winston Churchill carried on a vitriolic campaign in Parliament and outside, against his own party leader Chamberlain and his Munich approach, yet no one suggested that he was "denigrating the institution of Prime Minister".

When British Prime Minister Anthony Eden embarked on his ill-conceived Suez adventure, BBC offered its forum to the leader of the opposition, Hugh Gaitkskell, and allowed him to administer a bitter tongue-lashing to the Tory Government. No one castigated the BBC for being unpatriotic even though the Labour Party's broadside was, without doubt, a serious damper for the Goverment's war effort.

Johnson's Vietnam policies provoked some of the biggest mass rallies America has witnessed in recent years. Youth and Negro organisations carried on a searing and raging campaign, characterised Johnson's policies as stupid and perverse and accused him of sacrificing the flower of America's youth at the altar of a senseless war. But no one accused these organisations of spreading sedition in the armed forces.

More recently, when a powerful campaign mounted by the *Washington Post* and other American newspapers against the Watergate crimes of Richard Nixon snowballed into a national outcry for his impeachment and ultimately led to his ouster from office, no one—Nixon and his cronies excepted, of course— thought that the American Press was doing something unpatriotic.

Looking at all these episodes of modern history in retrospect it would seem that if Winston Churchill, the BBC, the youth and Negro organisations of America and the U.S. Press had not acted as forthrightly, as they did, the democratic conscience of the world certainly would have held them guilty of a grave sin, albeit of omission. Both these countries have emerged stronger as a result of these iconoclastic, anti-governmental activities.

Whether dissent or criticism by the opposition weakens or strengthens society is a moot question. The answer will depend entirely on the values to which one subscribes.

When Brezhnev asked Madhu Limaye an Indian opposition leader who met him at New Delhi, "What is the need of an opposition", the remark was not surprising coming as it did from a communist leader.

But when Indira Gandhi seeks to justify censorship of the Indian Press on the ground that its writings were weakening the nation's morale, democrats the world over feel baffled. Indira Gandhi's complaint that President Ford, the BBC and the Western Press criticise Indira Gandhi for authoritarianism but not Mao, is neither relevant nor fair—at least not while India continues priding herself as a parliamentary democracy.

Shortly after the proclamation of emergency in June, the *National Herald* of New Delhi, which is very close to Indira Gandhi, editorially commended adoption of the African one-party model. Following the bloody coup of Bangladesh of August 15, its enthusiasm for such one partyism seemed to diminish. In an editorial on the same subject on August 25, even while reaffirming its view that a one party set up was desirable, it said that this should not be forced, but should be allowed to emerge 'by natural evolution'—whatever that may mean.

It is difficult to say to what extent the *National Herald* was reflecting the official mind. It may have been a command performance, or merely a trial balloon. Whatever that be, Indira Gandhi is on record saying that she has no intention of changing the democratic multi-party character of the Indian Constitution. In the same breath, however, she has been saying that there is no question of returning to the pre-emergency period of licence and irresponsibility.

This charge of licence and irresponsibility has been levelled against Jayaprakash Narayan and the opposition parties on the one hand, and against the Press on the other.

In the case of J.P. and the opposition parties, Government can possibly dupe, or at least confuse public opinion by maintaining, that it has in its possession evidence to prove that they were conspiring to overthrow the Government by subversive means, but that it would not be in the public interest to reveal the evidence. Hitler had said just that with regard to the Reichstag fire.

But in the case of the Press, such chicanery is not possible. The role and performance of the Press is an open book.

Journalists the world over regarded the Indian Press as extremely sober and restrained. In fact, opinion in the world of journalism has been inclined to regard the Indian Press as too sober, and too responsible bordering on timidity and docility.

It is, therefore, a travesty of truth to say, as some Ministers have been saying these days, that the Indian Press is sensation-mongering. Indira Gandhi too has been totally off the mark when she complained about the Press supporting the opposition and being against the Government.

The fact is that an overwhelming majority of newspapers in the country are dependent for their very existence on Government advertisements. They cannot, therefore, afford to be against the Government even if they want to. The main issue of political debate in the last eighteen months has been the movement led by Jayaprakash Narayan. Most papers have been critical of it even though, barring pro-CPI papers, all of them even pro-Congress dailies, have held him personally in high esteem.

The Press has divided the opposition parties. If they come together, they are a motley crowd. If they stress their respective stances, they are a weak and divided opposition.

One, therefore, wonders which newspapers Indira Gandhi has been talking about when she describes the Indian Press as anti-Government. In one of her speeches she went to the extent of saying that the Press has been so for nine and a half years, that is, ever since she became Prime Minister. Assuming, however, for a moment that this is so, is that a crime? For autocrats it may be so. But no democrat is going to buy this argument of Indira Gandhi's. The Britishers had democracy at home, but in their colonies they practised the worst form of autocracy. But even under the British rule never did the Indian Press suffer such draconian censorship orders as Indira Gandhi's Government has imposed.

When Gandhiji was arrested just before the 1942 satyagraha, Mirabehn (Margaret Slade) is said to have remarked: "At the dead of night, like thieves they came to steal him away".

On the night of June 25-26, 1975 Jayaprakash Narayan, the Mahatma Gandhi of today's India, was whisked away in an identical manner, with one difference.

The British Government never sought to prevent people from knowing that their beloved leader had been arrested nor did they suppress the news of even Bhagat Singh's hanging. Newspapers all over the country flashed the news of Mahatmaji's arrest with eight column banner headlines.

Under Indira Gandhi's rule, from June 26 onwards J.P. and Morarji, Charan Singh and Vajpayee have just ceased to be. They have become 'non-persons'. That J.P. is in jail is today a top state secret and its publication would attract severe penalties. It is only under a Hitler or a Stalin that such stupidity can even be conceived of. In totalitarian countries, the media of mass communication have no role except to be subservient to the aims of authority. All media including the Press are virtually limbs of the state. But the function of the Press in a democracy is entirely different.

I remember a former press secretary of the U.S. President, Bill Moyers, saying once:

> Government and the Press are not allies, they are adversaries. One has the mandate to conduct the affairs of state, the other the privilege to find out all it can about what is going on. It is the nature of democracy to thrive upon this conflict without being consumed by it.

As has been already made out, the Indian Press has never been an adversary of Government, it has been an ally, albeit an unwilling one. Why then has it been so severely punished, it may be asked. The truth is that there is a very solid basis for Indira Gandhi's pique against the Indian Press.

It is a common characteristic of all despots that while they may be willing on occasion to condone criticism of Government, they cannot lightly overlook criticism of their person. The true reason for Indira Gandhi's wrath against the Indian Press is that after the Allahabad verdict, the Press showed a rare unanimity in holding that the verdict warranted her resignation till it was reviewed by a superior Court. Indira Gandhi is unwilling to forgive this.

Censorship has naturally made newspapers dull and drab. They read like official handouts, inane and insipid.

This happened in Nazi Germany also, following the imposition of censorship. At one stage, Goebbels himself told editors not to be too timid, and not to make their papers so monotonous.

A Berlin editor, Welke took Geobbels seriously. In his next issue, he came out with a sarcastic piece chiding the Propaganda Ministry for its red tape, and for the heavy hand with which it held down the Press and so made it dull. Within days of this publication, the journal was suspended, and the editor was carted off to jail.

Something similar has been happening these days in New Delhi.

Encouraged by repeated declarations by the Prime Minister that press censorship had been relaxed, some pressmen, particularly foreign pressmen, have been trying to relay something other than the colourless press notes of the PIB. But this has only landed them in trouble. During the past weeks Reuters and U.P.I., both international news agencies, have had their telephone and teleprinter lines disconnected for alleged violation of censorship rules.

If one single attribute were to be identified as the hallmark of democracy, it is freedom of expression. Madison has very aptly said:

A popular government, without popular information or the means of acquiring it, is but a prologue to a farce or a tragedy, or perhaps both. Knowledge will forever govern ignorance, and a people who mean to be their own governors must arm themselves with the power which knowledge gives.

Shortly after Hitler came to power, the Nazi leader Joachim Ribbentrop (who later became Hitler's External Affairs Minister) spoke of the need for a new legal system.

The old system, Ribbentrop said, needed to be replaced because under this earlier system, "Adolf Hitler, too, like any other common mortal, could be tried under the same paragraph of the penal law".

Addressing a convention of lawyers Dr. Hans Frank, Commissioner of Justice and Reich Law Leader said: "There is in Germany today only one authority and that is the authority of the Fuehrer".

Is there much difference between Ribbentrop's and Dr. Frank's idolatry of Hitler, and Deva Kant Borooah's hallelujah-chanting that "Indira is India and India is Indira"? The outcome in both cases has been similar.

The Constitution and the law were amended to mutilate the concept of the rule of law, and to place the executive head of the country above the law. As part of the same process the judicial review was whittled down.

With regard to the position of judges in Nazi Germany, William Shirer has recorded:

> . . .under the Weimar Constitution, judges were independent, subject only to the law, protected from arbitrary removal, and bound at least in theory by Article 109 to safeguard equality before law. Most of them were sympathetic to National Socialism (Nazism) but they were hardly prepared for the treatment they soon received under its actual rule.

The civil service law, relating to Government employees, empowered the Reich to remove any one "who indicated that he was not prepared at all times for the National Socialist State". This law was already being used to rid Government of Jews. On April 7, 1933, the law was made applicable to judges also.

In 1935, the orders and actions of the Gestapo (Hitler's secret police) were made "not subject to judicial review". The basic Gestapo law promulgated by Government on February 10, 1936, put the secret police organisation above the law. Courts were prohibited by law from interfering with its activities.

Indira Gandhi's attitude towards detenus held under MISA during the emergency has been absolutely identical to this approach.

In 1937 the German Reich framed a new civil service law which provided for the dismissal of officials including judges for political unreliability.

Even a cursory look at the business transacted by the so-called Emergency Session of Parliament held in July and August 1975, would reveal that the primary target of most legislative measures undertaken was the Courts.

The President had already suspended enforcement of Fundamental Rights under Article 14 (Equality before law), Article 21 (Protection of life and personal liberty) and several clauses of Article 22 (Protection against Detention).

As if this was not bad enough, a series of constitutional and statutory amendments were effected. To recapitulate, these were as under:

(a) Courts were barred from pronouncing on the validity of a proclamation of emergency or President's Rule or an ordinance.

(b) The MISA was amended to prevent Courts from giving relief to detenus even by virtue of common law or natural law.

(c) The Election Law was amended to bar Courts from adjudicating with regard to the date of appointment, resignation, dismissal, etc. of a Government employee.

(d) The judgment of the Allahabad High Court was declared null and void by 'Constitutional amendment'.

(e) Courts were stripped of their authority to deal with disputes relating to the election of President, Vice-President, Speaker and Prime Minister.

(f) The Representation of People Act and MISA were included in the Ninth Schedule and thereby made immune to judicial review.

(g) The Maintenance of Internal Security Act was amended so as to provide that those detained during the emergency need not be furnished the grounds of detention. They could be kept indefinitely in prison without having even the ghost of an idea why they had been jailed.

Some High Courts held the view that this bar on disclosure operated only between Government and the detenus. The Courts could not be precluded from examining the grounds and satisfying themselves that the detention was not arbitrary or mala fide. When Government still refused to give them grounds, as they did in editor Nayar's case, the Courts struck down the detention.

Taking umbrage at this interpretation, the Government had issued a fresh ordinance on October 17 amending the detention law for the third time since the emergency. The ordinance provided that the grounds of detention would be regarded as 'confidential' and so would not be available even to Courts for examination.

What do all these laws add up to? Firstly, an unabashed demonstration of the executive's distrust of the judiciary and, secondly, a determined bid on its part to attenuate the scope of judicial review, a concept which the Supreme Court has described as a basic feature of the Constitution.

The emergency proclaimed in June 1975 is thus an Evil Trident with which Indira Gandhi has sought to suppress simultaneously all the three democratic institutions which have been obstructing her assumption of absolute power. The detention of tens of thousands of political activists in action against the opposition, censorship of the Press, arrest of critical editors (like Kuldip Nayar and K.R. Malkani) and expulsion of almost all foreign correspondents (except those from Communist countries) are measures directed against the Press. The Presidential Order under Art. 359 and the string of laws passed recently are essentially anti-judiciary measures.

It might embarrass many Congressmen to know that if Indira Gandhi is proud of her 20-point programme, Hitler was prouder still of his 25-point programme, which he used to call 'unalterable'. It was at first a kind of personal creed; later, it became the Nazi party's official programme.

Under Hitler's regime too, there used to be daily demonstrations of faith in his 25-point programme. The participants were not just common folk but leaders of opinion in various walks of life. At one such demonstration of loyalty held in the autumn of 1933, some 960 professors of the Berlin University, including some renowned scientists and academicians, participated.

Roepke, a senior professor, wrote later, "It was a scene of prostitution that has stained the history of German learning". Another teacher Julius Ebbing, wrote in 1945:

> The German Universities failed. While there was still time to oppose publicly with all their power the destruction of the democratic state. They failed to keep the beacon of freedom, and right, burning during the night of tyranny.

India too is passing through a night of tyranny. This razzle-dazzle talk of discipline cannot deceive anyone.

What we see in the country's climate today is not discipline. It is servile sycophancy and cowardly conformism. Indira Gandhi today commands awe, not respect. It is fear that holds sway, not duty or honesty.

Hitler had created even greater awe, and so was able to secure even stricter compliance with rules. He framed regulations providing that workers absenting themselves from work without satisfactory reasons would be imprisoned.

In Government offices today, under the pervasive umbrella of the emergency, all safeguards against arbitrary action have been suspended. No one is in a position to assess in how many cases the action taken by superior authorities is justified, and in how many cases it is motivated by ulterior or collateral considerations.

Yet, all that this is known to have achieved is to make peons and *babus* scurry to office in time. It was Benito Mussolini, the Italian dictator, who had once boasted that trains had started running on time because of his fascism.

Well, if the cost of punctuality is democracy—and countries like the U.K. and Japan show that it is not—then this country would rather compromise with unpunctuality.

There can be no two opinions that the country needs to build up the virtue of discipline consciously and deliberately. But is it not ironic that an individual whose own spurt to political supremacy owes primarily to an act of gross and indefensible indiscipline, should be waving this rod of discipline at a person like Jayaprakash Narayan, steeped *manasa, vacha, karmana* (in thought, word, and deed) in the highest traditions of Gandhian discipline?

In fact, the indiscipline and irresponsibility that has been evident during the past few years not only in Government offices and industry but in all walks of life can be traced directly to the populist slogan-mongering initiated by Indira Gandhi herself in 1969.

On the institutional plane, if there is one organisation in the country which has made the maximum contribution towards character-building and discipline-building, it is the Rashtriya Swayamsevak Sangh. Literally millions of young men have imbibed their basic grounding in patriotism, integrity and discipline from this body. Yet, the R.S.S. has been outlawed. Why? Presumably because its leader commended J.P.'s leadership and idealism and said that Swayamsevaks were free to participate in the movement.

It ill behoves a Government which seeks thus to suppress the most efficacious non-official mechanism for inculcating discipline to talk about discipline.

Indira Gandhi's attitude to workers, to their right of collective bargaining and to trade unionism also bears a close resemblance to Hitler's.

One can appreciate conscious efforts being made to make trade unions more responsible and production-conscious. But what is being done now under cover of the emergency is virtually to destroy the workers' rights of collective bargaining, and in the name of production to give a free rein to the owners of industry.

Hitler banned strikes. He abolished trade unions. He replaced them by a governmental body, the Labour Front. The chronicler of Nazi Germany, Shirer, has commented:

All the propagandists in the Third Reich, from Hitler on down were accustomed to rant in their public speeches against the bourgeoisie and capitalists and proclaim their solidarity with the workers. But a sober study of the official statistics revealed that the much maligned capitalists, not the workers, benefited most from Nazi policies. . . .

No section has been more thoroughly exposed by the emergency than the C.P.I. They have meekly acquiesced in all the anti-labour misdoings of Government. Their supine surrender to the Establishment has proved, if any proof is necessary, that the C.P.I. has no real concern for the workers.

As long as New Delhi-Moscow relations remain what they are, the C.P.I. has no role in Indian politics except to act as a palanquin bearer of the ruling party.

To revert to the historic parallel which is our main theme here, it would be worthwhile to quote Shirer again on the role of Communists in Nazi Germany:

> The Communists, at the behest of Moscow, were committed to the silly idea of first destroying the Social Democrats, the Socialist trade unions and whatever middle class democratic forces there were on the dubious theory that although this would lead to a Nazi regime, it would be only temporary and would bring inevitably the collapse of capitalism, after which the Communists would take over.

Everyday we read in the papers and hear on the radio that so many officials or employees in the States have been sacked or compulsorily retired because of corruption or inefficiency.

Day in and day out the the radio keeps blaring news about raids on industrialists and businessmen by income-tax officials. An impression is sought to be given that a relentless campaign has been launched by Government to root out corruption in the administration, in industry and in commerce.

In all these four months, have we heard of even one single Minister being sacked or one single Congress M.P. or M.L.A. being proceeded against either on account of corruption, or tax dues, or any other?

This may be surprising, though significant. It is an undisputed fact that the roots of all corruption, administrative, industrial and commercial, lie in political corruption. The Santhanam Committee and the Administrative Reforms Commission have examined the problem in depth and suggested several sound measures to deal with political corruption. The main attack of J.P.'s movement was directed against this evil but Government stubbornly refuses to do anything about it.

Corruption among party colleagues has never bothered Indira Gandhi. Hitler too always showed supreme unconcern in this respect. Shirer has tartly remarked:

> He, who was monumentally intolerant by his very nature was strangely tolerant of one human condition, a man's morals. No other party came near to attracting so many shady characters as the Nazi party. Hitler did not care so long as they were useful to him . . .

The inescapable conclusion which can be drawn from this is that the seemingly strong arm measures adopted with regard to the bureaucracy, industry, business and workers are not honestly meant to clear society of its filth. They are essentially part of a political design to tighten the party stranglehold on the country. It is one more exercise in authoritarianism.

In the first few weeks of the emergency there was a lot of talk about falling prices. After a short while the claims became muted. Lately it is being admitted that prices are once again showing an upward trend.

Statistics and data apart, the man in the street knows that so far as his economic hardship is concerned, the emergency has made not an iota of difference. Most opposition parties hold that the common man's lot cannot be improved except by a radical reorientation of policies to make them conform to a Gandhian framework of decentralised economics. Mere tinkering will not do.

The question raised by the emergency is not what specific economic pattern would suit the country best. That can be left to contending political parties to canvas at the appropriate time.

The question really raised by the present situation and this extends far beyond the frontiers of political competition is: Are we going to permit this nation's constitutional commitment to social, economic and political justice, to liberty of thought and expression and equality of status and opportunity, to be thrown overboard all because a single individual suffers from the hallucination that he or she is indispensable?

The concept of a person's indispensability and democracy go ill together.

For the last two years or so, Jayaprakash Narayan and his associates have been warning the country that Indian democracy is in great peril and that only a proper mobilisation of Lok Shakti can avert this danger.

A constant refrain of their campaign has been that the present regime will go to any lengths if it feels its own position is seriously threatened.

On June 12 last, two momentous events occurred. The Allahabad High Court unseated Indira Gandhi and disqualified her from contesting elections for a period of six years. The same day the people of Gujarat voted the ruling Congress out of power and installed in its place the Janata Front constituted by parties supporting the J.P. movement.

The Court verdict and the electoral verdict added up to a grave threat to Indira Gandhi's position as Prime Minister. It was this political threat and not any threat to state security, which has brought about this emergency.

In his excellent analysis of the Watergate episode, "The fall of Richard Nixon", Theodore H. White has made this perceptive observation:

> The true crime of Richard Nixon was that he broke the faith that binds America together and for this he was driven from power.
> The faith he broke was critical—that somewhere in American life there is at least one man who stands for law. The faith holds that all men are equal before the law and are protected by it; and no matter how the faith may be betrayed elsewhere by the ugly compromises of daily striving, at one particular point, the Presidency, justice is beyond the possibility of a fix.

Indira Gandhi has described the emergency as 'a shock treatment', an objective totally alien to the purpose of emergency conceived by our Constitution makers. But a shock it has no doubt been. It has shocked even sceptics into realising the truth of J.P.'s prognostications. More sadly, however, it has shaken the faith of many in the future of Indian democracy.

Restoration of this faith is the task to which every thinking Indian needs to address himself. How to do this is a matter

which each one of us has to decide for himself. But all of us
can do one thing in common: shed fear and speak the truth as
we   see it. This in   itself will be no mean contribution to the
cause of democracy.

When Disobedience to Law is a Duty

An Open Letter to AICC Delegates at Chandigarh

by

A Detenu

(December, 1975)

It is our first duty to render voluntary obedience to law: but when law fosters untruth, it becomes a duty to disobey it.

MAHATMA GANDHI

I am not of the opinion of those gentlemen who are against disturbing the public repose; I like a clamour wherever there is an abuse. The fire-bell at midnight disturbs your sleep, but it keeps you from being burnt in your bed.

EDMUND BURKE

When in the early hours of August 15, 1975 some soldiers of the Bangladesh Army sneaked into the Dacca residence of President Mujib and massacred him and his family in cold blood, they were avowedly carrying out the orders of their immediate superior, Major Dalim.

The Major's orders were patently illegal. If any soldier had refused to obey them, he would have been performing not only a patriotic duty, but would have been fulfilling a constitutional and legal obligation as well. He may have had to forfeit his life at the Major's hands on that account. He may have been martyred along with Mujib, but no one could have found fault with him for defying his superior officer. Even Indira Gandhi would have lauded his martyrdom.

Yet curiously, the most serious charge which Indira Gandhi's Government has levelled against Jayaprakash Narayan is that he has been continuously counselling armymen and policemen not to obey the illegal orders of their superiors.

It is a preposterous lie to say, or even to suggest, that J.P. had been inciting the army and the police to revolt. The constant refrain of J.P.'s speeches has been that armymen and policemen must hark to the voice of their own conscience and so must not feel obligated to carry out any illegal orders.

The Government of India has published a White Paper under the title "Why Emergency", in which a full chapter has been devoted to this charge. The chapter is misleadingly captioned, "Incitement to Policemen, Armed forces and Government Employees", but the newspaper reports which have been cited, themselves give the lie to the charge.

Some of the news reports quoted in the White Paper read as follows:

"On 1st August, 1975 at Patna:

Denying that he (J.P.) had ever incited policemen to revolt, he stated that he had advised policemen to *disobey wrong orders* of their superiors".

"On 2nd August, 1974 at Muzaffarpur:

He urged the policemen *not to obey illegal orders of their superiors*".

"On 15th December, 1974 at Sitamarhi:

He appealed to policemen including the CRP and BSF *not to go beyond their duties* as they were essentially the servants of the people".

"On 15th February, 1975 at Delhi:

Addressing a meeting of Government employees, he stated that democratic institutions were weakening in the country and asked Government employees to *resist all measures which could* weaken democracy. He advised the Government employees *to remain faithful to the Constitution and not to a particular party or person*".

"On 23rd February, 1975 at Meerut (U.P.):

He urged policemen *not to obey orders which were illegal or against* their conscience".

"On 26th February, 1975 at Karnal (Haryana):

He appealed to the policemen *not to obey illegal orders*".

"On 27th February, 1975 at Gwalior (M.P.):

He called upon the police personnel not to *obey illegal orders* of their superiors but to work according to their conscience".

"On 28th February, 1975 at Agra (U.P.):

He urged policemen *not to obey unlawful orders* of their senior officers and *to remain loyal to the country only*".

"On 2nd April, 1975 at Calcutta:

During these discussions with the Nav Nirman Samiti leaders, when he was asked about his utterances regarding the army and the police to rise in revolt, J.P. explained that *if any illegal or unjust orders were given to the police or the military personnel it would be within their competence to defy them*".

"Replying to a question after addressing a workers' rally in Hyderabad on May 2, 1975 he stated that just as the army was bound to safeguard the security of the country and the honour of the national flag, in the same way it was bound by law to safeguard and defend the Constitution against threats from totalitarian trends. He added that in the face of such threats, the army would be doing its duty if it refused to cooperate with those in authority if they acted in defiance of the Constitution.

He stated that there was nothing illegal or immoral about what he had said and that constitutional experts had advised him that such a call to the armed forces did not amount to treason".

"On 12th May, 1975 at Cochin (Kerala).

He denied that he had given a call to the army and the police to revolt. He had only urged them to protect democratic principles and the Constitution of India as it was their duty, even if they were violated by the Prime Minister. He asserted that the police had been asked *only to disobey immoral or illegal orders*".

"Replying to a question at a press conference in Bangalore on May 18, 1975 he stated that the fundamental duty of the armed forces under the Supreme Commander (President) was to defend democracy irrespective of the party which was in power. He added that the army should rise to the occasion of defending the constitutional rights of the people without being the servants of the ruling party".

These above are excerpts from the Government's White Paper which speak for themselves. There is no need to elaborate the written elucidations J.P. has given earlier of his stand on this point.

In all his exhortations to the army, the police, or the Government employees, J.P.'s unvarying theme has been: Be loyal to the country, preserve and protect the Constitution, but refuse to indulge in any acts against either the country, or the Constitution, even if ordered to do so by the authorities.

Tested by any touchstone whether of patriotism, or of pure constitutional law, J.P.'s utterances are totally unexceptionable. He repeatedly challenged the Government to try him for treason if it thought that his speeches were actionable. The Government, of course, was conscious that J.P.'s observations were legally unassailable. So, even though J.P. had been making these speeches for nearly a year, they kept quiet.

When in June last Government decided to act, even then it dared not indict him for any of these speeches. Instead, it clapped him behind bars under the lawless law that is MISA, kept him incommunicado for months, and in the meanwhile published a spurious chargesheet against him in the shape of this White Paper.

Incidentally, a significant book has appeared during these very months relating to India's struggle for independence from

British rule. It is D.P. Mishra's autobiography titled "Living an Era". In this book Mishra, the erstwhile Chief Minister of Madhya Pradesh, and Indira Gandhi's principal political adviser at the time of the Congress split, has reminisced about the British Government's bid to slander Mahatma Gandhi and has, inadvertently, we must presume, sketched for us a remarkable parallel to recent events.

Mishra has recalled:

Wilful propaganda against one's opponents need not be based on facts and Linlithgow ordered Richard Tottenham to damn Gandhiji and the Congress in the eyes of the world. The command performance was published in the form of a White Paper under the title 'Congress responsibility for the Disturbances'.

Churchill had already declared that "Gandhism and all it stands for will have to be grappled with, and finally crushed". His disciple Linlithgow was anxious to deny Mahatma Gandhi even a glorious death. He had written to Amery that Gandhiji "would fast and try to go out in a cloud of glory". But with a view to prevent Gandhiji dying in a cloud of glory, the Viceroy timed the publication of the Tottenham circular with the fast of the Mahatma, which commenced on February 10, 1943.

But this ignoble and melancholy attempt at dishonouring Mahatma Gandhi met with miserable failure. There was a chorus of condemnation both in India and outside. Even a London paper, the *Nation* disapproved of it in unmistakable terms: "The Government of India has done a questionable thing in publishing a White Paper of 76 pages, which is from first to last a personal indictment of Mr. Gandhi. It is a propaganda document primarily designed, we presume, to damage him in American eyes.... This attack is made on a man who is after all, one of the world's greatest personalities, but who is not in a position to reply or defend himself. Again, if the graver charges are well founded, ought not the Indian Government to have tried Mr. Gandhi before a Court of law, instead of holding him silent and isolated in internment by an administrative act?"

The only difference between what happened in 1942-43 and what has happened in 1975 is that while in Gandhiji's case, the Churchill Government's cussedness evoked "a chorus of condemnation" from the Western and Indian Press alike, in J.P.'s case the Indian Press has been stifled into silence, and totally incapacitated from speaking out against the Indian Government's outrage. Western papers like the *New Statesman* have had to wage a war against New Delhi all on their own.

R everting to the main theme of this (pamphlet), it is today accepted in all democracies that official imprimatur on any order, or even enactment does not necessarily make it the last word.

In the United States Courts have repeatedly held that the American citizen has the right to ignore not merely an executive order if he considers it illegal, but even a law if he thinks it is unconstitutional. Whether the order is in fact illegal, or the statute is actually ultra vires the Constitution would, of course, be a matter for judicial determination. To that extent, he who disregards an order or law runs a risk. But his right to run such a risk is conceded by law.

It may surprise many to know that so far as U.S. servicemen are concerned, this right has been given formal, statutory sanction.

Articles 90 to 92 of the Uniform Code of Military Justice specifically confer on U.S. armymen "the absolute right to disobey any unlawful order of a superior officer".

A t the Nuremberg trials which followed the second world war, many Nazi officers had pleaded that, in respect of the crimes against humanity with which they had been charged, they were only carrying out orders. This plea was not regarded as a valid defence.

The Charter governing the decisions of the Nuremberg Tribunal was later referred to the General Assembly of the United Nations which affirmed the principles recognised by the Charter and asked the International Law Commission to reformulate them.

The Commission did so and codified them in the shape of seven principles, one of which is that a person who commits an act which is a crime under international law cannot be absolved from liability because he was carrying out the orders of his Government or his superiors. These principles now form part of the corpus of international law.

These facts have been referred to stress that whether it be municipal law, or international law, the soldier or policeman's duty is limited to carrying out lawful orders. To try to depict J.P.'s utterances in a manner as if they were speeches of an irresponsible seditionist or anarchist is thus an act of wilful slander, far more reprehensible than that indulged in against Mahatma Gandhi by the Britishers.

This discussion has been confined to J.P.'s remarks with regard to the army and the police and it has been shown how what was said was perfectly lawful. It was J.P.'s legal right to appeal to the army and police as he did. But steeped in the Gandhian tradition, J.P. would never hesitate even to violate a law if he felt that to be his moral duty. Gandhiji described one's voice of conscience as "the highest law". Of course, in such a situation he would readily accept the penalty the law imposed on him for such a violation.

The American statesman Thoreau who had a profound influence on Gandhiji's thinking, refused to pay the town tax because he disapproved the purpose for which the money was to be spent. For this, he had to spend a night in jail. This brief spell of incarceration resulted in Thoreau's famous essay on civil disobedience in which he wrote:

> Under a Government which imprisons anybody unjustly, the true place for a just man is a prison.

Under Gandhiji, Thoreau's idea of civil disobedience flowered into a systematic science of satyagraha. Gandhiji described Daniel and Socrates, Prahlad and Mirabai as ideal satyagrahis. They had refused to subordinate their conscience to the will of the Establishment, and had voluntarily accepted the penalty for such insubordination.

Despite his advocacy of civil disobedience, individual as well as mass, Gandhiji was not an anarchist. He once said that satyagrahis were friends of the state and so philanthropists. He pointedly mentioned that Daniel and Socrates were model citizens, that Prahlad was a model son, and Mirabai a model wife.

The Mahatma wrote in his *Young India*: "I have found that it is our duty to render voluntary obedience to law, but whilst doing that duty, I have also seen that when law fosters untruth, it becomes a duty to disobey it". He added that civil disobedience was the "purest form of constitutional agitation".

The White Paper published by Government has made a lot of hullaballoo over the nation-wide civil disobedience proposal made to the national coordination committee by George Fernandes, the Socialist leader. The committee was still to take a decision in that regard. Thanks to Indira Gandhi and her emergency, the nation-wide satyagraha being thought of then has now become a reality.

At the time of writing this, the satyagraha has entered its second month. More than 35,000 satyagrahis who hold that the emergency proclamation of June 1975 fosters untruth of the most despicable nature and so deem it their duty to defy it, have already courted arrest. Never before, perhaps not even in the days of the British had the number of satyagrahis swelled so rapidly in the very first fortnight.

Viewed against the background that all satyagraha news reports are totally taboo, and that for five months preceding the satyagraha, the voice of dissent has been completely gagged, the number of satyagrahis who have courted arrest provides us with a measure of the strong sentiment the people feel against the emergency. The myth assiduously propagated that the emergency is popular stands exploded.

Towards the end of December 1975, the ruling Congress will be holding its plenary session near Chandigarh. A news report says that the session is going to cost Rs. 50 lakhs. Obviously, the razzle-dazzle of wealth is intended to divert public attention from the ugliness of the sins committed during the past months.

Indeed, the crimes are too heinous for history to forgive. Democracy has been decimated; Parliament has been paralysed; the Press has been pulverised.

Liberalism and liberty, hitherto regarded as the most cherished attributes of our body politic, have become anathema to the Establishment.

When Benito Mussolini took over as the dictator of Italy, one of his first pronouncements was a contemptuous fling at liberty. Men are weary of liberty, they have had a surfeit of it, he declared and added, "At this new dawn of history there are other words which move more deeply; the words are: Order and Discipline".

Eulogies heard these days to the "new dawn of history" ushered in by the emergency are nothing other than echoes of Mussolini's boast. In the name of order and discipline, liberties have been trampled under foot, and autocracy and arbitrariness rule the roost.

Grave damage has been done to democratic institutions and values, to the primacy of Parliament, to the freedom of the Press, to the rule of law, to the independence of the judiciary, and to civil liberties. Sustained efforts will need to be made by the people. The cost in terms of sacrifice and suffering may be considerable, the struggle may be long and protracted. But democracy will ultimately triumph, of this there can be no doubt.

However, in the immediate present, what causes limitless agony to all patriots is the serious and irreparable damage which the powers-that-be have done to the health of Jayaprakash Narayan. Today J.P. is the embodiment of the conscience of democratic India. He is the hope and heartbeat of millions. Five months ago he had entered prison far more healthy and vigorous and active than any person of his age. When he emerged, he was virtually on his death-bed.

Millions in the country are today praying that J.P. be restored to health and be granted many more years to serve and lead the country. If J.P. survives the physical ordeal that he is having to go through, it will be by virtue of his own sheer will power, and the grace of the Almighty. It will certainly be in spite of the Government of India.

Anyone who has had any experience of prison life knows that the harshest punishment that can be inflicted on a prisoner is solitary confinement. When J.P. was arrested on the night of June 25-26, he had requeste dthat his secretary or any other colleague of his be allowed to accompany him. The British Government always used to permit Kasturba, Mahadev Desai and Gandhiji's close associates like Sushila Nayyar to be detained along with him. But J.P.'s request was refused. For all these five months he was kept in a small room in total isolation from the rest of the world.

What was worse was that the country was kept entirely in the dark about his failing health. It is now known that ever since July, there has been a continuing deterioration in his health. Repeated statements were being made at home and abroad that all leaders in detention were in good health and were being well looked after.

As late as on November 6, Home Minister Brahmananda Reddi told the Parliamentary Consultative Committee attached to his Ministry that all detenus were in normal health.

Indeed, the manner of J.P.'s release reflects an attitude not much different from that of Viceroy Linlithgow towards Gandhiji. As indicated by D.P. Mishra's account quoted earlier, Linlithgow's sole concern was that the Mahatma should be prevented from dying "in a cloud of glory". J.P.'s release seems motivated by exactly the same consideration.

Jayaprakashji's brother R. Prasad met J.P. on November 7 and found his condition very disturbing. Without J.P.'s knowledge, Prasad addressed a letter to Indira Gandhi giving her his own impression about J.P.'s health. In his letter dated November 9, Prasad wrote:

> I have very serious apprehensions that if his condition continues like this, he might not survive for more than two months. This is causing us great anguish. l have not discussed my anxiety with J.P. nor mentioned that I would be writing to you, but I must apprise you about his condition so that you can make your own assessment. Apart from the great personal tragedy that his loss would mean to our family, it is for you to decide whether it would be in the best interest of the Government, if J.P. dies in jail.

On November 12, Jayaprakash was released. The nexus between Prasad's letter and J.P.'s release is very clear. J.P. was released not because of any genuine concern for his health. He was released because it would not have been in Government's interest if he had died in jail. Whatever the Government's motivations, J.P.'s release was a wise act. What is sorely distressing about it is the gracelessness and the rather mischievous boorishness of the announcement.

A cryptic P.T.I. message announced that J.P. had been released "on parole". There was not a word about his health, the sly suggestion being that J.P. had secured conditional release for himself. No wonder that J.P. was taken aback when he was told that he was being released on parole. "Who asked for parole?" he asked angrily. Of course, the release order was unconditional. It only said that J.P. would have to surrender himself to the police after 30 days. Later, as J.P.'s condition kept worsening, the detention order was revoked absolutely. The parole news item given to the Press was like adding insult to injury.

It is ironical that Congressmen from all over the country will be assembling this month at Chandigarh itself where J.P. had been incarcerated for five months. No one has any doubt that any overwhelming majority of those who gather at this conclave will dutifully ditto the resolutions drafted for them by the drafting committee. Hallelujahs will be sung to Indira Gandhi, hymns will be recited in praise of the emergency and damnation sought from the gods for the right reactionaries and the left adventurists.

About 40 years ago—in April 1936 to be precise—the Congress held its annual session at Lucknow. That session was presided over by Jawaharlal Nehru. It would not be out of place to remind delegates to this Chandigarh conference what Nehru had said to the Lucknow session. In the course of his presidential address he said:

Comrades, being interested in psychology, I have watched the process of moral and intellectual decay and realised, even more than I did previously, how autocratic power corrupts and degrades and vulgarises.

Of one thing I must say a few words, for to me it is one of the most vital things that I value. That is the deprivation of civil liberties in India.

A Government that has to rely on the Criminal Law Amendment Act and similar laws, that suppresses the Press and literature, that bans hundreds of organisations, that keeps people in prison without trial and that does so many things that are happening in India today, is a Government that has ceased to have even a shadow of justification for its existence.

I can never adjust myself to these conditions; I find them intolerable. And yet I find many of my countrymen complacent about them, some even supporting them, some who have made the practice of sitting on the fence into a fine art, being neutral when such questions are discussed.

Judging the British Government by its onslaught on civil liberties, by its suppression of Press freedom, by its outlawing of organisations, and by its incarceration of people without trial, Nehru declared it to be bereft of even "a shadow of justification for its existence". Nothing that the British Government did in 1936 in the matter of civil liberties can match the crimes committed against democracy by the present regime.

Nehru expressed dismay over the process of intellectual and moral decay and over the debasing influence of autocratic power. He felt pained that while all this was happening, some Indians had made a fine art out of fence-sitting.

One wonders what he would have felt about today's Congressmen most of whom whisper their unhappiness over the present scene in private but who indulge in loudmouthed sycophancy in public.

The excesses of British rule drew forceful protests even from those who differed with the Congress—litterateurs like Tagore renounced their knighthood, leaders like Aney and Mookherji quit the Viceroy's Executive Council. But Congressmen of today are tongue-tied even on an issue like J.P.'s health.

The sins of these last six months are not those of Indira Gandhi alone. In retrospect, it would be deemed a collective guilt of all those Congressmen who supported her policy actively as well as of those who acquiesced in it by remaining silent. Bhishma and Drona were as much responsible for the disrobing of Draupadi as were Duryodhana and Dushasan.

Nehru felt the despotic conditions of 1936 to be intolerable. He said he could not adjust himself to them. But at least he could give expression to this righteous indignation of his. In 1975, even that is not possible. Can any conscientious Congressman reconcile himself to such a situation?

The country today knows at least five brave souls who have refused to do so. They have had to suffer for that. Chandra Shekhar and Ram Dhan have been clapped behind bars; Lakshmikantamma, Krishna Kant and Mohan Dharia have been ostracised from the party. But they have fearlessly held their ground, and are worthy of emulation by their party colleagues.

This is an appeal to the conscience of Congressmen. It is a plea to them to pause and ponder. Let them not think in terms of Government versus the opposition. That is not the issue at hand. The issue is democracy; the issue is civil liberties; the issue is a free Press.

If at Chandigarh even a single voice is raised boldly for these issues, if there is one delegate who speaks up fearlessly against the cruel and callous treatment meted out to J.P., that single voice would be heard loud and clear over and above the din that may be created by stooges and sycophants, by flunkies and flatterers.

Gandhi's favourite song used to be Tagore's *Ekala Chalo:*

> If they heed not your call,
> Walk alone, walk alone.

Not Property, but Democracy is her Bugbear

by

A Detenu

(February, 1976)

We must respect the Judiciary, the Supreme Court and other High Courts in the land. As wise people, their duty is to see that in a moment of excitement, even the representatives of the people do not go wrong. In the detached atmosphere of the Courts, they should see to it that nothing is done that may be against the Constitution . . . it is important that judges should be people of the highest integrity, if necessary people who can stand up against the Executive Government and whoever may come in their way.

JAWAHARLAL NEHRU

At its Chandigarh conference, the ruling Congress has called for a second look at the Constitution.

None of the opposition parties has any quarrel with this proposal. In fact, if one were to go through the election manifestoes of various political parties in the 1971 poll, one would find that it is some of the opposition parties which have committed themselves to constitutional reform, and not the ruling party. The Socialist party, for instance, favoured the convening of a new constituent assembly, while the Jana Sangh advocated setting up a commission on the Constitution.

It is our charge that the ruling Congress has never been earnestly interested in constitutional reform. When its spokesmen speak of constitutional change, they do so for two ulterior purposes—one negative and the other positive.

The negative purpose is to project the Constitution as a scapegoat for the Government's own failure on the economic front. Their positive interest in raising this issue is to create a propaganda smokescreen behind which democracy can be destroyed, and an authoritarian polity set up in its place.

For years, the Supreme Court's judgment in the Golak Nath case was being flaunted as a major road-block on the path of progress. By this judgment the Supreme Court had declared that Parliament had no right to abrogate or abridge any of the fundamental rights.

One of the fundamental rights under our Constitution is the right to property. As the judicial constraint on Parliament's amending power protected the right to property also, the Government went hammer and tongs at the judgment, and maintained that all its progressive schemes had been hamstrung because of this judgment.

Then came the Twenty-fourth Amendment, seeking to undo the Golak Nath judgment. The Amendment conferred on Parliament the right to amend any provision of the Constitution including those which related to fundamental rights.

During the debate on this proposal some opposition members who held that inclusion of the property in the chapter of fundamental rights was in itself an initial error, objected to the sweeping powers sought to be acquired by Parliament by this Amendment. They suggested that while Parliament may be empowered to abrogate or abridge Art. 31 pertaining to property, the other fundamental rights, such as, freedom of expression, freedom of religion, etc. should remain inviolable.

The validity of this Amendment was challenged. The case that ensued, the Keshavananda Bharati case, has now become a landmark in Indian Constitutional History.

The Court, however, did draw up a *Lakshman Rekha*—a thus-far-and-no-further limit. It held that, Parliament was not empowered to abrogate or emasculate any of the essential features of the Constitution.

The Keshavananda Bharati verdict was delivered in April, 1973. If the Government had honestly believed that the right to property was obstructing any of its welfare measures, it could have gone ahead and abrogated it without much ado. The highest judicial tribunal in the country had given it the necessary clearance.

The Government has done nothing of the kind. All that it has done during the three years since, is to unleash a fresh campaign projecting the Keshavananda Bharati judgment as the newest hobgoblin, holding back the economic bounties Indira Gandhi's Government is yearning to shower on the people.

By a clever propaganda alchemy, Government has preserved in the public mind a link between Golak Nath, Keshavananda Bharati and property rights. It has thereby tried to create the illusion that by crusading against the Keshavananda Bharati judgment, it is only continuing its battle against property rights.

The fact, however, is that the issue of property is altogether irrelevant to the new context. According to the Golak Nath judgment, the right to property guaranteed under Art. 31 could not be repealed. It could not even be abridged. But after the Keshavananda decision, it can be scrapped altogether if Parliament so desires.

During the Keshavananda Bharati hearing, Government counsel were put searching questions from the Bench as to what exactly they meant when they claimed an unfettered amending power for Parliament. Government counsel were very frank and forthright in their replies. Summing up these replies, Justices Hegde and Mukherjee recorded in their joint judgment:

According to the Union and the States, that power, inter alia, includes the power to :

(1) destroy the sovereignty of this country and make this country the satellite of any other country;

(2) substitute the democratic form of government by a monarchical or authoritarian form of government;

(3) break up the unity of this country and form various independent States;

(4) destroy the secular character of this country, and substitute the same with a theocratic form of government;

(5) abrogate completely the various rights conferred on the citizens as well as on the minorities;

(6) revoke the mandate given to the state to build a welfare state;

(7) extend the life of the two Houses of Parliament, indefinitely; and

(8) amend the amending power in such a way as to make the Constitution legally, or at any rate practically, unamendable.

The Supreme Court very rightly refused to accept this contention. It felt that this was like empowering Government even to scrap the Constitution, if it could somehow manage the requisite majority in Parliament.

Justices Hegde and Mukherjee noted :

At one stage, counsel for the Union and the States had grudgingly conceded that the power conferred under Art. 368 cannot be used to abrogate the Constitution, but later under pressure of questioning by some of us they changed their position and said that by 'abrogation' they meant repeal of the Constitution as a whole. When they were asked as to what they meant by saying that the power conferred under Art. 368 cannot be used to repeal the Constitution, all they said was that while amending the Constitution, at least one clause in the Constitution must be retained; though every other clause or part of the Constitution including the preamble can be deleted and some other provisions substituted. Their submission, in short, was that so long as the expression Constitution of India is retained, every other Article or part of it can be replaced.

On this aspect of the question, Justice Khanna, whose judgment became the decisive ratio for this case, made this very crisp observation:

> ...nor can Art. 368 (Article relating to the amending procedure) be so construed as to embody the death-wish of the Constitution or provide sanction for what might perhaps be called its lawful *harakiri*.

The Government of India has never been happy with this judgment. But, of late, it seems to have become totally exasperated with it.

Government's annoyance with the verdict was officially proclaimed when in October last, Chief Justice A.N. Ray of the Supreme Court announced that in deference to a request made by the Attorney-General of India, he had decided to constitute a full Bench of the Court to review the Keshavananda Bharati judgment.

The announcement surprised everyone. To members of the Bar it appeared odd, to say the least, that a review Bench was being created only because the Government wanted it.

But if the constitution of the Bench was a surprise, its abrupt winding up just two days after the hearing commenced was an even greater surprise. It was a personal triumph for Nani Palkhiwala who was the main counsel for the petitioners in the Keshavananda Bharati case, and who at this hearing raised a preliminary objection that the review decision was uncalled for. He argued that it was against established precedent. The objection, brilliantly spelt out, hit the bull's eye.

A few days after this, Umashankar Dikshit a senior member of the Union Government (since kicked up to gubernatorial status) declared that if the present limitations on Parliament's power of amendments are not removed, a constituent assembly would have to be convened to frame a new Constitution. It sounded more like a threat than a statement.

Let it be clearly understood that the Government of India is angry with the Keshavananda Bharati decision not because it protects property (which it does not) but because it defends democracy (which it does).

The tirade against the Keshavananda verdict is not aimed at economic iniquities; it is directed against democratic liberties. The present hullabaloo about constitutional change has nothing to do with the interests of the underdog; it betrays a concern for the security of the overlords.

The famous American critic James Russell Lowell has said very aptly about democracy:

Democracy has a habit of making itself generally disagreeable by asking the powers-that-be at the most inconvenient moment whether they are the powers-that-ought-to-be.

For Indira Gandhi, this most inconvenient moment arrived on June 12.

Before this, J.P. and the parties participating in his movement had been expressing the view that Indira Gandhi's Government was fast losing its legitimacy.

On June 12, the judiciary in Allahabad and the ballot box in Gujarat simultaneously posed a very disagreeable question to the P.M. "Indira Gandhi, should you not quit?"

During the fortnight that followed, the same vexatious question reverberated in literally hundreds of editorial columns all over the country. Even papers traditionally pro-Congress, who commented that the Allahabad judgment was harsh, opined that so long as the judgment stands, Indira Gandhi should quit.

Indira Gandhi refused to quit. Instead, on June 25, she launched an operation aimed at making democracy quit.

Hitler had used the emergency provisions in the Weimar Constitution to foist a dictatorship on Germany. Indira Gandhi rode on the same path and adopted identical tactics.

With regard to the emergency provisions, the Weimar and

Indian Constitutions are similar. In the Constituent Assembly, the veteran socialist leader H.V. Kamath, had drawn pointed attention to this disturbing similarity. But one important difference between the two is that while judicial review is an essential feature of the Indian Constitution, in the Weimar Constitution, this feature was altogether absent.

It might be noted here that Huge Preuse, the father of the Weimar Constitution, had strongly pleaded for the inclusion of judicial review in the Constitution. But his view in this regard was not accepted. So, later, by a ruthless exercise of emergency powers, Hitler was able to bend the German judiciary to his will as easily as he could subordinate the German Parliament, the political parties and the Press.

In India, on the other hand, by using its emergency powers Government has succeeded in stultifying Parliament, political parties and the Press; but the fourth institutional check on its authoritarianism namely, judicial review, continues to operate, be it though to a limited extent.

During the emergency, the executive becomes empowered to suspend the enforcement of any of the fundamental rights.

Availing of this power, the President has suspended four provisions; Art. 14 (Right to equality), Art. 19 (the seven-fold Freedoms of expression, assembly, association, trade, movement etc.), Art. 21 (Protection of life and personal liberty) and Art. 22 (Detenu's right to be furnished grounds of detention etc.).

These provisions embody a citizen's democratic liberties Incidentally, it is significant that Art. 31, the provision guaranteeing right to property has not been suspended. And this, despite the fact that the present emergency is sought to be continued o the pretext of carrying out the 20-point economic programme This is glaring proof, if proof be needed, that Government is no a bit worried about property rights.

Ever since the proclamation of emergency in June 1975, th watchword for all has been "Indira is India". All limbs the state have been required to honour this maxim scrupulousl Parliament itself did so when it dutifully passed the 39 Amendment.

The 39th Amendment was an outrageous enactment. I this, Parliament arrogated to itself what was patently a judic function and peremptorily declared the Allahabad High Court verdict on Indira Gandhi's election as null and void.

The validity of this Amendment was tested in the Supreme Court. The A.I.R. and other Government media have trumpeted a lot that the Supreme Court had upheld Indira Gandhi's election. But the really important facet of the Supreme Court's judgment in Indira Gandhi's case was its striking down of the Constitutional amendment validating her election. The election was upheld on the basis of the changes made in electoral law.

The observations made by the Supreme Court about the 39th Amendment add up to a pointed rejection of the "Indira is India" thesis. Justice Chandrachud observed:

I find it contrary to the basic tenets of our Constitution to hold that the amending body is an amalgam of all powers—legislative, executive and judicial.

Whatever pleases the emperor has the force of law is not an article of democratic faith. The basis of our Constitution is a well-planned legal order . . .

Sharply reprimanding Parliament for this encroachment into the judicial domain, Justice Chandrachud wrote:

. . .The function of the Parliament is to make laws, not to decide cases. The British Parliament in its unquestioned supremacy could enact a legislation for the settlement of a dispute, or it could with impunity, legislate for the boiling of the Bishop of Rochester's cook. The Indian Parliament will not direct that an accused in a pending case shall stand acquitted or that a suit shall stand decreed; Princely India, in some parts, often did it. . .

Indira Gandhi must have been rudely shocked by this judgment. If she had the slightest inkling that this Amendment may be struck down, she would never have agreed to it. After all, by simply moving this Amendment, the Law Minister had ripped the mask off Indira Gandhi's pretence that the emergency had nothing to do with the Allahabad judgment.

The Law Minister must have assured Indira Gandhi that the Constitution Amendment was absolutely fool-proof. He may have also pointed out to her that four out of the five judges hearing her appeal—Chief justice Ray, Justice Mathew, Justice

Beg and Justice Chandrachud—were among the dissenting
judges in the Keshavananda Bharati case. Gokhale's calculations went all awry, except in the case of Justice Beg. By striking down a measure directly concerning Indira Gandhi, and in
regard to which she had even risked world opprobrium, the
Supreme Court clearly demonstrated that unlike Parliament, the
judiciary was not prepared to abdicate its responsibility, and to
prostrate itself before the executive.

The same bold awareness of the judiciary's constitutional
obligations has been evident at the High Court level as well.

In all cases arising out of emergency laws, the Government's
stand has been that as fundamental rights have been suspended
by the President under Art. 359, Courts cannot give relief to
citizens, whatever be the nature of injustice which the executive inflicts on them.

The Attorney-General put this point very strikingly in the
Supreme Court when he argued that even if a MISA detenu is
shot dead by an official to settle a personal score, Courts cannot
intervene.

The Bombay High Court took judicial notice of a similar
argument, advanced by Government counsel. In that case some
detenus had challenged their conditions of detention. The
Government counsel had argued that conditions of detention
being merely different facets of personal liberty whose enforcement had been suspended, if the conditions of detention include
a clause that detenus are not allowed to eat food, even such a
clause could not be challenged during the emergency.

Till now, neither the Supreme Court, nor any High Court,
has accepted Government's preposterous contention.

The Allahabad High Court, in a forthright denunciation of
the Government's stand, has said:

> The learned Advocate-General has stated that (because of
> the Presidential orders under Art. 359) the right to personal
> liberty has come under eclipse, and that in the resulting
> darkness the executive has become empowered to take any
> action it pleases.
> This would mean a kind of darkness in which the spectre of
> Hitler would be stalking the land, terrifying people and toy-
> ing with their lives, their liberty and their reputation.

The President could never have imagined that this would be the outcome of his orders under Art. 359 suspending enforcement by Courts of Articles 14, 21 and 22.

Court after Court has thus continued to intervene on behalf of civil liberties, and declared that suspension of fundamental rights enforcement by the President does not mean suspension of the rule of law.

In July, the eminent journalist Kuldip Nayar was detained under MISA. The Government was angry that he had organised a meeting of pressmen to protest against the censorship. More than that, even after the emergency, he had continued to write articles strongly criticising authoritarian trends be it in the context of Pakistan or America or other countries. The hint was too obvious to be missed.

Nayar's wife filed a habeas corpus petition in the Delhi High Court. At the hearing it came out that the official who had signed Nayar's detention order and who was supposed to have personally satisfied himself that his detention was impera-tive for the country's security, was ignorant even of the fact that Kuldip was a journalist. Nayar's detention was declared illegal. The Delhi High Court thus became the first to strike a blow on behalf of citizens' rights. The Government had been able to sense the Court's mood during the hearing itself. So it tried to retrieve its position by releasing Nayar four days before the judgment was due to be delivered and then plead with the Court not to pronounce judgment as the detenu had already been set free. The High Court refused to oblige, and formally quashed the detention order.

In the earlier weeks of the emergency, MISA detenus were allowed to have interviews with family members once a week. Towards the middle of July, under instructions from the Centre all interviews were stopped. Some relatives of the detenus (more notably the daughter-in-law of Morarjibhai Desai) filed writ petitions in Courts arguing that detentions under MISA were preventive in nature and could not be made punitive. This ban on interviews made it punitive. The High Courts admitted the writs and issued notice to Government to explain. The

Government sulkily amended the rules, and permitted interviews to be resumed.

In Bombay, a journalist wrote articles dealing with the law of emergency and censorship. The censors forbade their publication. The journalist went to court against the restriction. The Court held the censors' orders were wrong. It also forbade the censors from blacking out reports of Court hearings about the case.

In Bombay again, lawyers had planned a Civil Liberties Conference in November. The former Chief Justice of the Supreme Court Justice J.C. Shah and former Union Minister M.C. Chagla had agreed to address it. The State Government refused to permit it. They relied on a blanket ban they had imposed in Bombay on gatherings of five persons or more.

The lawyers went to court, and the Court struck down the ban order itself as bad. Earlier, a Kavi Sammelan organised in Bombay on Gandhi Jayanti was also prohibited and could be held only because of Court intervention.

In the Karnataka High Court, writ petitions were filed by four opposition leaders in Parliament, A.B. Vajpayee, Shyam Nandan Mishra, Madhu Dandavate and L.K. Advani alleging that their detention was mala fide. The Government of India sought to have these petitions dismissed "at the threshold". Home Minister Brahmananda Reddi filed an affidavit saying he had personally satisfied himself that their detention was necessary. The Attorney-General and his aides waged a fierce battle spread over weeks somehow to spike these petitions.

The Karnataka High Court overruled the Government's objections, and in their 95-page judgment held that notwithstanding the Presidential orders under Art. 359, the petitions were maintainable. Even while the High Court was considering this matter, the Government of India twice went to the Supreme Court to secure a stay of proceedings. The Supreme Court declined to grant stay.

On the question of maintainability of habeas corpus petitions by MISA detenus, similar judgments have been delivered by the Allahabad High Court (excerpt cited above), the Jabalpur

Bench of the Madhya Pradesh High Court and the Nagpur Bench of the Bombay High Court.

The Nagpur Bench has also held that notwithstanding the ordinance declaring grounds of detentions as confidential, Courts are empowered to call for files relating to detentions under MISA.

Against this background one can well imagine how furious the Government must be feeling about the judiciary these days. Parliament has been tamed, the Press has been muzzled, but the Courts continue to bark—this may well be the mood in the PM's Secretariat.

On November 22, *Mainstream*, a pro-CPI weekly of Delhi carried the text of a paper on changes proposed in the Constitution. The paper was described as having the blessings of senior Congressmen.

The changes envisaged made the President, instead of the Prime Minister, the keystone of the political set-up. However, it was not to be a Presidential system. The Prime Minister was to continue though half the Cabinet was to be from outside Parliament. The worst feature of the plan was the obliteration of an independent judiciary. The apex body for the law Courts would be not the Supreme Court, but a body described as the Superior Council of the judiciary. This was to be headed by the President himself. The writ jurisdiction of the Court was to be abolished. Its present authority to pronounce on the validity of Parliamentary enactments also would go.

Despite all constraints and curbs on criticism, the publication of this draft evoked a sharp reaction in all concerned quarters. A number of leading newspapers in the country wrote editorials disapproving of the scheme.

The Bar Council of India convened an emergency meeting and opposed any drastic changes being made in the Constitution. It pointed out that social justice did not require abridgement of any citizen's rights other than that of property.

The Bar Council specifically attacked the draft paper and said if adopted it would lead to the destruction of democracy, and usher in authoritarianism.

So powerful and spontaneous was the reaction that Government beat a hasty retreat. The Bar Council held a meeting on December 27, 1975. On December 28, Prime Minister

Indira Gandhi declared that changes in the Constitution would be made only after a public debate. On December 29, Law Minister Gokhale disowned any official connection with the draft paper. This disclaimer, it is important to note, came more than a month after the paper's publication.

This paper, I believe, was a trial balloon. Seeing that it failed to take off, Government has decided to abandon it, at least in its present form. But the main considerations which had given birth to this scheme continue to condition their thinking.

During the past few months a series of Government-sponsored lawyers' conferences have been held in various parts of the country. Most of them have been poorly attended despite the high-powered publicity they have received. These conferences have occasioned a lot of woolly-headed and diffuse talk about constitutional changes to make the Constitution "an instrument of social change". But in terms of specifics, the conferences have yielded little other than pinpricks against judges and suggestions to clip the powers of the judiciary.

The Law Minister himself has gone on record saying that Courts have been abusing their power to issue writs. He, perhaps, forgot that less than three years back, in an essay, "The Constitution in operation," he himself had paid rich tributes to Courts for the manner in which they had been exercising their writ jurisdiction. The exercise of this jurisdiction, Gokhale wrote, had "produced socially desirable consequences" and had generated "tremendous public confidence in the Constitution".

The country's super Law Minister, Siddhartha Shankar Ray (it was he who accompanied Indira Gandhi to Rashtrapati Bhawan on June 25 evening to advise the President about the emergency) told a meeting of Congress lawyers in Madras recently that the power of judicial review was "preventing the emergence of a new economic order".

It would be in place here to recall what B.R. Ambedkar, the chief architect of the Indian Constitution, had said about Articles 32 and 226, the provisions comprising writ jurisdiction of Courts.

Speaking in the Constituent Assembly on December 9, 1948, Ambedkar commended Art. 32 (this refers to the Supreme Court, and Art. 26 to the High Courts) in these words:

If I was asked to name any particular article in this Constitution as the most important, an article without which this
Constitution would be a nullity—I would not refer to any
other article except this one. It is the very soul of the Constitution and the very heart of it.

It is this heart and soul of the Indian Constitution which the
Government of India is now itching to destroy, or at least to
cripple.

Taking note of this desire, Justice Krishna Iyer of the
Supreme Court (who, even Gokhale would have to agree, is no
'reactionary' judge) remarked in the course of a recent judgment (December 18, 1975):

Speaking in critical retrospect and portentous prospect the
writ power has, by and large, been the people's sentinel; and
to cut back on or liquidate that power may cast a peril.

Summing up, the Government's intentions, when it speaks of
constitutional change, are as follows:

(a) All official talk about egalitarianism and common man
    interest, and a new economic order is irrelevant to this
    debate about Constitutional amendment; the Right to
    Property can be abolished; all land reform legislation
    becomes protected when included in the Ninth Schedule.
    No wonder, the President has not suspended the Right
    to Property even during the emergency. In fact, the egalita-
    rian argument is only a cover and veneer for ulterior
    ends.
(b) The Right to Property does not irk government but the
    other fundamental rights do. It is these that enshrine
    democratic freedoms. During the emergency, these
    freedoms have been suspended, and political activity and
    press freedom have been curbed. But these curbs (laws
    like the Objectionable Press Matter Act, for instance)
    cannot survive the emergency unless the Constitution is
    amended.
(c) The right of judicial review conferred on Courts by the
    Constitution has become a serious irritant for the
    Government. Their writ jurisdiction has become a

headache. The Government would very much like to see
the Constitution amended so as to repeal it or attenuate it.
(d) Unfortunately for Government, both in respect of democratic rights as well as the right of judicial review, the
Keshavananda Bharati decision solidly bars any curtail-
ment. It is therefore that the Government wants this
decision to go.

At Chandigarh the other day, Indira Gandhi approvingly
quoted Thomas Jefferson's well known dictum about the
desirability of reviewing a country's Constitution every twenty
years or so. She twitted the opposition for opposing constitutional change now though they themselves had been earlier
pressing for it.

It was a pleasant surprise to hear her quote Jefferson. For the
past several months quoting Western liberals seemed to have
become *passe*, if not altogether retrograde and reactionary.
However, now that she has chosen to quote Jefferson at us in
the context of constitutional change, we feel tempted to quote
Jefferson back at her in the matter of many issues relevant to
the present scene.

Jefferson was a dedicated libertarian. A recurring theme in
his writings was that political society can naturally be divided
into two kinds of parties: one which trusts the people and so
would like Government to impose the minimum of curbs on the
people's liberties, and the other which distrusts people and so
holds that unless they are held in leash by a powerful Government, there can be no social progress.

Political India too has become divided today into two camps,
one led by Indira Gandhi and the other by J.P. The first distrusts
the people, and relies on a shackled Press, parties, Parliament
and the judiciary; the second trusts the people, and believes with
Jefferson, that Governments degenerate and that the people themselves are its only safe depositories.

One of Jefferson's major contributions to liberal political
thought was his insistence that every citizen had a right to defy
an unconstitutional statute. He himself regarded the Alien and
Sedition laws (resembling our MISA, DIR) as unconstitutional
when he became President of the U.S. in 1800 and his first
executive act was to release all prisoners arrested under these
laws. He said on the occasion:

I consider this law to be a nullity, as absolute and palpable as if Congress had ordered us to fall down and worship a golden image.

I regard it as much my duty to arrest its execution as it would be to rescue from the fiery furnace those who should be cast into fire for refusing to worship the image.

Jefferson was the author of the American Declaration of Independence proclaimed in 1776. If Jefferson had been living in India in the year of grace 1976, there is little doubt that his fervent writings would have landed him in gaol under MISA. J.P. has never said anything more seditious than what Jefferson once wrote to a friend: "God forbid, we should ever be twenty years without a revolution".

Anatomy of Fascism

by

A Detenu

(April, 1976)

Cure the evils of Democracy by the evils of Fascism? Funny therapeutics. I have heard of their curing syphilis by giving malaria, but I have not heard of their curing malaria by giving the patient syphilis.

SINCLAIR LEWIS

Discipline must come through liberty. We do not consider an individual disciplined only when he has been rendered artificially silent as a mute, and as immovable as a paralytic. He is an individual *annihilated*, not *disciplined*.

MARIA MONTESSORI

Indira Gandhi never tires of branding her opponents as 'fascists.' Apparently she thinks that by sheer repetition, people will come to believe her. But 'fascism' has a precise meaning and connotation. Besides, there is historical experience of how 'fascists' behave and what the purpose of 'fascism' is. This should serve to show who are 'fascists', Indira Gandhi or her opponents.

President Franklin D. Roosevelt of the U.S.A. once identified "the essence of fascism" as "ownership of Government by an individual". The liberty of a democracy, he clarified, is not safe if people tolerate the growth of personal power to a point where it becomes stronger than their democratic state itself.

Roosevelt, of course, was a sworn enemy of fascism. But even the protagonists of fascism never denied the basically anti-democratic character of their creed.

Hitler himself used to denounce democracy as being "the nourishing soil for the plague that is Marxism". In the future Nazi State, he wrote that there would be no 'democratic non-sense', and that the Third Reich would be ruled by the leadership principle.

Mussolini similarly, boasted that under fascism the "noxious theories of liberalism would be thrown upon the rubbish-heap." He scoffed at the talk of civil liberties and held that it was for the state to decide what measure of freedom an individual citizen should be allowed to enjoy. The fascist state, he declared, organises the nation, leaves to the individual "as much liberty as is essential", but deprives him of "all useless and possibly harmful freedom". Mussolini added:

When (under fascism) a group or a party is in power, it is its duty to fortify and defend itself against all.

This sawdust Caesar declaimed that men were now weary of Liberty; the words that move them more deeply are Order and Discipline.

The attitude of fascism to the question of trade union rights, workers' rights of collective bargaining, and to strikes, was the logical outcome of this contempt for individual liberty, and an obsession with collective order.

Harwood Brown, the American essayist who made an in-depth study of fascism and fascist techniques, has noted:

> One of the first steps which fascism must take in any land to capture and keep power is to disrupt and destroy the labour movement. It must rob trade unions of their power to use strike as a weapon.

Spain's dictator Francisco Franco called strikes 'a crime' and the right to strike as indicative of "the law of jungle and primitive societies". On the other hand, Samuel Gompers, a prominent leader of the trade union movement in the West, remarked sharply:

> Show me the country where there are no strikes, and I will show you that country in which there is no liberty.

Unlimited state power, concentrated in the hands of an individual or group, and suppression of civil liberties and trade union rights, constitute the pith and substance of fascism. It has no other meaning.

Outside the arena of state power, fascism has no meaning. It is absurd to hurl the epithet at the RSS, which, despite its immense organisational weight, has scrupulously kept away from politics for all these years. It is meaningless also to fling the word at the opposition parties in the J.P. movement, who have been, generally speaking, far removed from the acquisition of power let alone wielding it to suppress civil liberties.

Indeed, it is significant that Tamil Nadu and Gujarat, the two States where till recently non-Congress parties were in office, were the only two islands where, despite the emergency, citizens' rights remained inviolate and where opposition parties feel free to attack and arraign the Government—a freedom that is anathema to a fascist.

In Nazi Germany, fascism in action developed two other distinctive characteristics : firstly, adoption of propaganda as a key instrument of state policy; and secondly, the systematic development of a demonology to keep the masses in a mood of perpetual tension and hysteria.

Mathews and Shellcross, two specialists in the field of advertisement, have observed in their book, "Partners in Plunder":

> Advertising, in its spirit and purpose, is germinal fascism. Hitler was the first European politician who saw the significance of the techniques of commercial advertising for politics. In MEIN KAMPF he used the distinctly, commercial word *reklame* (advertising) to describe his political method.

The Information & Broadcasting Ministry (designated, under the Nazis, as the Ministry of Popular Enlightenment and Propaganda) was, for Hitler a pivotal branch of the Government. Hitler entrusted the portfolio to one of his closest confidants, Paul Joseph Goebbels, whose name has now become synonymous with high-voltage, mendacious propaganda.

Hitler frankly spelt out his own concept of the use to which propaganda would be put. Through clever and constant application of propaganda, he wrote, people could be made to see paradise as hell, and hell as paradise.

The second thrust of Hitler's regime was creation of a demonology to whip up mass passions to justify its own perpetuation. Thus, for the German masses, the Jewish community was painted as a diabolical ogre responsible for all their sufferings and misery. Legal suppression of this community, and later, even its extermination, was projected as not only legitimate but even imperative in the national interest.

This, then, is the anatomy of the fascist creed. Its main ingredients are:

(a) Concentration of state power in the hands of one individual or a group.
(b) Suppression of civil liberties.
(c) Extinction of trade union rights.
(d) Use of propaganda as a key instrument of state policy.
(e) Reliance on demonology.

Let anyone apply these objective criteria to the Indian scene, and the answer to the question, who a fascist is, would become obvious. The so-called anti-fascist *tamashas* being organised lately with the help of governmental money and CPI hirelings cannot deceive anyone.

Since June 26, 1975, when Indian democracy was shoved into cold storage, all the essential features of the fascist state are being absorbed into the Indian body-politic piece by piece. Its democratic superstructure alone is sought to be retained; its content has become fascist. After all, let us remember that Hitler did not alter the democratic complexion of the Weimar Constitution.

The Government of India has recently published a pamphlet describing the RSS as the Indian version of fascism. The pamphlet is a string of lies and half-truths crudely put together by a person who suffers from some kind of pathological hatred for the RSS.

One of the grounds mentioned in this pamplet to sustain its slander against the RSS is the fact that this organisation is pyramidical in structure, with the Sar Sangh Chalak (RSS President) at the apex. The non-elective nature of this office is also cited to dub the organisation as fascist.

Several social, cultural and religious organisations in the country are pyramidical in structure and have non-elective heads. The Sarva Seva Sangh and the Ramakrishna Mission may be mentioned as two prominent illustrations. In these cases, the heads generally represent not just the majority, but what Acharya Vinoba has commended—a unanimity of opinion in these bodies.

A democrat can have no objection to a pyramid, as such. All presidential systems are pyramidical. What is unacceptable to a democrat, and what a fascist set-up truly resembles, is an inverted pyramid, standing on its apex. The Indian state, today, is just that.

No one can seriously dispute the fact that in the Government today, nobody matters, except Indira Gandhi. Some say that her son Sanjay Gandhi also matters. Perhaps that is so; but that does not alter the basic proposition that we have put forward.

So, if you can mentally equate India with the Government of India, you will have to concede that Congress President Devakant Borooah is not wrong when he says that "India is Indira, and Indira is India".

Political idolatry of this kind, vulgar and uncouth, is the first and foremost trait of the fascist state—Winston Churchill characterised it as the "fetish worship of an individual".

There is, of course, nothing very original about Borooah's chant. It is only an echo of what has been heard over and over again under dictatorships, sometimes from the dictator himelf, sometimes from his cronies. *L'etat c'est moi* (I am the State), so said Louis XIV. The law, the will of the Fuehrer, are one, proclaimed Goering. Hitler himself told a Nazi Congress in 1935: "The Fuehrer is the Party; and the Party is the Fuehrer".

From a premise of this kind, suppression of the opposition, of dissent, and so of civil liberties, is just one jump ahead.

In a democracy, the function of the opposition is to expose the Government's failings ruthlessly. It is not merely a right, nay it is the duty of the opposition to be vigorous enough to make those in office feel politically insecure unless they acquit themselves ably.

A democrat welcomes trenchant criticism as essential for a healthy democracy. A fascist, on the other hand, regards a threat to his own security, or that of his party, as a threat to national security. He looks upon political opponents as enemies of the country, and, so, underserving of any political freedom. For him a 'responsible' opposition means opposition comprised of yes-men.

The trauma, inflicted on the country in June 1975, is the direct manifestation of such authoritarian thinking. The agitation or satyagraha threat by opposition parties had nothing to do with it.

The Gujarat agitation ended in February, 1974. The Bihar agitation passed its peak in November 1974. Gradually, the political parties in the J.P. movement had started shifting attention to preparations for the electoral battle ahead. Joint participation in the movement, however, had brought about a rare cohesion among them which unnerved the ruling party. J.P.'s movement against corruption and for a saner polity had created an enormous fund of public goodwill for all those involved in the movement.

The Gujarat poll offered them an opportunity to test how enduring this unity would be, and whether despite the ruling party's advantage of governmental and financial resources, popular support to the J.P. movement could be converted into electoral gains. The smooth formation of the Janata Front and its subsequent victory showed that the opposition had passed the test on both counts. And when simultaneously with the announcement of the Gujarat results came the Allahabad verdict, the Government in New Delhi began to be jittery for once.

In some of her speeches and interviews during recent months, Indira Gandhi has clearly revealed that it was the threat to her own position and to that of her party which worried her, and which made her take the subsequent steps.

On March 12, 1976, the Prime Minister gave an interview to Swedish TV, excerpts from which were reproduced in the Indian Press. In this interview she said categorically (for the first time, perhaps) that the opposition parties were not opposed to her as a person. Earlier, she had been saying that opposition parties have been opposed to her, to her family, to her friends and supporters.

"They opposed me", she said in this interview, "because I became the symbol of certain things, of certain programmes. Along with the programmes, I was also somebody who was holding the country together. My party is the only all-India party, and *it is the only party that can keep the unity* and stability of the country. Now, when you threaten that party and you have nothing to put in its place, then you are threatening the unity and perhaps the very survival of India as it is".

What conceit! What megalomania! In the fifties and the sixties, a pet theory with Western analysts of Indian affairs used to be that after Nehru, India would go to pieces. But Nehru himself never claimed that after him, there would be the deluge! Indira Gandhi has evidently no need for such modesty.

Had it been a question only of immodesty of expression, it may not have mattered much. But when paranoia of this kind in the leader is combined with acquiescence by his party and by Parliament, in the suppression of liberties, the upshot is a fascist state.

Never before in living memory has there been in India as thorough a clamp-down on citizen's freedoms as has been imposed in this recent emergency. All the fundamental freedoms have been suspended, something that was never found necessary in any of the earlier emergencies.

With shamelessness, which would outrage even the Nazis, the Government of India has told the Supreme Court that according to their understanding of the law as they have amended it, even if a detenu is shot dead by a Government official simply to settle a personal score, the Courts cannot intervene.

Indira Gandhi is never tired of repeating that no political party has been banned. Technically, she is not lying. But she knows better than anyone else that in effect, India has already become a one-party state. No opposition activity can be reported by the Press. Even speeches by opposition members in Parliament cannot be covered unless the censor clears them. And the censor clears, if at all, only such excerpts that are anaemic and colourless, or which convey an impression quite contrary to that intended by the speaker.

In recent months, the censored Indian Press has been treating us to occasional statements by foreign visitors praising the emergency. So far as visitors from communist countries are concerned, their comments do not surprise anyone. Nor indeed the remarks by leaders of some Afro-Asian countries where democratic liberties are considered a nuisance. But complimentary comments, few though these may be, made by observers from Canada, UK and such countries which have a long history of democratic traditions may appear baffling to some.

It would not be out of place to recall that before the Second World War, Hitler's fascism too had its quota of admirers in the democratic world. And this happened even though Hitler's Germany, till before the War, was far more open to the probing gaze of the foreign Press, and of foreign visitors, than Indira Gandhi's India today.

In his famous work "The Rise and Fall of the Third Reich", William Shirer has noted:

Apparently, the Nazi leaders had nothing to hide. A

foreigner, no matter how anti-Nazi, could come to Germany and see and study what he liked—with the exception of the concentration camps and, as in all countries, the military installations. And many returned, who, if they were not converted, were at least rendered tolerant of the 'New Germany' and believed that they had seen, as they said, 'positive achievements'.

Even a man as perspicacious as Lloyd George, who had led England to victory over Germany in 1918, and who, in that year, had campaigned with an election slogan of 'Hang the Kaiser' could visit Hitler at Obersrlzberg in 1936, and go away enchanted with the Fuerhrer and praise him publicly as 'a great man' who had the vision and the will to solve a modern nation's social problems. . .

Off and on, particularly in her interviews with Western correspondents critical of the curbs on civil liberties and the large-scale detentions, Indira Gandhi has been suggesting that the present restraints on individual and Press freedom are temporary. But on many occasions, she has also stressed that Indian politics will never be allowed to return to the pre-June 1975 position.

These two stances can be reconciled only in one way. The emergency, as such, would be temporary. But the attributes of the emergency will be made permanent. The present stringent restrictions on Press freedom and civil liberties will be made part of the normal law of the land: passing of the Objectionable Press Matter Act is a clear indication of this. Plans are in the offing to curtail drastically the power of the Courts. Thus, the three main democratic checks on the arbitrariness of the executive— political parties, the Press and the judiciary—are thus proposed to be crippled altogether.

In many of the statements made by Indira Gandhi and other official spokesmen about the gains of the emergency, one would find invariable reference to the fact that there has been no strike during this period. How is this an achievement? No totalitarian country permits strikes!

If the Government were to give us statistics to show how the living conditions of the working class have improved during this period, that would have been something. But the *de facto* extinction of the workers' right to strike for their just demands is a thoroughly retrograde development from the point of view not only of the workers, but also of industrial growth. It took decades for trade unionists to establish that bonus in a country like ours should be deemed a deferred wage. In a trice, the emergency wiped out this achievement.

Industrialists, understandably, have generally backed fascists and dictators everywhere. Harold Laski has taken note of this fact in his "Introduction to Politics":

> The history of the establishment of the fascist regime in Italy, the Nazi tyranny in Germany and the Franco dictatorship in Spain is the record of a deliberate alteration of the whole constitutional arrangements of the state, encouraged and supported by the employer's class because it would involve, among much else, the destruction of trade-union organisations.

In India too you find the same phenomenon being repeated. Indira Gandhi rose to the pinnacle of power in 1971 mainly with the support of the working class and the trade unions. Her main backers, today, however, are industrialists and big businessmen. Having first ensured that trade unions have been rendered powerless Government has had not the slightest qualms in jettisoning worker interests.

At a seminar held recently in Bombay on the subject "Disciplined Democracy", Indira Gandhi is reported to have restructured the title of the seminar as "Discipline is Democracy"!

One may have no quarrel with the new slogan if discipline is Vinobaji's *'Atmanushasan'*. But when Indira Gandhi talks of discipline, she merely means the absence of strikes, of agitations, of opposition to Goverment policies and so on, achieved by state coercion. And if discipline means no strikes, no political resistance to governmental wrong-doings, no political opposition and dissent, Hitler's Germany, Mussolini's Italy and Franco's Spain would have to be regarded as more democratic than U.K., Japan, U.S.A. and many other countries.

As mentioned earlier, fascism lay immense store by propaganda. Hitler has given us a very candid record of his
views on the subject. Some 'rules of the game' he has put down
are as follows:

> All propaganda must be on such an intellectual level that
> even the most stupid of those towards whom it is directed
> will understand it. Therefore, the intellectual level of the
> propaganda must be influenced by it.

If you tune in any day to some of the political broadcasts by
AIR against J.P. and the opposition parties, you would easily
realise that this dictum of Hitler's is being followed by V.C.
Shukla very religiously. It sometimes does appear, however,
that these propaganda pieces are meant, not "even for the
stupid", but "only for the stupid".

> Propaganda has to confine itself to little and to repeat
> that eternally.

Government propagandists use the phrase, 'Twenty-point
Programme' as a kind of *mantram* to be chanted over and over
again. No one cares to spell out what those twenty points are.
Indira Gandhi, of course, mentioned these 20 points in her
July 1, 1976 broadcast. However, even Ministers have per-
haps forgotten it since.

> Propaganda must not serve the truth, especially not insofar
> as it might bring out something favourable to the opponent.

So Government spokesmen scrupulously refrain from giving
out the names and figures of those arrested. Even mentioning
names would create sympathy for those opponents. So, following
Hitler's advice, the Government under the circumstances, has
behaved in a manner in which even the Britishers did not, or
rather, would not.

Hitler then goes on to propound his theory of the big lie:

> The size of the lie is a definite factor in causing it to be
> believed. . . The primitive simplicity of the people's minds
> renders them a more easy prey to a big lie than the small

one for they themselves often tell little lies but would be ashamed to tell big ones.

Let us examine at some length how this big lie theory is being followed in India today.

Speaking in the Lok Sabha on July 22, 1975, Indira Gandhi said:

> Yesterday, another member of the opposition wanted to know what fascism was. Fascism does not mean merely repression. Over and above everything, it is the propagation of the big lie. It is the use of whispering campaigns, the search for scapegoats.

This definition of fascism given by the Prime Minister meant two things. Firstly, she tried to play down the coercive content of fascism by saying that it does not rely "merely" on excessive force, not merely detentions. Not "merely", no doubt, but surely, State coercion is an inseparable feature of fascism. She underplayed it because this charge can be levelled only against Government and by no stretch of imagination, against a voluntary body like the RSS.

Even so, the second part of Indira Gandhi's statement showed awareness of the fact that the cornerstone of fascist propaganda is the big lie. One wishes that, having made this charge against the RSS, she had also substantiated it.

Neither the PM, nor anyone else in the Government, has ever cared to produce even a shred of evidence. They just keep repeating bald and bland accusations of this kind, smug and secure in the knowledge that tens of thousands of RSS men are now in jail and in no position to answer back. Moreover, even if anyone did reply to the charge, it would not be published.

Indeed, in season and out, the RSS has been sought to be depicted as a secret, sinister organisation which believes in violence and which trains its members in the use of lethal weapons.

As proof of this charge, dozens of TV films and documentaries have been produced, and photographs published on front pages of dailies purporting to show "huge caches of unlicensed arms and ammunition recovered from RSS offices". These films and pictures show some petty police officer proudly posing in front of the RSS office, an assorted pile of not-clearly-identifiable articles lying beside him. The only objects distinguishable in this heap would be some dummy swords.

In the Lok Sabha debate, Jana Sangh Leader Jagannath Rao Joshi, neatly punctured this propaganda bubble by challenging the Government to deny that all those recovered were dummy swords. The P.M.'s reaction to this was amazing. She could not refute Joshi's assertion but instead of admitting the unfairness of the libel, she glibly remarked: "The next speaker (Joshi) said that the sword of the RSS was a wooden sword. What is the point in having a toy sword? What games are they going to play with it?"

What is all this, if not the technique of the big lie? One could reel out a long chain of the fibs which the Government has been circulating during this past year, some of those over and over again. Here are some of the more glaring examples of the official canards, particulary those that can be documented.

To begin with, the proclamation of emergency itself is rooted in an egregious lie.

The emergency is supposed to have been Government's response to the decision of the opposition to launch a movement from June 29, 1975, demanding Indira Gandhi's resignation on grounds of 'political propriety'. The Joint Resolution adopted by the executives of five parties in the presence of eminent leaders like J.P. and Morarji Desai stressed that the movement would be in the nature of a 'peaceful satyagraha'.

But according to Indira Gandhi (and she has nothing to offer in support of this lie save her own word) the emergency was proclaimed because from June 29,

> opposition parties had chalked out a programme of country-wide bandhs, gheraos, agitations, disruption and incitement to industrial workers, police and defence forces, in an attempt wholly to paralyse the Central Government. (AIR broadcast on June 27, 1975, quoted from Democracy and Discipline, Speeches of Indira Gandhi published by I & B Ministry, GOI.).

It should be noted that the charge is not about the satyagraha possibly deteriorating into violence. The charge is straight, of planning disruption. If you are to tell a lie, why not a big lie— that is the simple logic.

Not satisfied with the size of this initial lie, the PM has subsequently been indulging in even bigger fantasies to justify her crimes against democracy.

On September 19, 1975, Indira Gandhi addressed a conference of so-called Educators for Secularism, Socialism and Democracy at Delhi. Here once again she referred to opposition plans for June 29 and made this preposterous statement:

> I do not want to comment on what system or what persons other countries have within their borders. We have always been scrupulously correct in this matter. But I would like to pose a question! *Would this country be considered more democratic had large numbers of people been killed after the 29th of June? Myself, my family and all those Chief Ministers and others who support me, had they been annihilated, would this country be considered more democratic?* (P.111 "Democracy and Discipline: Speeches of Indira Gandhi" GOI publication. Italics added).

So the charge against the opposition becomes a plot to assassinate the PM, her family and her supporting Chief Ministers! In no other country in the world would a person occupying such a responsible position have made so grave a charge with such irresponsibility.

On one occasion while referring to the Western Press, Indira Gandhi has used the phrase "big lie". Interviewed on September 29, 1975, by Dr. Kronzucker and Dr. Scharlav of the North German TV, Indira Gandhi spoke bitterly about writings in the German, British and American Press, and said: "What they write is absolutely a figment of somebody's imagination. One cannot even say that things are exaggerated, many of them have no foundation whatsoever".

Pressed by the interviewers to give some concrete instance of such baseless reporting, this is what the PM replied:

For instance, one very big lie that is propagated is that the whole emergency and so on is run by a some small group including my son, which is absolutely false.

The decision was taken by the Chief Ministers of this country and they were the ones who have to manage the states.

You see this is more like a federal set-up... So the decision was taken by the Chief Ministers, with our senior colleagues, and so on.

(P. 166, "Democracy and Discipline, Speeches of Indira Gandhi", GOI Publication)

So, as illustration of the kind of "big lies" the Western Press has been indulging in, the worst that Indira Gandhi was able to think of was their report that the emergency was decided upon by a small group, and that Sanjay Gandhi was one of them. And, this was the "big lie" that Indira Gandhi peddled.

With sources of information in India as clogged as they are, it is simply not possible even for those in India to say with certainty what Sanjay Gandhi's role has been in the imposition of the emergency, and then, in its working. For the foreign Press, with its own correspondents mostly expelled, it is even more difficult. Even so, any perspicacious journalist abroad who has been merely following reports in the Indian Press, and who has not omitted to read the numerous speeches, statements, and interviews, of Sanjay Gandhi, can very reasonably infer that Sanjay had quite a lot to do with both the declaration of emergency, as well as its subsequent direction.

If the Western Press is wrong in drawing such a conclusion, the blame lies not on them, but on Sanjay's own loud-mouthed, flamboyant replies at scores of meetings he has been addressing. At these meetings the PM's son himself has been putting on airs as though he was the originator of the emergency idea. Neither the foreign journalists, nor anyone else, has any solid ground for disbelieving the claim.

At worst, the Western Press can be dubbed guilty of drawing wrong inferences. It is unfair to accuse them of lying.

But can the same be said about what Indira Gandhi has stated in the second half of her above reply? The emergency decision may, or may not, have been Sanjay Gandhi's. Nevertheless it is a patent lie to say, as she has done, that the emergency decision was taken by the Chief Ministers.

The Chief Ministers had nothing to do with it. They did not even know about it. In fact, even the Union Cabinet was not consulted when Indira Gandhi took the decision to declare the emergency.

On the evening of June 25, Indira Gandhi went to Rashtra-pathi Bhawan and asked President Fakhruddin Ali Ahmed to declare an emergency. The few who possibly were aware of this development were Law Minister Gokhale, West Bengal Chief Minister Siddhartha Shankar Ray, and perhaps Sanjay Gandhi. The Union Cabinet was blissfully ignorant about this.

The President dutifully signed the proclamation papers, affixed the date also as "June 25, 1975", and thus set in motion the constitutional distortions that followed.

Members of the Central Cabinet came to know about this only on the morning of June 26. They were woken up in the early hours, hustled to the PM's residence for a Cabinet meeting fixed for 6.00 A.M. According to a Press Trust of India release, duly approved by the censors and carried by the Press, at this hurriedly convened meeting, the Union Cabinet "considered the situation, and approved the recommendation to the President for the declaration of emergency".

The Press report makes it clear that the Cabinet did not recommend proclamation of emergency, it merely approved a a recommendation which had already been made by the PM.

In the Lok Sabha debate on July 22, 1975, Mohan Dharia, a former member in Indira Gandhi's Government strongly condemned what he called "this monstrous operation" of emergency and added :

I am not charging the whole Cabinet because I know that even the Cabinet was told about it after the operation was already initiated.

Neither the Prime Minister, who intervened in this debate, nor Food Minister Jagjivan Ram who had moved the motion of approval of the emergency proclamation, denied this charge made so categorically.

Here is one more example from Indira Gandhi's own utterances. Immediately after the Allahabad verdict against her, a series of Government-sponsored demonstrations were

organised in New Delhi in front of her residence. At these
rallies, apart from hymns sung to her, angry speeches used to
be made against Justice J.M.L. Sinha who gave the adverse
verdict. It was once reported that the judge's effigy was burnt.
It is not known if the report was true. No one from the
opposition spoke about it.

The compilation of Indira Gandhi's speeches and interviews
put out by the Ministry of Information and Broadcasting,
reproduced an interview of hers. The *Times of India* report on
July 3, 1975 reads:

> A campaign of hate and calumny was unleashed against
> me in 1969. But most of our Press did not protest at all.
> There was no comment when effigies of the Chief Justice
> were burnt by opposition parties some time ago . . .

True, there was no comment, the simple reason for this was
that there was no such burning.

A nother important matter is the question of political detentions.

Generally speaking official spokesmen refuse to give figures
either of arrests or of releases. Since September 1975 they have
started talking about percentage of releases. If we recall
aright it was Home Minister Brahmananda Reddi who started
this release canard. He started with 25 per cent; within a fortnight or so he improved the percentage to 35!

On October 24, Indian newspapers published Indira Gandhi's
interview with the Communist Central News Information in
which she said that only top leaders actually engaged in plans
to paralyse Government had been detained. The rest were all
free !

The same day the *Hindu* of Madras carried a Government
inspired news-story saying that 40 to 50 per cent political detenus
have already been released, and that State Governments have
been directed to continue review of detention cases.

If one were to judge the pace of releases from these ministerial statements, one would be inclined to think that by now
more persons have been released than were actually detained.
The fact, however, is that out of the about twentyfive thousand
held under MISA (the number of those arrested under DIR

may exceed one lakh) barely a hundred or so have been released.

Occasionally, official spokesmen have given out figures of arrest. And when they have done so, they have taken to the big lie technique with a brazen face that would make even the Nazis blush.

On November 1, 1975, T.N. Kaul, India's Ambassador in the U.S. addressed a ladies' club meeting in Washington. That evening the Voice of America carried a longish report on the event. The Ambassador, VOA reported, was asked repeatedly about the number of political arrests made in India. He first evaded giving numbers. But when pressed, he cheekily replied: "Fifteen leaders and about one thousand followers".

To impress his audience, Kaul added that the fifteen leaders arrested were those who had participated in the June 25 meeting where the anti-government conspiracy was hatched. Of these fifteen, three had been released. Of the one thousand followers arrested, some 300 has been let off. So, according to Kaul, as on November 1, the total number of political prisoners in the country were 712!

This same Kaul, shortly after the proclamation of emergency, made a statement that "political leaders have been kept under house-arrest, and only the 'bad characters' have been jailed"!

When the emergency was first proclaimed, all that Indira Gandhi had in mind was the political threat that had emerged to her position. As explained earlier, the government was not worried about agitations. What disturbed it was the threat of electoral ouster in Gujarat and the growing momentum of the J.P. movement after Allahabad. For the first time after Independence, the possibility of the incumbent Government in New Delhi being dislodged had become real.

In this electoral calculus weighing on Indira Gandhi's mind on the eve of the emergency, the RSS naturally did not figure. Incidentally, this is indirect recognition by officials of its non-political and non-electoral character. The initial crack-down on June 25 touched only J.P. and the constituents of the Janata Front. The ban on the RSS came a few days later, partly, it seems, as part of a demonology-tactic, but also because the Government knew that this youth-based, idealistically-oriented body could provide the sinews to any national resistance movement that may be organised against its authoritarianism.

The Jamaat-e-Islami has had to suffer perhaps only to maintain a communal balance. On the other hand, the Naxalites may have been dragged in to keep a left-right symmetry.

So far as the Anand Marg is concerned, J.P. and all others in the movement have always felt intrigued by official references to the Marg. The Anand Marg has never had anything to do with the J.P. movement, but was a very convenient scapegoat and whipping boy.

In the context of the J.P. movement, therefore, bracketing of the Anand Marg's name with the others has always been a case of deliberate misjoinder.

It may be interesting to note that need for demonology of sorts is felt by all politicians with an authoritarian streak—even by those functioning in a democracy. The commitment of such politicians to democratic values being fragile, they have no scruples about means, so long as those means help them hold on to power.

Theodore N. White, noted author of "The Fall of Richard Nixon", has given us a remarkable insight about this category of politicians, which of course, includes Nixon.

Describing Nixon as the product of a "new style of politics" nurtured in California, White says that this new style "which was ultimately to corrupt the White House" depended for its execution on a "new breed of political manipulators, who were to take over, without even understanding it, the delicate meeting ground of politics and Government".

White adds: "The principle of the new Californian politics was simple: the best kind of campaign is an attack; in any campaign, an enemy has to be invented against whom the voters can be warned . . . ."

The new politics of India too, initiated in 1969, has been based on similar principles: political manipulation becoming the substitute of political policy, and invention of bogeys to mobilise mass support.

According to Indira Gandhi's calculations, the incessant tirade against the RSS, would influence, if no one else, at least the 70 million Muslims in the country.

Every system has its plus and minus points. Even dictatorships, and military regimes. A mature evaluation of any system must necessarily take its totality into consideration.

Early in 1975, Indira Gandhi herself said: "Some totalitarian systems have put all their people to work, and have eliminated all sorts of dissenters, but many a dictatorship had failed to solve the basic problem. When the choice was open to us, we deliberately chose the democratic system, although we knew it was slower". (Quotation recalled by N.B.C. interviewers in live telecast on August 21, 1975. P. 129, "Democracy and Discipline," Speeches of Indira Gandhi).

The choice, it may be pointed out, was based upon a certain set of values in which the right to offer satyagraha for what you hold as the truth, the right to strike and all such rights were inherent. Today, the Establishment regards these values as subversive, and against national interests. This was in the main in accordance with the principle enunciated by the Mahatma: "Reject the system that crushes the people".

Someone once said to Gandhiji that after all the British Government is not all evil. It had also been doing a lot of good to the people. Mahatmaji's reply was clear and categoric. He said:

There is no state run by Nero or Mussolini which has no good points about it; but we have to reject the whole. There are in our country, grand public roads and palatial educational institutions. But they are part of a system which crushes the nation. I should have nothing to do with it. They are like the fabled snake with a brilliant jewel on its hood, but which has, of course, poison.

Gandhiji's observation is as much relevant today as it was then.

Not An Amendment, It's a New Constitution

The Constitution (44th Amendment) Bill

by

A Detenu

(September, 1976)

The sanction of a truly democratic system consists in certain generally recognised standards of conduct which cannot be abrogated by any party in power, by any voluntary association of citizens or even by the unanimous vote of a popular assembly.

Shri Shankaracharya has said somewhere that the power of the Almighty Himself is limited in the sense that He cannot break His own laws, and that this very limitation constitutes His omnipotence. In the same way the life lines of democracy cannot be overthrown even by the united will and sovereign power of the whole human population.

DADA DHARMADHIKARI

(*In his Preface to Acharya Vinoba's* Democratic Values *published in 1962.*)

Unlike earlier Constitution Amendment Bills, the Constitution (Forty-fourth Amendment) Bill 1976, is not just one single amendment. It comprises some 57 different amendments, all lumped together in an omnibus Bill. In a way, thus, with the enactment of this Bill, the Indian Constitution would have undergone one hundred modifications in all. One hundred modifications in twenty-six and half years, and two-thirds of these, the contribution of the fifteen-month-old emergency!

The contents of this Bill apart, there are three preliminary, but weighty, objections why the present Parliament should not even consider this Bill.

The present Lok Sabha was elected in March, 1971. On March 17, 1976, its mandate expired. Ordinarily, therefore, under Art. 83 of the Constitution, the Lok Sabha would have become automatically dissolved on that date. If it continues to survive, it is solely because of the emergency proclamation, which has made it possible for the majority party in the House to give the Lok Sabha an extended tenure.

The emergency itself is phoney, and the proclamation malafide. That apart, a Lok Sabha which has given itself an extended tenure for avowedly emergency reasons is essentially a caretaker Parliament, politically competent to undertake only routine legislation. A major constitutional metamorphosis such as this one is certainly outside its ken.

The second objection is that at the moment, more than thirty senior members of Parliament are in jail, detained without trial. They do not know why they have been jailed. They cannot even go to Court. The only reason they can guess is that the gigantic fraud that is this emergency can be palmed off on the people only when all the three main sources of

popular enlightenment—the Parliament, the Press, the platform—are blacked out.

In his classic work on democracy entitled, "Democracy and
the Organisation of Political Parties", noted political scientist
M.Y. Ostrogorski has very correctly identified the soul of
democracy in these words :

> The mainspring of representative government is not in
> machinery, however perfected; it is the light that it sheds on
> the acts of the rulers; it is the publicity which attaches to all
> their sayings and doings.

Very true, snuff out the source of publicity and you have
really choked off the mainsprings of democracy.

Some time back, questioned about the number of MPs in
detention, Indira Gandhi glibly said that the number was
not large; "perhaps not even twenty", she added. In point
of fact, the number is thirty-three, and not less than twenty
as claimed. It is rather surprising that Indira Gandhi
should be ignorant of this. Or was she? What really matters
in this context is not how many have been detained, but who
has been detained.

The thirty-three MPs behind bars are drawn from seven
different parties: the ruling Party, the Congress (O), the Jana
Sangh, the Socialist Party, the BLD, the DMK, and the Akali
Dal. Among them are Morarji Desai, former Deputy Prime
Minister and now Chairman of the Congress (O) Parliamentary
Party, Shyam Nandan Mishra, Congress (O) leader in the
Lok Sabha, Ram Dhan, Secretary, Congress (R) Parliamentary
Party (elected just a month before the emergency, but expelled
from the party since), A.B. Vajpayee, leader of the Jana Sangh
Parliamentary Group, L.K. Advani, Party President and leader
of Jana Sangh in the Rajya Sabha, Samar Guha, leader of the
Socialist Party in the Lok Sabha, and Rabi Ray, leader of the
BLD in the Rajya Sabha.

The list of detained MPs also includes a galaxy of distinguished parliamentarians like Madhu Limaye (he has since
resigned), Madhu Dandavate, Mohan Dharia, K. Chandra
Shekhar and Murasoli Maran. Then, there are in this list these

two irrepressible, unrelenting and uncompromising critics of Indira Gandhi's Government—Raj Narain and Jyotirmoy Basu. Altogether, the MPs in jail make a formidable array of parliamentary talent and vigour.

To mark the completion of 25 years of the Constitution's working, the Lok Sabha Secretariat brought out last year an excellent commemorative volume titled "The Constitution and the Parliament in India". This volume carried a special section on the working of Parliament. The main article in this section is the one contributed by the Secretary-General of the Lok Sabha, S.K. Shakdher, captioned, "Parliamentary Initiatives". This article gives an interesting account of how Parliament enforces the responsibility of the executive to itself and to the people, "by exercising its unlimited right of information and criticism". It is noteworthy that in this well-documented account of Parliament's achievements in recent years, several of the above names keep recurring over and over again.

During these past fifteen months, a sustained campaign has been carried on by Government agencies that opposition MPs, particularly in detention, have been abusing the forum of Parliament, and indulging in "irresponsible obstructionism". There can be no greater lie than this. As this article by Parliament's topmost official amply bears out, it is these opposition MPs who have imparted vitality and verve to Parliament as an institution and made it possible for Parliament to exercise control over the executive, control which, in Shakdher's words, is "genuine, strict, and total". Visitors to Parliament these days have invariably returned with the impression that in the absence of these alert and vigilant members, Parliament has the looks of a 'mortuary'.

The third objection is that major amendments of the nature proposed must be preceded by a free countrywide debate. The validity of this contention is conceded in theory by the Government. But they glibly affirm that a free debate on the issue is actually going on! "Thousands of articles have been written and thousands of meetings have been held", a minister said the other day. He might have added: "Of course, in support of the amendments".

There is an apocryphal story about a group of American tourists who visited the Soviet Union in Khrushchov's days. At the end of their trip they called on Khrushchov, and said: "Everything seems all right, except that your curbs on liberty are suffocating". One of the Americans quipped : "In Washington we feel so free that we could stand right in front of White House and shout, 'Kennedy is a blackguard and a rascal', and would be none the worse for that". The story goes that Khrushchov stared at the American, and said coolly: "I do not know how you have gathered that impression that there is no such freedom. I give you my solemn assurance that you might stand in the centre of the Red Square, and shout at the top of your voice, 'Kennedy is a blackguard and a rascal' and no one is going to raise even a little finger at you".

The free debate going on in the country today is no different from the 'freedom' assured by Comrade Khrushchov to the American tourists. Towards the end of September our former External Affairs Minister M.C. Chagla addressed a meeting at Bombay in which he made a fervent appeal to the Government to put off the Bill till after the elections. What Reuter, BBC and other foreign media found remarkable about this was the fact that "even the official news agency 'Samachar' gave a few lines to this speech which was critical of Government's proposal, something that has not happened till now".

Jayaprakash Narayan constituted a committee to study the proposed amendments and organise seminars and symposia to discuss them. The committee comprised distinguished public men and jurists like M.C. Chagla, K.S. Hegde, V.M. Tarkunde, Shanti Bhushan and Krishan Kant. The committee, however, could not function effectively. No seminars or symposia were permitted.

The committee did, however, study the Swaran Singh Committee's recommendations in depth, and produce a learned report. But even this was dismissed by the official 'Samachar' in a few anaemic lines.

Introducing the Bill in the Lok Sabha, Law Minister Gokhale said that it did not alter the basic structure of the Constitution. The Law Minister, we are sure, knows better. A more honest statement on his part would have been: "We know that this Bill if enacted, will alter the basic structure of the Constitution; we know that this Bill runs counter to the Supreme Court judgment in the Keshavananda Bharati case; but we feel confident that with the present Supreme Court, we can violate the Keshavananda Bharati judgment with impunity, and yet get away with it".

However, since Gokhale has chosen to take this stand, namely, that the Bill does not militate against the Keshavananda Bharati judgment, we might start with the most important clause of this Bill, and see how it is in blatant violation of that judgment.

Clause 55 of the Bill reads :

In Art. 358 of the Constitution, after clause (3), the following clause shall be inserted, namely:

No amendment of this Constitution (including the provisions of Part III) made or purporting to have been made under this article (whether before or after the commencement of section 55 of the Constitution Forty-fourth Amendment Act, 1976) shall be called in question in any court except upon the ground that it has not been made in accordance with the procedure laid down by this Article.

By this provision, Parliament seeks to clothe itself with complete immunity from judicial scrutiny, in so far as amendments to the Constitution are concerned. At present, Parliament does not have any such immunity. Clause 55 enlarges Parliament's power. But how does Gokhale explain the rationale of this clause? In the "Notes of Clauses", the Law Minister says that Clause 55 "seeks to amend Art. 368 to clarify the true scope of that Article".

The explanation is thoroughly mendacious. The true scope of Article 368 has been discussed at considerable length in the Keshavananda Bharati case, and the law has been very clearly delineated. The Supreme Court held that :

(a) *The amending power of Parliament was wide, but limited*:
Parliament has no power to abrogate or emasculate the basic elements of the fundamental features of the Constitution such as the sovereignty of India, the democratic

character of our polity, the unity of the country, the essential features of the individual freedoms secured to the citizens. Nor has Parliament the power to revoke the mandate to build a welfare state and egalitarian society. These limitations are only illustrative and not exhaustive. Despite these limitations, however, there can be no question that the amending power is a wide power and it reaches every Article and every part of the Constitution.

(Justices Hegde and Mukherjee)

(b) *That a limited amending power cannot be made unlimited*: Article 368 cannot be amended so as to change its identity completely. Parliament, for instance, could not make the Constitution uncontrolled by changing the prescribed two thirds majority to simple majority.

(Chief Justice Sikri)

The effect of limitless amending power in relation to amendment of Art. 368 cannot be conducive to the survival of the Constitution because the amending power can itself be taken and the Constitution can be made literally unamendable by providing for an impossible majority.

The amending body has been created by the Constitution itself. It can only exercise those powers with which it has been invested. And if that power has limits, it can be exercised only within these limits.... Art. 368 cannot be so amended as to remove these limits.

(Justices Shelat and Grover)

(c) *Constitutional amendments are not immune from judicial review*: There is no constitutional matter which is not in some way or other involved with political, social or economic questions, and if the Constitution makers have vested in this Court a power of judicial review, and which so vesting, have given it a prominent place describing it as the heart and soul of the Constitution, we will not be deterred from discharging that duty merely because the validity or otherwise of the legislation will affect the political or social policy underlying it. The basic approach of this Court has been, and must always be, that the legislature has the exclusive power to determine

the policy and to translate it into law, the constitution-
ality of which is to be presumed unless there are strong
and cogent reasons for holding that it conflicts with the
constitutional mandate.

(Justice Jaganmohan Reddy)

The position in law thus, is that clause 55 of this Bill is
manifestly ultra vires. The Government is not unaware of it,
hence it first sought to have the Supreme Court revive the
Keshavananda Bharati verdict. That attempt ended in a fiasco.
It has, therefore, embarked on its present course, in a way taking
the Supreme Court's acquiescence for granted.

In the statement of Objects and Reasons appended to this Bill,
the Law Minister had said that the Bill aims at "removing
the difficulties which have arisen in achieving the objectives
of socio-economic revolution, which would end poverty and
ignorance and disease and inequality of opportunity". One
wished the Law Minister could enlighten the nation in precise
terms how the Constitution, as it is, impedes socio-economic
changes. The plethora of speeches and statements made till
now from the Prime Minister downwards about the need
for constitutional change have failed to throw any light on this
question.

Until 1973, that is, until before the Keshavananda Bharati
verdict, Art. 31 relating to the Right to Property was constantly
being projected by Government spokesmen as a roadblock in
the way of socio-economic progress. The Golak Nath judgment,
it was argued, had made the property right unassailable. Fortified
by this judgment, vested interests were able to obstruct progressive legislation relating to land reforms, bank nationalisation and so on, ran the argument. The Constitution (24th
Amendment) Bill was enacted in 1971 with the declared object
of removing this "roadblock". The Keshavananda Bharati
judgment was a sequel to this.

While discussing the Keshavananda Bharati case these days,
it is often forgotten that in that particular case the Supreme
Court decided in favour of Government, and against the petitioners who had challenged the validity of the Twenty-fourth
Amendment. By this judgment, the 24th Amendment was
upheld, the Golak Nath verdict was upturned, Parliament was

held competent to amend any provision of the Constitution including the Fundamental Rights provisions, and the Right to Property was declared as not being an essential feature of the Constitution.

A proviso was added to this verdict, however, by the majority judgment. This proviso was that Parliament cannot alter the basic democratic, federal and secular character of the Constitution.

Government has never concealed its unhappiness with the basic structure theory. Actually, if Government had been honestly concerned with socio-economic reforms, it would have been completely satisfied with the Keshavananda Bharati judgment. The basic-structure-theory does not in any way come in the way of socio-economic legislation leading to egalitarianism. But it does impose constraints on political legislation leading to authoritarianism. That is precisely why Government has been angry with it.

Even the minority judgments in the Keshavananda Bharati case have brought out this fact very clearly so far as socio-economic changes go. Government can no longer complain of any constitutional barriers. Justice Chandrachud, for instance, did not subscribe to the basic-structure theory. He delivered a judgment sharply dissenting from the majority view. But he too felt that the judgment had invested Government with all the powers it needed to achieve what it had been talking about. The last but one paragraph of his judgment is in fact a grim warning to the Government, administered in ringing words thus:

> We are all conscious that this vast country has vast problems and it is not easy to realise the dream of the Father of the Nation to wipe every tear off every eye. But, *if in spite of the large powers now conceded to Parliament*, the social objectives are going to be a dustbin of sentiments, then woe betide those in whom the country has placed such massive faith (emphasis added).

The basic-structure theory has held the field for more than three years now. Let Gokhale cite even a single law, constitutional or statutory, central or State, which aims at any socio-economic reform, but which has got which bogged down because of this theory. He cannot, simply because there is none.

The Constitution Amendment Bill now on the anvil is certainly in jeopardy because of this judgment. The Indian Constitution, at present, apportions powers and authority to the executive, the legislature and the judiciary, to the centre and the States, to the President and the Governors, to institutions like the Election Commission and to the Comptroller and Auditor-General, in a manner so as to make them all add up to a harmonious system of checks and balances against arbitrariness, autocracy and authoritarianism by the state.

The 44th Amendment is an undisguised bid to destroy all checks and balances built into the Constitution. Depradations are to be made into the realm of all institutions except the executive, so as to transfer huge chunks of power now vested in those institutions, to the executive. The upshot of this would be that the Prime Minister would become a constitutional dictator.

The most rapacious encroachments proposed are those into the sphere of the judiciary. Reference has already been made to the provision under which amendments to the Constitution would become immune to judicial scrutiny. Even in the matter of ordinary legislation though a majority of judges on the Bench may regard a law as ultra vires, the law remains unaffected unless two-thirds of the Bench holds that view. So far as central laws are concerned, High Courts will be stripped of their present jurisdiction to adjudge their validity.

One of the major remedies available to the common citizen against executive excesses has been his right to invoke the writ jurisdiction of High Courts under Art. 226. Gokhale himself is on record having noted in an article that it is the availability of this remedy "which has generated tremendous public confidence in the Constitution, and the institutions functioning under it". The 44th Amendment proposes to curtail severely this writ jurisdiction of the High Courts.

Till now, under Art. 31C, only laws framed in pursuance of Art. 39 (b) and (c) that is, in order to give effect to directive principles of state policy pertaining to ownership and control of economic resources for the common good etc. were protected from judicial scrutiny, even though these laws might violate certain Fundamental Rights such as Art. 14 (Right to Equality),

Art. 19 (Right to Freedom of Expression etc.) and Art. 31 (Right to Property). When Art. 316 was being considered by Parliament, several opposition members were agreeable to giving limited protection to socio-economic laws in this category and in so far as Art. 31 was concerned favoured the official proposal. But they stoutly opposed that the state be permitted to violate Articles 14 and 19 under cover of socio-economic legislation. The Government rode roughshod over these objections, and Art. 31C was adopted in its entirety.

That was bad enough. But the change now proposed is several times more dangerous. Under the new amendment, Courts are to be ousted not only in respect of laws relating to Art. 39 (b) and (c), but in respect of laws relating to any Directive Principle of State Policy.

There are in all fourteen articles in the Constitution dealing with Directive Principles. It is theoretically possible to relate any and every law to one or other of these fourteen articles. Thus the Fundamental Rights provisions will become meaningless.

Articles 14 and 19 are the twin articles which give constitutional recognition to the concept of republicanism and rule of law. The 44th Amendment plans to administer a fatal blow to these concepts.

The proposed new Art. 31D is yet another mortal assault on democracy and civil liberties. This Article is to empower Parliament to frame laws to suppress "anti-national activities" and "anti-national associations". This article so defines "anti-national activity" as to bring even normal trade union activity and political opposition to the ruling party and its philosophy within the mischief of this provision.

As in the case of other anti-democratic provisions conceived during the emergency, this Article 31D is also to be made immune to judicial scrutiny even though it may violate Articles 14 to 19.

It is really a tragic irony that the prime instrument for this unending chain of anti-judiciary amendments introduced during the emergency is Gokhale, himself a former judge.

The Comptroller and Auditor-General of India is an independent authority under the Indian Constitution charged with ensuring that the accounts of the Union as well as the States are in order. The Constitution contains several provisions which enable him to carry out his functions effectively. Thus under Art.150, the form in which accounts are to be kept is to be prescribed by him. Now this power is to be assumed by the President. This change can have serious political implications in financial management. If, for instance, Government decides that certain lump sum allocations need not be shown in the accounts with details and voucher, it can constitutionally do so.

When it first sponsored the idea of a Fundamental Duties Charter, the Swaran Singh Committee had suggested that Parliament be empowered by the Constitution to frame laws to punish breach of these duties. The Committee's proposal, to say the least, was odd and quaint. The duties enumerated in the proposed Part IV A include obligations such as that Indian citizens shall (*i*) "cherish and follow the noble ideals which inspired our national struggle", (*ii*) "value and preserve the rich heritage of our composite culture", (*iii*) "protect and improve the natural environment", (*iv*) "develop the scientific temper, humanism and the spirit of inquiry and reform", and (*v*) "strive towards excellence in all spheres of individual and collective activity".

Now, how does one have laws to penalise failure to discharge duties such as these? The proposal to have statutory sanctions has, therefore, been dropped, which is welcome as far as it goes. Unfortunately, it does not go far.

The Swaran Singh Committee's plan of legal sanctions was not concerned with duties. It had an ulterior motivation. The intention was to forge an instrument for political suppression. That object has been accomplished by introducing the provision against so-called "anti-national activities" (something not at all conceived by the Swaran Singh Committee). The legal sanctions are therefore no longer needed.

As it stands, Art. 51A which embodies this Duties Charter sins by omission rather than commission. It lays down Ten Commandments for the ruled, but not for the rulers, who, one would think, need them more. A country's Constitution is essentially a political document; a code of political ethics for ministers and legislators would, therefore, be more in place than the charter now proposed.

A tirade against the judiciary, of course, has been going on for several years now. But not even once prior to the formation of the Swaran Singh Committee had any Congressman ever suggested that a five-year term for the Lok Sabha and the State Assemblies was inadequate. All of a sudden this wonderful discovery has been made. And post-haste the Constitution is going to be amended to give the Lok Sabha and the State Assemblies a six-year term.

The parity rationale now being canvassed (that the change is to bring the Lower House's term on par with the Upper House) is an afterthought. The initial argument given was that five years were insufficient. Actually the original proposal was to have the Lok Sabha and Assembly terms for seven years. It need not be forgotten that with an even-numbered term for the Upper House members, the Constituent Assembly consciously prescribed a five-year term for the directly elected House.

How long is long enough? In George Bernard Shaw's play "Back to Methuselah" the Barnabas Brothers propound the thesis that "the term of human life must be extended to at least three centuries"! "Can't you see", argues one of the brothers, "that three-score-and-ten, though it may be long enough for a crude sort of village life, isn't long enough for a complicated civilisation like ours?"

A five-year term may have appeared adequate to our Constitution makers with their "crude" conceptions, but it is hopelessly insufficient to measure up to the "complicated" claims of this twenty-point era—that is perhaps how our rulers today feel. There is no knowing, however, where this logic will ultimately lead. Even so, it needs to be noted that in Britain, a four-year term is deemed long enough. So also in Japan and Switzerland. Even the Supreme Soviet of the USSR and the National People's Congress of China have a lifespan of just four years. In Australia, the lower House of Parliament has a term of three years only. In the US elections to the House of Representatives (Lower House) are held every two years.

Against the background of this experience the world over, in democratic as well as non-democratic countries, how can it be said that five years are inadequate for India?

The true roots of this particular Amendment lie in the elementary urge in all autocrats to cling to power. But in this case it seems political expediency also has played a part. Indira Gandhi may be wanting to keep her options open about holding a Lok Sabha election in February 1977. At the same time she wants to ensure that even if she does have a Lok Sabha poll, she does not have to hold Assembly elections simultaneously. The delinking of Lok Sabha and Assembly elections effected since 1971 has been advantageous to the ruling Congress, particularly because of the financial factor.

The 44th Amendment proposes to make several changes in Part XVIII of the Constitution, the Part dealing with emergency provisions. A major amendment of Art. 352 was made just after the clamping of emergency last year. By the 38th Amendment, the declaration of emergency by the President or its continuation, was made non-justiciable. There is no knowing when, and for how long, and indeed whether democracy and federalism would be kept in cold storage for ever (these were the effects of the emergency). This is a matter which, by virtue of this Amendment, it will be left entirely to the sweet will of the executive. The additional amendments now proposed are intended only to bolster the same purpose.

There is no doubt whatsoever that the emergency provisions in the Indian Constitution do require to be changed, and that too drastically. When the Constitution was being formed several members of the Constituent Assembly had expressed grave doubts about the wisdom of having these provisions. The Socialist member H.V.Kamath had recalled how Hitler had used similar provisions in the Weimar Constitution to destroy democracy. We have not seen the Germany of the thirties. But we have witnessed the India of the seventies. And it makes us ardent admirers of Kamath's foresight.

During the months preceding the promulgation of the June 1975 emergency, a campaign had been gathering momentum to have these provisions modified. Non-official bills had been tabled in Parliament seeking to make the imposition of emergency contingent upon some objective criteria instead of the arbitrary opinion of Government. At a seminar at New Delhi, the late Subba Rao, former Chief Justice of the Supreme Court, made a powerful plea that the emergency provisions be amended to give the judiciary and legislature the right and authority to restrain the executive when it declares or continues an emergency without justification.

Instead of moving in the direction desired by the people, the 44th Amendment would have us move in quite the opposite direction. On the face of it, the proposal to empower the President to impose an emergency only in a part of India and not in the entire country seems innocuous. By itself, clause 48, which provides for this is not objectionable. But clause 49 lays bare the true intent of the Government. This clause provides that even though the emergency proclamation may be in force oaly in a part of the country, the central Government's executive powers to issue directions to States, and Parliament's powers to frame laws relating to subjects in the State list, will extend to the entire country. For all practical purposes, this would mean an emergency in the whole country.

The changes proposed in provisions relating to the imposition of President's Rule in a State also are changes contrary to the change actual experience warrants. In the Constituent Assembly opponents of this provision relented only when Ambedkar assured them that this Article would be invoked by the central Government very rarely, in times of grave constitutional crises, and that too after the President had exhausted all other avenues trying to resolve the crisis. Ambedkar went on to express the hope that this Article would remain "a dead letter".

But far from being "a dead letter", Art. 356 has been one of the most recurringly used provisions of the Constitution. It has not been used rarely, only in times of grave constitutional crises as promised, but over and over again, for reasons of pure party expediency. During the last 26 years it has been used more than 40 times. If Art. 356 and related articles need to be amended, it should be to impose powerful curbs on this repeated abuse. The amendments being made serve only to enfeeble further the weak restraints that already exist. Thus, today, a proclamation of President's Rule is required to be approved by Parliament every six months. The 44th Amendment seeks to make an annual approval sufficient.

Art. 357 of the Constitution relates to laws framed by Parliament for a State while that State is under President's Rule Under this Article, laws which but for the imposition of President's Rule, Parliament would not be competent to make would cease to have effect on the expiration of one year after the end of President's Rule.

This Article recognises that Art. 356 is an emergency provision and the authority which Parliament derives by virtue of this is an ad hoc authority. Legislation in respect of State subjects is the State's exclusive preserve and any trespass into that sphere by Parliament has temporary validity, justified by emergency circumstances. Laws framed by Parliament survive only if the State legislature after revival wishes them to. This article thus honours the federal concept.

The new Amendment, however, seeks to reverse the position. It provides that all such laws framed by Parliament will continue to prevail unless changed or repealed by the State legislature. No explanation is offered for this inversion of the original scheme.

Clause 43 of the Bill constitutes a still graver assault on federalism. This clause seeks to empower the Government of India to deploy its armed force in any State "for dealing with any grave situation of Law and Order".

Hitherto, Law and Order has been an exclusively State subject. States have been dealing with Law and Order problems on their own. On occasion, they have sought and secured from the centre the help of the armed forces; but the responsibility has always been the State's. Never has any problem arisen in this sphere, control over which gives to States some feeling of autonomy. It is uncalled for, and entirely unwarranted. It only betrays New Delhi's distrust of the States. It can be conveniently used as an instrument for central intervention in the administration of States without even having to go throught the formalities required by Art. 356.

The same distrust of States is evident in clause 57 of the Bill which transfers several State subjects such as Administration of Justice and Forests to the Concurrent List.

Encroachments made by this Bill into the judiciary's realm, or into the domain of States, are unabashed. Less overt though, inroads have been planned into the authority of legislatures also, Parliament not excluded. Clause 14 thus proposes to amend Art. 77 in a manner so to limit the authority of Parliament, though without mentioning Parliament. Art. 77 is the provision which empowers the President to frame rules for "the more convenient transaction of business of the Government of India, for the allocation among ministers of the said business". The Amendment is not just about the judiciary. Its sweep is wider. It reads: "No Court or *other authority* shall be entitled to require the production of any rules. . ." etc. (emphasis added)

Obviously, by this Amendment, not only Courts but Parliament and its Committees too, will be divested of their right to call for these rules. Today, high-powered Parliamentary Committees like the Public Accounts Committee, Estimates Committee and the Committee on Public Undertakings are able to discharge their duties effectively because their right to examine any official document is untramelled. This Amendment clips their powers too.

The phrase "or other authority" would cover also the Comptroller and Auditor-General, and the Election Commission, both independent authorities under the Constitution, and whose proper functioning may warrant examining these rules. A similar amendment made in Art. 166 would have an identical effect with regard to the State legislature.

The Election Commission comes in for direct devaluation also by virtue of two other clauses. These clauses amend Articles 103 and 192 relating to disqualifications of legislators. Under these articles, before asking a decision on the question of disqualifications of MPs or MLAs and MLCs, the President is required to obtain the Election Commission's opinion. That requirement is still to continue, but what is to be deleted is the key portion of the article, namely, that after obtaining the Election Commission's opinion, the President "shall act according to such opinion". Here too power shifts from the Election Commission to the executive.

A rt. 105 of the Constitution provides that until such time that Parliament by law defines its powers, privileges and immunities and those of its members, these shall be the same as those of the House of Commons. There is a similar provision regarding State legislatures and their members.

There has been a persistent demand, particularly from the Press, that parliamentary privileges should be codified. It has been argued that the present indefiniteness hampered the Press in its working. The codification demand was formally made by

the Press Commission in 1954. Various professional bodies of
newsmen have been voicing the same view.

Parliamentary opinion, however, has not favoured this course
of action. Presiding officers' conferences, held annually have
generally opined against codification. Perhaps, as a middle
course, Government had readily accepted Feroze Gandhi's Bill
giving complete immunity to pressmen with regard to coverage
of parliamentary proceedings.

Even while the debate about codification continues unresolv-
ed, the Bill protecting correspondents who report parliamentary
proceedings has been scrapped. In addition, the constitutional
provisions regarding parliamentary privileges are proposed to
be overhauled.

The amendment proposed omits the reference to the House of
Commons, and says that "the powers, privileges and immunities
of each House of Parliament, and of the members and the
committees of each House shall be such as may, from time to
time, be evolved by such Houses of Parliament".

The Press was urging codification because it felt that without
a definite law of privilege, the position was vague and obscure.
There was weight in the contention. Even so, there was then
at least a definite yardstick, the House of Commons. A positive
merit in that touchstone was that it made Indian legislatures
lean in favour of liberty and liberalism, which is the direction
privilege cases in Britain continue to move towards.

The new Amendment makes the position altogether unsettled
and uncertain, and so makes issues of privilege all the more easily
amenable to the arbitrariness of the executive. The victims of
such arbitrariness would be not only the Press and the common
citizen, but the legislators themselves.

Today, though there is no codified law of privilege, there is at
least a definite frame of reference—the body of decisions about
privileges taken by the House of Commons. This frame of
reference has been common for both Parliament as well as the
State legislatures. But after the 44th Amendment, the views of
the majority party at a given time, which means in effect the
whims of the executive, would be the sole determinant as to
whether a member, or a newsman, or any other citizen, charged
with contempt, or breach of privilege, is guilty or not. And for
absolutely identical cases, the decision will vary from State to
State, from State to Parliament, and may well be diametrically
opposite even for the two Houses of Parliament.

There is really no explanation for this kind of change except that the privilege article as now worded gives Parliament and its members ample power to make the executive behave responsibly. That Parliament has failed to exercise this power and has chosen to kowtow to the behests of the executive owes itself to other factors, not the least being the imprisoning of almost all active Parliamentarians. By this Amendment, even the power is proposed to be taken away.

The most massive enchroachment made by the executive into the realm of Parliament is that envisaged by the last clause of this Bill. Under this clause 59, for a period of two years the executive proposes to arm itself with the right to make any change in the Constitution on the plea that it was doing so in order to remove difficulties.

The provision is unheard of; it is atrocious. If Parliament acquiesces in it, it will only be putting a seal on its own humiliation and abasement. The analogy given by the Law Minister about statutory laws having a provision for removal of difficulties is irrelevant and absurd. This is not an ordinary statute. This is a constitutional amendment which Parliament is going to pass supposedly after due deliberation.

If any difficulty does arise in implementing its provisions it is for Parliament to reconsider the issue and decide what changes are called for. As with all constitutional amendments, these changes too would have to be effected by a two-thirds majority.

It is preposterous that what Parliament itself is not entitled to do except by a special majority, the President (which now officially is going to mean the Prime Minister) is to be empowered to do all on his own.

The other day, Minister of State for Law, Syed Mohammed justified this clause by saying that even the Government of India Act, 1935 had an identical provision. That was a tell-tale analogy, we think. The British wanted the Viceroy and not the central legislature to wield real power. The purpose of this clause is no different. Syed Mohammed may as well have recalled that Hitler also had made the Reichstag, the German Parliament, pass what he called "an Enabling Act", by which Parliament handed over its legislative powers to Hitler for a period of four years! Syed Mohammed could have said: "We are seeking powers for the President only for two years"!

This article is not a clause-by-clause analysis of the 44th Amendment Bill. It is an attempt essentially to show how the Bill can radically change the complexion of the Constitution. Thus, we have not dwelt on the proposal to modify the Preamble of the Constitution by introducing words like Socialist, Secular etc., because we do not think that amendment germane to this discussion. In the Government's overall strategy, these clauses have the role only of a red-herring; Government would very much like the debate to get bogged down in such emotive, image-building words, so that the dangerous anti-libertarian, anti-democratic content of the other amendments can sneak through with lesser discussion. Opponents of the Bill would do well not to oblige Government on this score.

Institutions, they say, are as fallible as those who man them. So also are Constitutions. No Constitution is perfect. Constitutional experts and jurists, however, have generally agreed that the Indian Constitution as drawn up by our Constituent Assembly is a well drafted, neatly balanced document. Indira Gandhi herself made the following comment about the Indian Constitution:

> Our Constitution has struck a fine balance between Centre and States, and between State and citizen. Changes in the Constitution have been made only to enable it the better to fulfil its own purpose.

This observation, be it noted, has been made just a month before clamping of the emergency. It is dated May 22, 1975, and is part of a message sent by the Prime Minister for the commemorative volume on the Constitution published by the Lok Sabha Secretariat.

In the Keshavananda Bharati case, several judges including Chief Justice Sikri referred to the present harmonious distribution of power between the executive, the legislature and the judiciary as a basic feature of the Indian Constitution.

Any attempt, pronounced Justice Jaganmohan Reddy, to change "the power relationship inter se three departments, the federal character or the States and the rights of the citizen vis-a-vis the State", and to substitute in their place "new institutions, power relationships and fundamental features" would amount to abrogation of the Constitution, and so cannot be done. In their own words, Justices Shelat and Grover have emphasised this very thing.

It is quite clear then that the Constitution (44th Amendment) Bill, 1976, offers to the country not a new Amendment, but a new Constitution. The balanced democratic Constitution we have had till now is to be replaced by an executive, authoritarian set-up. That the Parliament and Courts will still continue is neither here nor there.

When in 1933, Adolf Hitler made the German Reichstag pass the Enabling Act (referred to earlier) transferring its legislative authority to Hitler's Cabinet, one of the clauses of the Act ironically read "No Law shall be enacted that affects the position of the Reichstag". Let the Indian Parliament, if it may, indulge in similar delusions about its own position: the people can have no such illusions. If Parliament does pass this Bill, the Constitution which they, the people of India, gave unto themselves on January 26, 1950, would have been buried fathoms deep. A new Constitution will usurp its place.

PART THREE

Some Letters and Notes from Jail

MEMBER OF PARLIAMENT   Bangalore
(Rajya Sabha)   December 12, 1975

Dear Shri Bhandariji,*
    I had received your letter and got all the information. Contact could not be maintained later. Please send a detailed report on the progress of the satyagraha. In this State the response has been very good.
    You have asked my opinion on the question of an election symbol. If elections do come upon us the Gujarat plan may be repeated. All units of the Janata front may adopt the election symbol of any one of them. To me, however, the possibility of elections being held seems remote.
    Personally I am of the view that against the background of the happenings of the past 5 or 6 months we should have no hesitation whatsoever in forming one party.
    I am sending herewith a letter addressed to Raj Mataji. Kindly arrange to have it delivered. Please go through it yourself also. If you so feel you may not send it.
    How is Atalji? I was glad to learn that (after his operation) he is now in a position to move about a bit.
    Has anyone met J.P. these days? Swamiji may be sent to him. It would be good if Eknathji can meet him on behalf of the Sangh.
    I am sending a pamphlet herewith. It has been drafted keeping the Chandigarh session of the Congress in mind. If it can be printed in time it may be sent to the Sarvodaya Conference at Paunar also. It would be good if we could do it. Shri Krishan

---

*Translated from the Hindi.

Kant or Shri Dharia may be asked to write to some of the delegates participating in the Chandigarh session.

At the next session of Parliament we must be able to form a Janata front inside. We should try to include the D.M.K. also in this. If releases take place by then Shri Morarji Bhai and Shri Nana Goray may be the leaders in the Lok Sabha and Rajya Sabha respectively. If the present position continues Shri Mohan Dharia and Shri Goray respectively may be the leaders in the two Houses. Please give thought to this suggestion.

As had been feared steps have been taken to paralyse and cripple the Press permanently. This will be the biggest impediment for our future plans. Some consultations must be held with friends from the Press and a plan of action devised. Apart from our own people Abu Abraham, Nayantara Sahgal, Puri and Mankekar may be consulted.

All here are fine.

With respects and regards,

Yours

Sd/- Lal

P.S. In the pamphlet enclosed there is a quotation from Pt. Nehru's presidential speech on page 11 which may be published separately in the form of a wall poster and used at Paunar and Chandigarh.

Shri Sunder Singh Bhandari

Republic Day, January 26, 1976
Central Jail,
Bangalore

My dear Dada,

Pranams. We here have just read with admiration your piece in the *Indian Express*, "Chapter from History". Only you could have done such an incisive and succinct summing up. The parallel you have drawn is so apt. And the *"Jehnum men jeo"* reference reflects very exactly the mood of those inside.

Along with Shri Shyam Nandan Mishra, Shri Madhu Dandavate and many others, I have been enjoying the very pleasant climate of Bangalore for the past several months. We three had come here for a parliamentary Committee meeting on June 25 and had planned to stay here for two days. But the two days have stretched into months. The period may well become years. We are all set for the possibility . After all, the prospect of leaving a small jail only to enter a bigger one is not particularly enticing.

Shyam Babu and Madhuji convey to you their respects and regards. We all wish you many more years, and good health, in the service of the nation.

Sincerely yours
Lal

To
Shri Jiwatram B. Kripalani
Sarvodaya Enclave,
Mehrauli Road,
New Delhi.

MEMBER OF PARLIAMENT   Bangalore
(Rajya Sabha)   February 27, 1976

My dear Shri Virendraji,

I understand that Shri Deve Gowda suggested to you yesterday that release of detenus be demanded who were in the Rajya Sabha, and whose term was due to expire this April.

This is to convey to you that I personally do not agree to any such move. It is, of course, for you to decide what to do. But I for one would be happy, and grateful, if this is not done.

In fact, no one from the opposition should suggest any selective release of detenus—of M.P. detenus, for example. In this case, it would be particularly embarrassing for me, and, I think, also for the one or two Rajya Sabha members in detention whose term is about to expire.

With regards,

                                    L.K. Advani

Shri Virendra Patil
Bangalore

L.K. Advani   Central Jail
Member of Parliament   Bangalore
Rajya Sabha   April 19, 1976

To
  The Chairman,
  Rajya Sabha,
  New Delhi

Hon'ble Sir,

Following my re-election to the Rajya Sabha, I was due to take oath on April 3, 1976. However, because of my detention, I could not do so. Article 99 of the Constitution imposes on me an obligation to take oath, and so I would like to do so at the earliest. But in the meanwhile, I hope that because of this forced incapacity to complete the formality of oath taking, I shall not be denied my right to receive all parliamentary papers, borrow books from the Parliamentary Library, secure the assistance of the Research and Reference Section, and avail of all such facilities as have been open to me even during detention.

Also, I hope that my inability to take oath will not entail a punishment for my family in the matter of residential, telephone, medical and other facilities which have hitherto been available to them in spite of my incarceration, and to which I continue to be entitled for another term.

You, Sir, are the custodian of the rights and privileges of members. I am hereby approaching you as such, with two alternative requests.

In the first place I would like to request that you use your good offices with Government to ensure that members of the

Rajya Sabha, re-elected or newly elected, who could not take oath on April 3 because of detention, are enabled to do so when the House meets next on May 10, 1976.

Incidentally, I may mention that going through Shri D.P. Mishra's autobiography "Living an Era", I have come across the case of one Shri S.C. Mitra, who in 1927 was elected un-opposed to the Central Legislative Assembly even while he was under prevention detention in far-off Mandalay. When the Central Legislative Assembly met, Pandit Motilal Nehru, who was leader of the opposition at that time strongly protested against Shri Mitra's detention and demanded his immediate release. The British Government stoutly resisted the demand. But the Speaker Shri Vithalbhai Patel pulled his weight in favour of the opposition demand, and ultimately, the Government had to yield. Shri Mitra was released.

I have referred to this precedent only to stress that in so far as executive actions against members of Parliament are concern-ed, Presiding Officers have never been unconcerned or disinterest-ed. In Shri Mitra's case, the issue was release of the detenu, because he had been elected. What I have suggested to you is far simpler—facility to take oath for detenus who had been elected.

In case you find yourself unable to accept this suggestion, or if the Government is reluctant to heed your advice, my alterna-tive request is that you take steps to see that the facilities of detenu M.Ps. and the facilities of residence etc. to which their families are entitled even after their detention are not denied to them simply because of this formal omission regarding oath-taking.

I am enclosing herewith a copy of a letter I have already addressed to the Chairman, Housing Committee, Rajya Sabha, with regard to my residence.

Thanking you, and with respects,

Yours sincerely,
Sd/-
(L.K. Advani)

Bangalore
May 13, 1976

Dear Shri Tyagiji,*

I am informed that members of the Jana Sangh Working Committee who are out will be meeting in Delhi this week. This is to convey my warm greetings to all of them and to share with them some thoughts.

Perhaps this meeting has been convened mainly to consider the issue of party unification. From what I have been able to gather till now, among Jana Sangh circles all seem to be agreed that one party must be formed. This I think is as it should be.

The Bihar agitation was launched in March 1974. Shri J.P. led the movement and all opposition parties supported it. Ever since, the Jana Sangh has been steadily moving towards opposition unity. The resolutions we have adopted on this issue at Hyderabad (September 1974), Jammu (November 1974), Ahmedabad (January 1975), Delhi (March 1975) and Abu (June 1975) may be deemed firm and definitive steps taken in this direction.

At our annual session in March 1975 we had stressed the desirability of a national alternative. We had also maintained that a unified opposition party should emerge not out of summit talks but out of unity established at the level of cadres. We felt that this cadre level unity would develop out of joint activity, out of joint campaigning in elections and out of a joint struggle.

---

* Translated from the Hindi

Om Prakash Tyagi M.P. was Acting President of the Bharatiya Jana Sangh during the emergency period.

The joint agitation launched in respect of Shri Morarji Bhai's fast, the formation of the Janata Morcha in Gujarat, the joint election campaign undertaken in that State and the formation of the Janata Front Government were developments indicative of the progress made in this direction.

With the declaration of emergency in June 1975 a new chapter has commenced. Democracy has come under eclipse. Those who believe in democracy have had to undergo many kinds of suffering and have had to make sacrifices. As a result of this the cordiality, closeness and mutual trust generated during this last one year among parties and persons committed to democracy could not have been ordinarily created even in one decade. The emergence of a strong unified opposition party with democracy as its main plank should be regarded as a natural culmination of this chain of events.

I feel that our Working Committee should endorse the statement adopted at the Bombay meeting (convened by J.P.).

I learn that at the meeting held in Delhi on April 19 certain practical difficulties were pointed out. Some possible solutions also were perhaps mentioned and discussions on these are said to be on. If because of these difficulties all formalities of unification cannot be completed, what can be done by the 4 parties is, firstly to declare themselves categorically in favour of unification on the one hand, and also announce that until such time that formal unification does take place, all of them will carry on their political activities on a common platform which may be called Janata Front.

It has become a fashion these days to say that democracy can be of various kinds and that democracy of the western pattern is not quite suited for India. The present regime has been talking of evolving a new form of democracy.

Whatever be the form of democracy anyone contemplates, a political system which does not permit freedom of expression is certainly not a democracy.

In India today it is not just freedom of expression that has been suppressed; there is no freedom of information too. It is said that no political party has been banned but there is no gainsaying the fact that India today is a de facto one-party set up.

We cannot reconcile ourselves to this present political suffocation. It does not matter how long we have to stay inside, how much the price we have to pay. Generally speaking this is the mood of those inside. I am sure that friends outside have the same resolve. We must be conscious of the fact that the path we have to traverse is not merely difficult it may be long also.

On the day following the Supreme Court's verdict in the Habeas Corpus case I had an occasion to address MISA friends here. A synopsis of the talk is being enclosed for your information. You must be meeting Shri Atalji. His guidance would be available to you for this meeting. If he can prepare a statement etc. for the meeting it would be fine. I hope his health is alright. Does he still have to go to the Institute? Convey my respects and regards to him.

Yours sincerely,
Sd/- Lal

Bangalore
June 28, 1976

My dear Asokji,

Thanks for your warm letter. Virendraji (Patil) has sent us a full report of the Working Committee deliberations.

All of us have greatly appreciated your opening remarks to the Working Committee, but felt sad that despite your persuasion, the Committee did not endorse J.P.'s one-party move.

We are anxious to know as to where do we go from here, that is, in so far as this one party move is concerned. Virendraji informs us that you have undertaken to talk to Charan Singhji, and have advised J.P. not to reply to Charan Singh's letter till then. Have you been able to meet him, and discuss the matter with him?

You may also have had occasion to discuss the developments with Atalji and Nana Saheb Gore. How do they view the situation?

We here strongly feel that J.P.'s announcement must not be falsified. Failure to bring it off would impair the credibility not only of J.P. personally but of the entire movement. The Conference scheduled for July may be put off say to August 9 or August 15 but there must be no postponement sine die.

To us it appears that linking up formation of one party with restoration of normalcy amounts to shelving the issue indefinitely. Tactically also, that may not be desirable, because from the Government's angle, this then would become an additional constraint factor on any inclination towards normalcy.

We are totally unware of J.P.'s thinking in the matter. You have had the occasion to discuss the question with him and so can enlighten us. Virendraji's own assessment has been conveyed to us thus:

> J.P. was not happy with the stand taken by the Congress (O) Working Committee and Shri Charan Singh, leader of the B.L.D. When I had met him he told me that he is not in a position to take much strain in view of his failing health. He feels that so far as he is concerned, he has made best possible efforts for a national alternative. Now it is for the leaders of all the parties to take further action in the matter.

Obviously, J.P. may not be inclined to do anything further in the matter on his own. If any fresh initiative is to be taken, it can only be by you personally. Even if that means convening yet another meeting of the Congress(O) Executive, we feel that ought to be done. The matter should not be allowed to dangle loosely; it should be clinched.

Both your letter to us, as well as your remarks to the Working Committee, show how strong is the urge in you to rejoin us behind the bars rather than submit to the choking curbs on liberty that now prevail outside. It is our considered view, however, that your presence outside would be of far greater use to the cause, particularly in the context of the follow up this unification issue calls for. We request you, therefore, not to court arrest voluntarily.

With warm regards,

Yours sincerely
Sd/- L.K. Advani
Sd/- Madhu Dandavate

Shri Asoka Mehta
New Delhi

Central Jail,
Bangalore-9
August 18, 1976

My dear Atalji,

Namaskars. Your letter of August 6 has reached me yesterday. It's really a pleasure hearing from you after such a long time. Kamala had omitted to give me your first letter. I am sorry that my failure to write earlier should have caused any misunderstanding.

I am in agreement with your main contentions. Firstly, that after January, all that we are carrying on is a struggle posture, and not a struggle, and that such a posture, by itself, is likely to be counter-productive. Secondly, that between one phase of the struggle and another, there must be a gap. And lastly, that if the present authoritarian set-up stabilises, as is likely, a change in the struggle pattern will have to be thought of.

However, I have been inclined to think that in a situation of the present nature, decisions about strategy can best be taken by those outside. Those inside are likely to be subjective in their thinking.

Prolonged incarceration tends to create in the detenus two contradictory frames of mind. In some, it causes despondence, and an eagerness to get out at any cost, while in others it inculcates a hard, inflexible attitude—an attitude which tells the authorities something like this: Keep us here for our entire life, if you may, but we'll not budge an inch from the position we have taken.

Some letters I have been getting—from Khurana, for instance —reveal this second mood very pointedly. He reacted very sharply even to the letter written to the P.M. by J.P. in February last suggesting that some of the detained leaders be released so that he could consult them. Here, too, Shyam Babu was unhappy about that letter. Madhuji and myself saw nothing wrong about that.

I have referred to this only to illustrate my point. This I have always felt that out of the three major aspects of emergency relaxation we should be concerned with—namely Press freedom, freedom of political activity and release of detenus—release is the least important. Also, that from the Government's point of view, detentions are the least paying. So, I have felt that bending backwards just to secure the release of prisoners may not be a desirable thing. But if by bending backwards there is even a possibility of relaxation in the other two spheres, I am all for it. Of course, a formal winding up of the movement in January-February, as you suggested, would not have been even a bending-backwards. It would have been just the normal thing to do. Now, it may involve a measure of retreat.

With J.P. released, and with you available for consultation, we inside have felt at ease that whatever decisions are being taken are the outcome of collective thinking on the part of all of you. I have had the impression that those outside have a better, and more sustained, communication with you, than they can possibly have with me, or any of the others inside.

Be that as it may, so far as the Jana Sangh is concerned, please feel free to take any initiative you feel fit—both with regard to broad strategy, as well as the one party issue. I am sure Madhavraoji, Thengadiji and other colleagues outside would also like you to do the same. I am conveying to them also my views in this regard. The only thing I would stress is that J.P. must be involved in whatever move is made.

I wonder whether J.P. was able to meet you when he came to Delhi in connection with J.J. Singh's funeral.

Shri Madhuji agrees with this. I had read out to him portions of your letter spelling out your views on the struggle aspect. He has written to Shri Surendra Mohan about this. Shri Hegde also has written to Shri Asoka Mehta.

The Parliamentary Bulletin received just now by Shri Dandavate says that Shri Piloo Mody has been released (on

August 12) on parole. Is he too confined to his house like
you? Hope his health is all right. Please give him my warm
regards in case he meets you.

Always yours
Lal

Bangalore-9
January 8, 1977

My dear Shri Madhavraoji,

I am in receipt of your letter dated December 26, 1976 and have noted its contents.

From our side we should always be ready for talks. Efforts in this direction also may continue. But from whatever information is available with us Government does not seem to intend to hold any meaningful talks. The Government's objective in this regard seems to be:

(i) to make the opposition parties endorse the political and constitutional changes that have taken place during the last $1\frac{1}{2}$ years;

(ii) to extract from the opposition some statement which could substantiate that proclamation of the emergency was justified;

(iii) to release leaders, M.P.s etc. in driblets so that an impression may be created that most prisoners have been released and, also that the Government is honestly moving in the direction of normalisation.

The resolutions adopted at the meeting of opposition parties' representatives last month are good. We can also think about announcing withdrawal of the movement. This announcement could be related to J.P.'s statement in which he had said that the movement launched on June 25 had a limited objective and was within a limited time-frame—until the Supreme Court decided the issue.

But we must not take any stand which creates even an impression that we have reconciled ourselves to the changes made, or which may seem to justify the emergency.

Today's *Express* has published the letters exchanged between the Prime Minister and Shri Asoka Mehta. The tone of P.M.s letter is mild, but the content of it cannot be accepted. Shri Asoka Mehta has not joined issue with her and has only stressed the need for a dialogue. That is alright. But I doubt whether she will talk. Through Shri Om Mehta etc., she is only trying to probe how far we are willing to adjust to the Government's intentions.

If, however, there is any occasion of negotiating with Government and the question of releases is discussed, our emphasis should be on the release of ordinary workers and not on the release of leaders and legislators. I have a suspicion that the Government, on its own, intends to release the leaders, legislators etc. and thus create an illusory atmosphere of relaxation under cover of which it can keep the rank and file behind bars for a prolonged period. If indeed this is their intention I should think that our interest lies in seeing that the prominent men inside continue to remain inside.

Some months back I had suggested that Statewise lists of MISA detenus should be drawn up. Maybe, this has already been done. Now, when every other day we see reports in the Press about so and so being released, these lists can be put to proper use. In Karnataka, for instance, it has been suggested to Virendra Patil that he may address a letter to Shri Om Mehta drawing his attention to the P.M's statement that Chief Ministers have been directed to release detenus and that releases are accordingly taking place. It may be pointed out in this context that out of the over 325 detenus in this State till date, only 15 have been released. Our M.Ps. outside in various States can write similar letters to Government. Figures for the entire country may be compiled and Atalji may write in that regard to the Prime Minister. In this way, in so far as releases are concerned a deliberate effort should be made to shift the focus of attention from the names of persons released to the number of persons released. These letters, figures, lists etc. can be given to the Press also. They may not be able to publish them but they would be posted with facts and their writings would be in a proper perspective. I have seen Shri Kuldip Nayar's report today which too gives the impression as if large numbers have been already set free.

Did the opposition meeting held in December consider the question of resignations from legislatures? I have written to Shri Ram Bhau to discuss the matter in the Jana Sangh Working Committee which I am told will be meeting this month to consider the question of unification.

We should try to avail of the slight relaxation that has been in evidence in the Press. At various press centres teams may be organised of people who can write letters to the Press. Letters-to-the-Editor columns in various papers should be flooded with letters giving out our view point positively. In yesterday's *Indian Express* I saw a very well-argued letter from Mrs. Amiya Rao on "Gujarat agitation and the opposition." It would be fruitful if this can be consciously done on a large scale.

What news about Shri Swamy?

All of us here are fine. If you happen to meet Shri Madhu Dandavate you will be able to get full information about us all.

In an earlier letter from Shri Bhandariji it was mentioned that my name was being proposed as General Secretary of the new party. I have written to him that if this responsibility is to be entrusted to someone among us Atalji's would be the most suitable name. Atalji himself may perhaps insist on my name but I am sure he would accept your guidance.

Yours
Sd/- L.K. Advani

Shri Madhavrao Muley

NOTES ADDRESSED TO PERIODICAL CONFERENCES OF UNDERGROUND WORKERS

July 10, 1976

Note for consideration

1. It is evident that Indira Gandhi has no intention of allowing the situation to return to the pre-emergency position.

2. This does not mean that the emergency will not be lifted. It will be lifted but after all the essential attributes of the emergency have become part of India's body-politic. Indira Gandhi's current moves on the constitutional front seem aimed at achieving this.

3. Normally the restrictions on the Press could not have been continued after the emergency. Now, those have been made statutory in the shape of the Press Objectionable Matter Act. As it is, the Act violates Art. 19 and so the moment the emergency ended would have been struck down as invalid. It has therefore, been included in the Ninth Schedule and made immune to judicial scrutiny.

4. The Swaran Singh Committee's latest proposal about having in the Constitution a chapter on fundamental duties seems yet another major step in this direction. A charter of eight commandments has been drawn up. Failure to carry out any of these duties will be punishable by law, and such law shall be protected from Courts, even though it may be violative of Fundamental Rights. Now, the eight duties taken together cover the entire gamut of legislation. Every law framed by Parliament or the state legislatures can be related to one or the other duty. Thus every law can become non-justiciable. Thus Fundamental Rights can become meaningless.

5. At present the R.S.S. has been banned under D.I.R. A separate law may be enacted in pursuance of the Duty requiring citizens to eschew communalism and the ban reimposed thereunder. If the S.S. Committee's recommendations are incorporated in the Constitution such a law will be non-justiciable.

6. Of course, the Fundamental Duties scheme itself, as conceived, appears to go against the Keshavananda Bharati judgment. But in view of growing judicial pusillanimity the Supreme Court cannot be relied upon. Even so, legal opinion on this question must be sought in advance.

7. Vinoba's decision to undertake a fast on the issue of cow-protection may be causing some worry in New Delhi. In the beginning, New Delhi feigned unconcern. In fact by sealing the *Maitri* press at Paunar, and confiscating copies of the journal, they seemed to serve a notice on V.B., that we do not care for your decision. Later, perhaps, there have been second thoughts and Government may be wanting to avoid a confrontation. The press has been reopened, and the copies seized restored. It realises, perhaps that if it takes an adamant stand, and Vinobaji sacrifices his life for this issue, the electoral consequences—if and when elections are held—can be pretty serious. It is possible that shortly before the fast is to commence, Indira Gandhi may send an emissary or go to Paunar herself and somehow try to buy time on some such plea as that consultations with Chief Ministers, minority representatives etc. are needed.

8. It is not clear why Vinobaji chose this issue. He could not have been concerned with its electoral potential. His argument that the emergency issue is a transient one does not carry conviction. After all, he was responsible for the Acharya sammelan. It was he who declared that if Government does not accept the *anushasan* of Acharyas, satyagraha would be justified. In private conversation he had repeatedly affirmed that if Government did not do anything (about the emergency, prisoners etc.) by October, he would himself offer satyagraha. I think it would be good if he could somehow be persuaded to link the Acharya sammelan decisions also with the *Go-Raksha* issue.

9. I have no information whatsoever as to where exactly the one-party issue stands now. The last we heard was after the Cong (O) Working Committee meeting. Shortly after that the issue appeared to have been shoved beneath the carpet. Shri Madhu Dandavate and I wrote a joint letter to

Asoka Mehta, expressing our reaction. The letter reflects my views on the subject. One factor which I thought it rather indelicate to write in a letter of that kind is my anxiety that this process of fusion should be complete while J.P. is healthy and active enough to participate in it. Uncertainty about J.P.'s health lends urgency to the question which otherwise may have been allowed to proceed at its own pace. I think efforts in this direction should be revived and Shri Asoka Mehta may be persuaded to spearhead the move.

10. Reports that have been received here off and on indicate that we have been able to restablish our organisational network. This is immensely gratifying. The struggle is obviously going to be long-drawn, and only an enduring mechanism of this kind can bear the burden.

I am sure conscious efforts must have been made to see that there is increasing involvement of students and younger sections in this regular working of ours. In the *bauddhik* food that we provide to these get-togethers, a commitment to democratic values ought to be consciously built up. In the pre-emergency days our emphasis has been almost exclusively and rightly so, on nationalism. Now it has to be a twofold emphasis—on nationalism and democracy.

11. I had mentioned in my last note about the need to revitalise and re-enforce whatever free media of communication are available, our Gujarathi *Sadhana*, has acquitted itself very well, so also the Marathi *Sadhana* and the English *Janatha* both connected with the Socialist party. Gorwala's *Opinion* (now being sent in cyclostyled form) and the *Seminar* also have been doing very good work. All papers falling in this category—there may be some at district level—should be popularised by us irrespective of their ideological affiliations.

I saw a cyclostyled bulletin *Satya Samachar* from Bombay area. It could be regularised.

I had suggested last time that an effort should be made to publicise even normal routine activities of opposition activists outside, that is, those who are not underground—such as J.P., Goray, Tyagi, Shanti Bhushan, U.L. Patil, Pandit etc. I hope our own papers have started doing this. The L.S.S. bulletins also should cover this.

12. When Parliament meets on Aug. 10, the emergency will be more than a year old. Important Constitution amendments would be on the agenda. Prominent opposition members would

not be in a position to participate in the debate. The Janata
Front members remaining would do well to consider whether it
would still be worthwhile participating in the debate or whether
a boycott (such as was done in the first session after the emergency) would not be more appropriate.

L.K.A.

November 7, 1976

Note for Consideration

1. My views on the one-party issue are contained in the letters exchanged last week with Shri Atalji (copies sent earlier).

2. Lok Sabha elections have been put off for another year. The announcement has given rise to two interpretations:

(a) Mrs. Gandhi has no intention of holding elections—neither now, nor ever.

(b) Mrs. Gandhi is afraid that an election now will not be favourable to her, and so has decided to wait for a more propitious moment.

I am inclined to agree with the second interpretation. It would not be correct to infer that Mrs. Gandhi has decided not to hold elections at all. This, of course, is true that the course she has embarked on may lead her to that position—namely, no elections at all.

3. As of today, I feel Mrs. Gandhi would very much like to hold elections, register a triumph over the opposition, and flaunt that victory in the face of her foreign critics. But this desire notwithstanding, she would like to have an election only if and when she feels that there is no risk whatsoever of her being worsted at the polls.

* Obviously, her own reports about the state of public opinion at the moment do not hold out any such assurance.

This, in itself, is a matter of considerable satisfaction for us. In fact, during the first three or four months of the emergency, Government spokesmen used to sound far more cocksure of themselves, than they do now, after seventeen months of unprecedented repression and concentrated, one-sided propaganda.

* With the passage of time Government's alienation from public opinion is likely to increase rather than decrease. May be, Government is wickedly looking forward to J.P.'s physical departure from the scene, and/or the collapse of opposition morale.

* Anyway, if we keep in mind that Government would always be desirous of acquiring electoral legitimacy, we will not be caught napping if at any time she orders a snap poll. Our efforts at political consolidation, therefore, continue to be relevant despite the postponement of polls.

4. I do not know if there has been any contact with Paunar lately. It would be worthwhile exploring that direction. An attempt may be made to have Vinoba Bhave revive the Acharya Conference. I believe he told Shri N.G. Goray and others after his talks with Mrs. Gandhi in February last that she had promised to hold elections in February 1977, and that she would release detenus around October.

5. We must now get set for the next phase of struggle. The timing may be tentatively fixed for June 26 next. That would synchronise with the opening of schools and colleges, apart from being the second anniversary of the emergency.

6. Judging from the figures of detentions, and releases, in this State, it seems that there have been no releases anywhere in any substantial measure, and that the bulk of our workers are still inside.

* If, however, there is any indication of relaxation (in terms of detenu releases) in other parts, or any reasonable expectation, we may wait for a couple of months before starting any overt mobilisation for the struggle.

* Unlike those who offered satyagraha, and so who voluntarily invited incarceration, several friends detained under MISA had really not bargained for it, and so have been feeling exhausted. If there is any relaxation, and such detenus go out, it would strengthen our overall position.

* All important workers of the Sangh and Jana Sangh should be mentally prepared to be behind bars for a long spell.

7. During the coming months the newly created forum,

People's Union for Civil Liberties, should be consciously activated and strengthened by our people all over the country. Even if hall meetings are not permitted, group meetings should be organised on a regular basis and youth and students sought to be involved in these discussions.

* It may be suggested to Shri Tarkunde that a fortnightly bulletin be published on behalf of the Union.

L.K.A.

PART FOUR

Appendixes

APPENDIX 1

IN THE HIGH COURT OF KARNATAKA
AT BANGALORE

———

SYNOPSIS OF PROCEEDINGS
WITH REGARD TO
WRIT PETITIONS
OF
ATAL BIHARI VAJPAYEE
SHYAM NANDAN MISHRA
MADHU DANDAVATE
LAL K. ADVANI

———

(Hearing adjourned on October 8 for resumption on October 20)

(Prepared on October 10, 1975)

Facts of the Case

A Resume

———

Sarvashri A.B. Vajpayee, S.N. Mishra and L.K. Advani had come to Bangalore to attend a meeting of the Joint Select Committee of Parliament considering the Anti-Defection Bill. Shri Vajpayee had reached Bangalore on June 23. Shri Mishra and Shri Advani had arrived on June 25. Shri Madhu Dandavate had come to Bangalore in the course of a tour of the Estimates Committee. He also arrived on June 25.

Following proclamation of the emergency, all these four M.Ps were arrested on June 26 and detained under MISA by orders of the Commissioner of Police, Bangalore.

The four detenus filed habeas corpus petitions in which they challenged the bonafides of the emergency and the validity of their detention. They alleged that the Commissioner of Police, Bangalore, had arrested them under instructions from the Government of India. A 2-judge Bench of the Karnataka High Court presided over by Chief Justice Sankara Bhatt admitted the petitions and posted them for hearing on July 17.

On July 17 morning under orders of the Central Government the four detenus were released. But immediately on their stepping out from prison they were re-arrested under fresh orders of the Central Government. In court that day, Attorney-General Shri Niren De appeared personally to make a statement that as the earlier orders of detention had been revoked by the Central Government, and fresh orders issued, the earlier petition had become infructuous. The Chief Justice, therefore, advised the petitioners to file fresh petitions.

When the petitioners pointed out the difficulty they were

experiencing with regard to legal aid etc., the Court directed
that all necessary facilities be made available to detenus so
that they could file their petitions afresh. The Attorney-General
assured the Court that its directions in this regard would be
carried out.

But that very afternoon (July 17), Shri Mishra, Shri Advani
and Shri Dandavate were hurriedly transferred to Rohtak. A
special Air Force plane flew them to Delhi from where they
were brought to Rohtak. Shri Vajpayee who had undergone
an operation for appendicitis on July 12 could not be similarly
transferred because the doctors would not permit it.

So on July 18 an application was filed in the High Court on
behalf of Shri Vajpayee who was in the Bangalore Hospital,
pointing out that the transfer order was a malafide act intended
to delay the detenus from re-approaching the Court. The High
Court took serious note of it and immediately issued orders
restraining the Government of India from transferring Shri
Vajpayee. Later, Shri Vajpayee, on his own volition, indicated
that he would like to be treated at the All India Institute of
Medical Sciences, New Delhi. Shri Vajpayee was accordingly
transferred to New Delhi on August 6.

Fresh writ petitions filed on behalf of the four detenus were
admitted on September 10 and posted for hearing on September
29. Sarvashri Mishra, Advani and Dandavate were brought
from Rohtak to Bangalore on September 22. They were
presently lodged in the Bangalore Central Jail. Shri Vajpayee
could not come because of his health.

The hearing commenced on September 29. A 2-judge Bench
comprising J. Chandrashekhar and J. Venkataswami is hearing
the case.

In this case, Shri Vajpayee is being represented by Shri M. C.
Chagla, Shri Madhu Dandavate by Shri Venu Gopal, Shri
Mishra by Shri N. Santosh Hegde and Shri Advani by Shri
M. Rama Jois.

The Government of India is being represented by Shri V.P.
Raman, Counsel from Madras who has recently been appointed
Additional Solicitor-General in place of Shri Nariman, and
the Government of Karnataka by Shri Byra Reddy, Advocate-
General.

At the outset, the petitioners had indicated to the Court their
desire to argue their cases in person.

When they so decided, Karnataka Advocate-General Shri Byra Reddy stood up to request that the presence of the petitioners in Court be dispensed with. Their presence in Court, he argued, entailed elaborate security and transport arrangements. Hundreds of policemen had to be deployed for the purpose.

Justice Chandrashekhar was unimpressed by the argument. "I fail to understand this over-sensitivity", he remarked. He added: "Surely, they are not going to run away. They may after all, like to instruct their counsel." So to the great chagrin of Government, orders issued to the jail authorities that the detenus be brought daily to Court for the hearing remained unaltered.

A more substantial rebuff came when the Court overruled a preliminary objection raised by Government of India counsel. Shri Raman contended that in view of the recent amendments made in the Constitution and in the Maintenance of Internal Security Act, and also in view of the President's suspension of various articles under Art. 359 of the Constitution, the petitioners had no right to seek redress from the Court and the Court had no right jurisdiction even to entertain the writs.

Arguments on this preliminary point went on for one and a half days at the end of which the High Court passed an order overruling the objection.

The Government of India then applied for leave to appeal to the Supreme Court against the order. The High Court declined to grant leave.

Next day (Oct. 1) Government of India counsel sought adjournment of the hearing for one week so that Shri Niren De, Attorney-General, could participate in the proceedings. The Court observed that they would very much like to have the benefit of the Attorney-General's views, but as this was a habeas corpus petition they would not like to adjourn the hearing.

The hearing continued up to October 8, but on this day because of the indisposition of one of the judges Shri Venkataswami, the hearing was adjourned till after the Dussehra vacation, that is, till October 20.

According to the affidavits filed on behalf of Government Union Home Minister Shri Brahmananda Reddi owned personal responsibility for the arrest of these four opposition leaders.

Likely course of events
during the next six months
(as seemed likely on Oct. 31, 1975)

POSSIBILITY A

1. Supreme Court verdict favours Mrs Gandhi
2. Release of detenus shortly thereafter
3. Relaxation of curbs on the Press, and on public activity only about a month or so before polls
4. Polls in February or March, 1976

POSSIBILITY B

1. Supreme Court verdict favours Mrs Gandhi
2. Release of detenus to start thereafter, but release to be phased out till upto a month before polls
3. Relaxation of curbs on the Press, and on public activity only about a month or so before polls
4. Polls in February or March

Both the above possibilities do not take into account the possible impact of the proposed November satyagraha. Taking satyagraha into account, the possibilities to be:

POSSIBILITY C: *Greatest likelihood*

1. Verdict in favour of Mrs Gandhi
2. No release until Government is able to assess response to satyagraha call
3. If satyagraha evokes good response,
—no release
—no elections

POSSIBILITY D
1. Verdict in favour of Mrs Gandhi
2. No release until Government assesses response to satyagraha
3. If satyagraha evokes a feeble response, elections in February-March will be announced at next Parliament session and simultaneously releases may start
4. Curbs on the Press, public activity to continue till about one month before the polls
5. Polls in February or March

All the above possibilities are contingent upon the Supreme Court pronouncing in favour of Mrs Gandhi, as seems most likely. In case, however, the unlikely thing happens and the verdict is adverse, possibility E would follow thus:

POSSIBILITY E
1. Verdict goes against Mrs Gandhi
2. No release, no removal of curbs
3. Election Commission to remove disqualifications
4. Mrs Gandhi to be elected to Rajya Sabha, to continue as P.M.
5. Polls to be put off

NON-VARIABLES FOR THE NEXT SIX MONTHS
1. No lifting of emergency
2. No lifting of ban on RSS and other organisations
3. Press freedom not to be restored to what it was before emergency. Statutory shackles to be derived to perpetuate subservience of the Press.
4. No withdrawal of warrants against underground workers. Punitive proceedings against them to continue.

No. II/15014/4/75-S&P (D-II)
Government of India
Ministry of Home Affairs
(Grih Mantralaya)

New Delhi-110001, the 8th November 1976

MEMORANDUM

In accordance with the provisions of sub-section (4) of section 16A of the Maintenance of Internal Security Act, 1971 (26
of 1971), as amended, the Central Government has re-considered
whether the detention of Shri Lal K. Advani S/o Shri Kishan
Chand D. Advani, in respect of whom a declaration was made
on the 16th July, 1975 under sub-section (3) of section 16A of
the aforesaid Act, continues to be necessary for effectively
dealing with the emergency. On the basis of the facts, information and materials in its possession, the Central Government is
satisfied that the detention of the said Shri Lal K. Advani
continues to be necessary for effectively dealing with the
emergency.

(By order and in the name of the President)
To
    Shri Lal K. Advani
    S/o Shri Kishan Chand D. Advani

(R.L. Misra)
Joint Secretary to the Govt. of India

Received a copy of this memorandum. November 8, the date
of this memo, happens to be my birthday. So, I take it to be a
birthday gift. Thanks.

L.K. Advani
17.11.76

ERRATA

Page 75 line 28 for *a la Caesar* read *, a censurer*

Page 79 footnote for *Appendix 4* read *Appendix 3*